Information Systems and Management

Information Systems and Management

Edited by Daniel Brody

CLANRYE
INTERNATIONAL
www.clanryeinternational.com

Clanrye International,
750 Third Avenue, 9th Floor,
New York, NY 10017, USA

ISBN: 978-1-63240-891-4

Cataloging-in-Publication Data

Information systems and management / edited by Daniel Brody.
    p. cm.
Includes bibliographical references and index.
ISBN 978-1-63240-891-4
1. Information resources management. 2. Management information systems.
3. Information technology. I. Brody, Daniel.
T58.64 .I54 2019
004--dc23

For information on all Clanrye International publications
visit our website at www.clanryeinternational.com

Contents

Preface VII

Chapter 1 **Applying GA and Fuzzy Logic to Breakdown Diagnosis for Spinning Process** 1
Jeng-Jong Lin, Che-Jen Chuang, Chih-Feng Ko

Chapter 2 **Ordinal Semi On-Line Scheduling for Jobs with Arbitrary Release Times on Identical Parallel Machines** 19
Sai Ji, Rongheng Li, Yunxia Zhou

Chapter 3 **Maze Navigation via Genetic Optimization** 29
David J. Webb, Wissam M. Alobaidi, Eric Sandgren

Chapter 4 **Predicting Optimal Trading Actions using a Genetic Algorithm and Ensemble Method** 44
Kazuma Kuroda

Chapter 5 **Business Process Analysis and Simulation: The Contact Center of a Public Health and Social Information Office** 51
Antonio Di Leva, Emilio Sulis, Manuela Vinai

Chapter 6 **Decision Support through Intelligent Agent based Simulation and Multiple Goal based Evolutionary Optimization** 68
Wissam Alobaidi, Eric Sandgren, Entidhar Alkuam

Chapter 7 **A Rule based Evolutionary Optimization Approach for the Traveling Salesman Problem** 85
Wissam M. Alobaidi, David J. Webb, Eric Sandgren

Chapter 8 **Brokers as Catalysts for the E-Health Market** 103
Vivian Vimarlund, Craig Kuziemsky, Christian Nøhr, Pirkko Nykänen, Nicolas Nikula

Chapter 9 **Application of the SECI Model using Web Tools to Support Diabetes Self-Management and Education in the Kingdom of Saudi Arabia** 115
Saleh Almuayqil, Anthony S. Atkins, Bernadette Sharp

Chapter 10 **Exploring the Benefits of an Agile Information System** 136
Pankaj Chaudhary, Micki Hyde, James A. Rodger

Chapter 11 **Agri-food Supply Chain Management** 159
C. Ganeshkumar, M. Pachayappan, G. Madanmohan

Chapter 12   **A Comparative Survey on Arabic Stemming: Approaches and Challenges**...................................188
Mohammad Mustafa, Afag Salah Eldeen, Sulieman Bani-Ahmad,
Abdelrahman Osman Elfaki

Permissions

List of Contributors

Index

Preface

The main aim of this book is to educate learners and enhance their research focus by presenting diverse topics covering this vast field. This is an advanced book which compiles significant studies by distinguished experts in the area of analysis. This book addresses successive solutions to the challenges arising in the area of application, along with it; the book provides scope for future developments.

An organized system that deals with the organization, collection, communication and storage of information is known as an information system (IS). It can also be used to describe a combination of software, hardware, data, business processes, people and feedback that can be used for the optimization and management of an organization. An information system seeks to support decision-making, operations and management. Information systems can be of various types such as decision support systems, learning management systems, transaction processing systems, database management systems, etc. Computer based information systems are also widely used. Its main components are software, procedures, networks, hardware and databases. The objective of this book is to give a general view of the different areas of information systems and their management. It traces the progress of this field and highlights some of its key concepts and applications. It aims to equip students and experts with the advanced topics and upcoming concepts in this area.

It was a great honour to edit this book, though there were challenges, as it involved a lot of communication and networking between me and the editorial team. However, the end result was this all-inclusive book covering diverse themes in the field.

Finally, it is important to acknowledge the efforts of the contributors for their excellent chapters, through which a wide variety of issues have been addressed. I would also like to thank my colleagues for their valuable feedback during the making of this book.

Editor

Applying GA and Fuzzy Logic to Breakdown Diagnosis for Spinning Process

Jeng-Jong Lin[1,2], Che-Jen Chuang[1], Chih-Feng Ko[1]

[1]Department of Tourism and Leisure Management, Vanung University, Taiwan
[2]Department of Information Management, Vanung University, Taiwan
Email: jjlin@vnu.edu.tw

Abstract

In this study, an effective search methodology based on fuzzy logic is applied to narrow down search range for the possible breakdown causes. Moreover a genetic algorithm (GA) is employed to directly find the intervals of solution to the inverse fuzzy inference problem during diagnosis procedure. Through the assistance of the developed intelligent diagnosis system, an inspector can be easier and more effective to find various possible occurred breakdown causes by judging from the observed symptoms during manufacturing process. An application of the developed intelligent diagnosis system to tracing the breakdown causes occurred during spinning process is reported in this study. The results show that the accuracy and efficiency of the diagnosis system are as promising as expected.

Keywords

Fuzzy Logic, Inverse Fuzzy Inference, Genetic Algorithm, Breakdown Diagnosis

1. Introduction

It is crucial for a manufacturing process to be of an intelligent diagnosis system to help effectively find out the occurred problems and eliminate them in no time when breakdowns occur. However, nowadays the inspecting & tracing process for the breakdowns causes during producing product in manufacturing industry still heavily depends on the expertise of an experienced technician. In general a junior inspector is lacking in the knowledge or the experience needed for tracing out break down causes from the occurred problems. Results of inspection and diagnosis are exclusively influenced with mental and physical conditions of an inspector. It is not only time-consuming but also economically infeasible for an enterprise to retrain a new operator to expert at the specific technical knowledge

of engineering, once the trained operator leaves the job. For the sake to help
solve the above-mentioned problems, an intelligent diagnosis system is developed by using fuzzy logic and genetic algorithm (GA) in this study.

A good diagnosis system should have the capability to help find the possible
causes incurring the defects of product. Fuzzy sets theory is a handy tool for expert information formalization while simulating cause-effect connections in
technical and medical diagnostic problems [1] [2]. The model of a diagnostic
object, as a rule is built on the basis of compositional Zadeh rule of inference
which connects input and output variables of an object (causes and effects) using
fuzzy relation matrix [3]. The problem of diagnosis can be formulated in the
form of the direct and inverse fuzzy logical inference.

The direct logical inference suggests finding diagnoses (output variables or effects) according to observable internal parameters of the object state (input variables or causes). At present, the majority of fuzzy logic applications to the diagnosis problems adopt the direct logical inference [4] [5] [6] [7]. Several diagnosis systems have been developed to trace breakdowns occurred during manufacturing. Xu *et al.* [4] treated vibration signals of machinery in unsteady operating conditions by using instantaneous power spectrum (IPS) and genetic programming (GP), generating excellent symptom parameters GP-SP for failure
diagnosis, and failure of machinery in unsteady operating conditions is diagnosed. Chen *et al.* [5] traced multi-fault state for plant machinery using wavelet
analysis, genetic programming (GP), and possibility theory. The wavelet analysis
is used to extract feature spectra of multi-fault state from measured vibration
signal for the diagnosis. Hsu *et al.* [6] developed a diagnosis system, which is
based on fuzzy reasoning to monitor the performance of a discrete manufacturing process and to justify the possible causes.

In the case of inverse logical inference some renewal of causes takes place (of
the object state parameters) according to observable effects (symptoms). The inverse logical inference is used much less due to the lack of effective algorithms
solving fuzzy logical equation system. It is required to develop a more effective
approach to finding solution to inverse fuzzy logic problem during diagnosing
breakdown causes. Although the effective algorithm for solving the inverse fuzzy
logic problem has been researched [8] [9] [10] and reported in many studies [1]
[2] [4] [5] [11] [12] [13], the proposed methods need proceeding with compli-
cate compare procedures. In order to solve the above-mentioned problems, in
this study, the search for the solution to fuzzy logical equation is of an optimization problem solved by genetic algorithm (GA) [14]. We present a GA-based
approach to directly find the intervals of solution to the inverse fuzzy inference
problem. Moreover an effective search algorithm based on fuzzy reasoning is
applied to narrow down search range for the possible breakdown causes. Through
the assistance of the developed diagnosis system, an operator can more easily
and effectively find various possible breakdown causes by judging from the observed symptoms during manufacturing process. Thus, the manufacturing efficiency can be improved dramatically because the occurred breakdowns can be

eliminated in no time based on the problem-incurred causes being effectively traced out.

2. Fuzzy Logical Equation

Let the relationship between symptoms and causes in a diagnosis process be represented as r_{ij}. Thus, the relationship between cause i and symptom j in a diagnosis system can thus be illustrated as that between i and j in an diagnosis situation when a relationship exists between breakdown cause i and symptom j, the r_{ij} is shown as 1; otherwise it is 0. Assume that matrix R is composed of elements r_{ij} of size $m \times n$, matrix A is a row matrix consisting of m elements, and matrix B is a row matrix consisting of n elements, respectively. The relationship between causes and symptoms in a diagnosis system can thus be shown as the following.

$$A \circ R = B \tag{1}$$

where

$$R = \begin{pmatrix} r_{11} & r_{12} & \cdots & r_{1n} \\ r_{21} & r_{22} & \cdots & r_{2n} \\ \cdots & \cdots & \cdots & \cdots \\ r_{m1} & r_{m2} & \cdots & r_{mn} \end{pmatrix}$$

$$A = \begin{pmatrix} a_1 a_2 \cdots a_m \end{pmatrix}$$

$$B = \begin{pmatrix} b_1 b_2 \cdots b_n \end{pmatrix}.$$

Calculated result from Equation (1) by max-min composition (Zadeh and Kacprzyk, 1992) yields

$$\underset{i}{V}\left(a_i \wedge r_{ij}\right) = b_j \tag{2}$$

where V: max, $\wedge$: min, $i = 1, 2, \cdots, m$, and $j = 1, 2, \cdots, n$.

The diagnostic procedure seems quite simple using given matrix A and matrix R to find the solution of matrix B because there exists only one specific solution. Yet using matrix B and R to find matrix A, which can fit the requirement of Equation (1), will be rather more sophisticated because more than one solution exists. Such kind of vague relations existing between breakdown causes and symptoms are called fuzzy relations. A fuzzy set, defined originally by Zadeh [15], is an extension of a crisp set. Crisp sets allow only full membership or no membership at all, whereas fuzzy sets [11] [12] [13] [16] [17] allow partial membership. The diagnostic procedure, usually proceeding with given matrices R and B to find the solution of matrix A that fits the requirements of Equation (1), is an inverse problem of fuzzy relation equation. If the solution of matrix A can be found, then the breakdown cause is obtained.

3. Solutions to the Inverse Problems

Assuming that matrices A, B, and R in Equation (1) are all fuzzy set [18] [19], to find the solution of matrix A in Equation (1) from given matrices B and R is an inverse problem of a fuzzy relational equation. For instance, when $m = n = 1$, the solution, represented as a^*, of the inverse problem of $b = a \wedge r$ can be shown as

$$\begin{cases} a^* = b & \text{if } b < r \\ a^* = [b,1] & \text{if } b = r \\ a^* = \phi & \text{if } b > r \end{cases} \tag{3}$$

Relationships between b, r, and a can be illustrated as in **Figure 1**, from which we can conclude that when $b < r$ and $b = r$, it is true for $a = b$ and $a = [b, 1] = [r, 1]$ respectively. But when $b > r$ because there is no a, the solution is ϕ. In accordance with the magnitudes of b and r, there exist three kinds of solutions (*i.e.*, point, set, and ϕ). From **Figure 1**, we can conclude that a solution exists for $b = a \wedge r$ unless the magnitude of r is less than that of b.

Finding of fuzzy set A amounts to the solution of the fuzzy logical Equations system:

$$\begin{aligned} b_1 &= \left(a_1 \wedge r_{11}\right) V \left(a_2 \wedge r_{21}\right) \cdots V \left(a_m \wedge r_{m1}\right) \\ b_2 &= \left(a_1 \wedge r_{12}\right) V \left(a_2 \wedge r_{22}\right) \cdots V \left(a_m \wedge r_{m2}\right) \\ &\cdots \qquad\quad \cdots \quad \cdots \quad \cdots \\ b_n &= \left(a_1 \wedge r_{1n}\right) V \left(a_2 \wedge r_{2n}\right) \cdots V \left(a_m \wedge r_{mn}\right) \end{aligned} \tag{4}$$

which is derived from Equation (2). The solution to the problem of fuzzy logical equations (*i.e.*, Equation 2) is formulated in this way. Vector $a = \left(a_1, a_2, \cdots, a_n\right)$, which satisfies limitations of $a_i \in [0,1]$, $i = 1, 2, \cdots, m$, should be found and provides the least distance between expert and analytical measures of effects significances, that is between the left and the right parts of Equation (2).

Minimizing

$$\sum_{j=1}^{n} \left(b_j - \bigvee_i \left(a_i \wedge r_{ij}\right)\right)^2. \tag{5}$$

In general, Equation (2) can have no solitary solution but a set of them. Therefore, according to Equation (5), a form of intervals can be acquired as the solution to the fuzzy logical equations system and illustrated as follows.

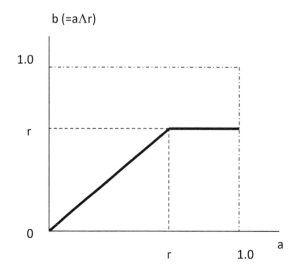

Figure 1. Graph of $b = a \wedge r$.

$$a_i = [a_i^l, \ a_i^u] \subset [0,1], \ i = 1,2,\cdots,m, \tag{6}$$

where $a_i^l \left(a_i^u \right)$ is the low (upper) boundary of cause a_i significance measure.

Formation of intervals $a_i \left(i.e., \left[a_i^l, a_i^u \right] \right)$ is done by way of multiple optimization problem solution to Equation (5) and it begins with the search for the null solution of it.

The null solution to optimization problem in Equation (5) is illustrated as $a^{(0)} = \left(a_1^{(0)}, a_2^{(0)}, \cdots, a_n^{(0)} \right)$, where $a_i^{(0)} \in \left[a_i^l, a_i^u \right]$, $i = 1,2,\cdots,m$. The upper boundary $\left(a_i^u \right)$ is found in range $\left[a_i^{(0)}, 1 \right]$ and the low $\left(a_i^l \right)$ in range $\left[0, a_i^{(0)} \right]$. Let $a^{(k)} = \left(a_1^{(k)}, a_2^{(k)}, \cdots, a_n^{(k)} \right)$ be some kth solution of optimization problem in Equation (5). While searching for upper boundaries $\left(a_i^u \right)$ it is suggested that $a_i^{(k)} \geq a_i^{(k-1)}$, and while searching for low boundaries $\left(a_i^l \right)$ it is suggested that $a_i^{(k)} \leq a_i^{(k-1)}$. It is shown in the **Figure 2** where the arrows correspond to direction of the search.

The upper and low boundary can be found as the following steps.

1) Randomly find an optimal solution (*i.e.*, $a^{(0)}$) based on Equation (5).

2) Search dynamics of upper solutions boundaries (*i.e.*, $a_i^{(k)} \geq a_i^{(k-1)}$).

{If $a^{(k)} \neq a^{(k-1)}$, then $a_i^u \left(a_i \right) = a_i^{(k)}$, $i = 1,2,\cdots,m$, $k = 1,2,\cdots,p$.

Else if $a^{(k)} = a^{(k-1)}$, then the search is stopped.}

3) Search dynamics of low solutions boundaries (*i.e.*, $a_i^{(k)} \leq a_i^{(k-1)}$).

{If $a^{(k)} \neq a^{(k-1)}$, then $a_i^l \left(a_i \right) = a_i^{(k)}$, $i = 1,2,\cdots,m$, $k = 1,2,\cdots,p$.

Else if $a^{(k)} = a^{(k-1)}$, then the search is stopped.}

4. Developing Search Mechanism

To solve a problem, the GA randomly generates a set of solutions for the first generation. Each solution is called a chromosome that is usually in the form of a binary string. According to a fitness function, a fitness value is assigned to each solution. The fitness values of these initial solutions may be poor; however, they will rise as better solutions survive in the next generation. A new generation is

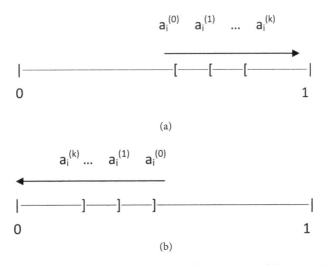

Figure 2. Search for upper (a) and low (b) boundary of the interval.

produced through the following three basic operations [14] [20].

1) Randomly generate an initial solution set (population) of N strings and evaluate each solution by fitness function.

2) If the termination condition does not meet, do

Repeat {Select parents for crossover.

Generate offspring.

Mutate some of the numbers

Merge mutants and offspring into population.

Cull some members of the population.}

3) Stop and return the best fitted solution.

4.1. Encoding and Decoding A Chromosome

In order to apply GAs to our problem, we firstly need to encode the elements of matrix A as a binary string. The domain of variable a_i is $\left[d_i^1, d_i^u \right]$ and the required precision is dependent on the size of encoded-bit. The precision requirement implies that the range of domain of each variable should be divided into at least $\left(d_i^u - d_i^1 \right) / \left(2^n - 1 \right)$ size ranges. The required bits (denoted with n) for a variable is calculated as follows and the mapping from a binary string to a real number for variable a_i is straightly forward and completed as follows.

$$a_i = d_i^1 + s_i \left(d_i^u - d_i^1 \right) / \left(2^n - 1 \right) \tag{7}$$

where s_i is an integer between 0 - 2^n and is called a searching index.

After finding an appropriate s_i to put into Equation (7) to have an a_p which can make fitness function to come out with a fitness value approaching to "1", the desired parameters can thus be obtained. Combine all of the parameters as a string to be an index vector, *i.e.* $A = (a_1, a_2, \cdots, a_m)$, and unite all of the encoder of each searching index as a bit string to construct a chromosome shown as below.

$$P = p_{11} \cdots p_{1j} p_{21} \cdots p_{2j} \cdots p_{i1} \cdots p_{ij} \quad p_{ij} \in \{0,1\}; \ i = 1, 2, \cdots, m; \ j = 1, 2, \cdots, n; \tag{8}$$

Suppose that each a_i was encoded by n bits and there was m parameters then the length of Equation (8) should be an N-bit ($N = m \times n$) string. During each generation, all the searching index sis of the generated chromosome can be obtained by Equation (9).

$$s_i = p_{i1} \times 2^{n-1} + p_{i2} \times 2^{n-2} + \cdots + p_{in} \times 2^{n-n} \ i = 1, 2, \cdots, m; \tag{9}$$

Finally the real number for variable a_i can thus be obtained from Equation (7) and Equation (9). The flow chart for the encoding and decoding of the parameter is illustrated in **Figure 3**.

4.2. Chromosome

A main difference between genetic algorithms and more traditional optimization search algorithms is that genetic algorithms work with a coding of the parameter set and not the parameters themselves [14]. Thus, before any type of genetic search can be performed, a coding scheme must be determined to represent the parameters in the problem in hand. In finding the solution (*i.e.*, matrix *A*) of a fuzzy logical inference problem, a coding scheme for the elements of matrix *A* must be determined and considered in advance. Suppose that matrix *A* is a row one of *n* elements. A multi-parameter coding, consisting of *n* sub-strings, is required to code each of the *n* variables (*i.e.*, elements) into a single string. In this study, a binary coding is utilized and the bit-sizes of the encoding for the elements of Matrix *A* are as follows. The bit-size of each element of matrix *A* is set to 7 bits. Thus a chromosome string consisting of $N(=n \times 7)$ bits can be formed and its layout is shown in **Figure 4**.

4.3. Fitness Function

The target is to minimize the distance between the observed values (*i.e.*, b_j) and the calculated ones (*i.e.*, $V_i\left(a_i \wedge r_{ij}\right)$) shown as Equation (5). The fitness of GA used in search mechanism can thus be set as Equation (10). This approach will allow the GA to find the minimum difference between them when the fitness function value is maximum (*i.e.*, approaches to 1).

$$\text{Fitness} = 1 - \sum_{j=1}^{n}\left(b_j - \bigvee_i\left(a_i \wedge r_{ij}\right)\right)^2 \tag{10}$$

where V: max, Λ: min, $i = 1, 2, \cdots, m$, and $j = 1, 2, \cdots, n$.

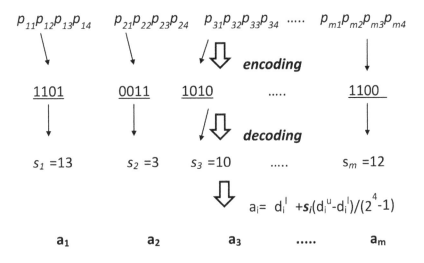

Figure 3. Flow chart for the encoding and decoding of a variable with 4-bit precision.

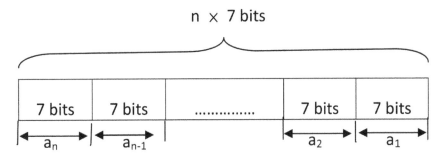

Figure 4. Layout of chromosome.

4.4. Make the Diagnostic Procedure More Effective

In order to develop a more effective diagnosis system, which is capable of tracing the possible breakdown causes from the categories of defects and providing an immediate response, it is necessary to sketch an effective searching algorithm for the diagnosis procedure. The methodology used in research [21] is employed in the study. Firstly, we define the following symbols:

$A_i = \{a_1, a_2, \cdots, a_m\}$ = cause set

$B_j = \{b_1, b_2, \cdots, b_n\}$ = symptom set

$R_{ij} = (r_{ij})_{mxn}$ = fuzzy relation matrix of size $m \times n$ between a and b

where

$a_1 - a_m$: m kinds of breakdown causes,

$b_1 - b_n$: n kinds of symptoms, and

r_{ij} : the fuzzy truth value between the ith kind of cause and the jth kind of symptom.

The fuzzy truth values of r_{ij}s are acquired empirically from experts of engineering using the following linguistic values [20] [22] (e.g., completely true, very true, true, rather true, rather rather true, and unknown) of the linguistic variable "truth." Their meaning is defined as follows.

1) completely true: Once a_i occurs then b_j appears.

2) very true: When a_i occurs, b_j will appear very definitely.

3) true: When a_i occurs, b_j will appear very probably.

4) rather true: When a_i occurs, b_j will appear probably.

5) rather rather true: When a_i occurs, b_j will appear seldom.

6) unknown: When a_i occurs, b_j will never appear.

Generally speaking, in a diagnosis problem, the symptoms can be divided into two kinds of categories, the positive symptom set (J_1), consisting of those symptoms that have been observed by the operator, and the negative one (J_2), consisting of those symptoms that have not yet been observed by the operator. When only certain symptoms have been observed by the operator, the diagnosis process can proceed. It is impossible for all the symptoms of the system to appear at one time, so that $J_1 \neq \phi$ and $J_2 \neq \phi$.

Actually during tracing a certain kind of breakdown cause through the observed symptoms, the reliability of diagnostic results should be very high as long as all possible symptoms for this kind of breakdown are all observed [19]. However, if there are many other symptoms (not the observed ones) that should have appeared but have not yet done so, then the reliability of diagnostic results of this kind of breakdown cause will be very low.

We can thus conclude that the diagnostic range can be narrowed effectively by neglecting those breakdown causes seldom noticed a_i. For instance, breakdown causes that are in accordance with the circumstance of

$$\underset{j \in J_2}{V} R_{ij} < \text{rather} \quad \text{rather} \quad \text{true}$$

should firstly be investigated. That is, the searching range of the diagnosis can be narrowed from $i \in I \left(= \{ i \mid i = 1, 2, \cdots, m \} \right)$ down to

$$i \in I_1 \left(= \left\{ i \middle| \underset{j \in J_2}{V} R_{ij} < \text{rather} \quad \text{rather} \quad \text{true} \right\} \right).$$

A relationship should occur between the breakdown causes searched a_i and the observed symptoms b_j. In other words, the condition of

$$\underset{j \in J_1}{V} R_{ij} > \text{unknown}$$

should be true. Therefore the searching range of diagnosis I_1 can be reconstructed as

$$I_1 = \left\{ i \middle| \underset{j \in J_2}{V} R_{ij} < \text{rather} \quad \text{rather} \quad \text{true}, \underset{j \in J_1}{V} R_{ij} > \text{unknown} \right\}.$$

In a practical diagnostic procedure in the real world, the members in I_1 are much fewer than those in cause set I (consisting of m members). Thus, an efficient searching method can be obtained.

Nevertheless, in a practical diagnostic procedure, while searching for the members of the set searching range I_1, the circumstance of $I_1 = \phi$ can happen. Then a wider searching range should be reset to search once again. Yet the wider the searching range is set, the less reliable the breakdown cause found through this diagnostic procedure is. In order to achieve both effectively narrowing the diagnostic searching range and specific reliability of the diagnostic result, the extension of the searching range in a diagnosis procedure should have a proper limitation. Therefore, there are three kinds of searching range selected in this study. These sets and their reliability are represented as

$$I_1 \left(= \left\{ i \middle| \underset{j \in J_2}{V} R_{ij} < \text{rather} \quad \text{rather} \quad \text{true}, \underset{j \in J_1}{V} R_{ij} > \text{unknown} \right\} \right),$$

which has the greatest reliability and from which the diagnostic result that is found can be regarded as the actual "cause";

$$I_2 \left(= \left\{ i \middle| \underset{j \in J_2}{V} R_{ij} < \text{rather} \quad \text{true}, \underset{j \in J_1}{V} R_{ij} > \text{unknown} \right\} \right),$$

which is less reliable than I_1 and from which the diagnostic result that is found can be regarded as "very probable"; and

$$I_3 \left(= \left\{ i \middle| \underset{j \in J_2}{V} R_{ij} < \text{true}, \underset{j \in J_1}{V} R_{ij} > \text{unknown} \right\} \right),$$

which is the least reliable, and from which the diagnostic result that is found can be regarded as "probable".

The flow chart of the system's diagnostic procedures is illustrated in **Figure 5**. Finally after searching for the members of the searching ranges I_1, I_2, and I_3 using the effective diagnostic procedure mentioned above, there probably exists the circumstance of $I_1 = I_2 = I_3 = \phi$. Then the system will select five a_is of greater L_i value as the suspected breakdown causes for further diagnosis:

$$L_i = \sum_{j \in J1} R_{ij} \tag{11}$$

where

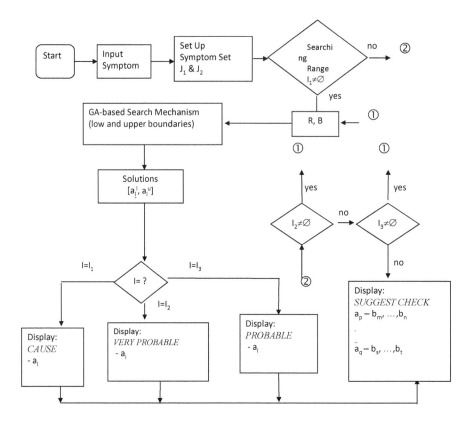

Figure 5. Flow chart of diagnostic procedure for diagnosis system.

R_{ij}: the fuzzy truth value between the ith kind of breakdown cause and the jth kind of symptom.

J_1: the positive symptom set.

5. Results and Assessment of the System

5.1. System Implementation

An application of the intelligent diagnosis system to tracing the breakdown causes occurred during spinning was reported in this study. There were 6 kinds of defects that are most likely found during spinning and 20 possible occurrence causes of these defects all chosen from and referred to the reports [22] on the occurrence causes and the effects of the defects in spinning.

1) Symptom Set and Cause Set

The cause set A and the symptom set B consist of the above-mentioned 20 causes and 6 kinds of defects respectively and the elements of each of the two are illustrated as below.

SYMPTOMS

b_1 smash

b_2 stick-out on the edge of cone

b_3 ribbon-shaped defects around cone's surface

b_4 ring-shaped defects

b_5 spindle-shaped defects

b_6 too much happening in yarn's cut-off

CAUSES

a_1 mal-set for Bobbin holder

a_2 mal-functioned pulley tension caused by neps or cotton trash

a_3 bobbin slipping from slot

a_4 gap occurred between bobbin and sketch

a_5 improper setting of skeleton

a_6 improper yarn's adjunction

a_7 big gap on top of cone

a_8 lack of yarn tension

a_9 defects in cylinder-slot

a_{10} too big gap between bottom of bobbin and cylinder

a_{11} forward shifting during bobbin's circulation

a_{12} un-smooth spindle-spinning

a_{13} too big gap on top of cone

a_{14} over-heavy tension pulley

a_{15} mal-positioned tension device

a_{16} mal-functioned back-forth motion

a_{17} too much yarn tension

a_{18} mal-positioned empty bobbin

a_{19} mal-positioned de-knotter

a_{20} mal-positioned plug base of bobbin

2) Fuzzy Relation Matrix

All the truth values of members of fuzzy relation matrix R are illustrated as **Table 1**. The fuzzy truth value of each r_{ij} in **Table 1** was acquired empirically from experts of textile engineering and technical references [22] [23] on causes and effects of the yarn defects in spinning. By using the linguistic values (e.g., completely true, very true, true, rather true, rather rather true, and unknown) of the "truth" linguistic variable, the fuzzy truth value of each r_{ij} in the fuzzy relation matrix R of the diagnosis system thus can be characterized. Furthermore, for making it feasible for the computer to execute the logic operation processing, the fuzzy truth value of each linguistic value (e.g., completely true, very true, true, rather true, rather rather true, and unknown) is characterized by specific weight value (e.g., 1.0, 0.8, 0.6, 0.4, 0.2, and 0.0) respectively and is listed in **Table 1**, in which A-E represent 1.0, 0.8, 0.6, 0.4, and 0.2, respectively and the blank represents 0.0.

5.2. Diagnosis Example

After the operator examines the defects (breakdown causes) occurred on the yarns, "ring-shaped defects" (*i.e.*, b_4) formed during winding process is found so that symptom "b_4" is input into the system to proceed with the diagnosis. According to the diagnosis procedure shown in **Figure 4**, the positive and negative symptom sets are $J_1 = \{b_4\}$, $J_2 = \{b_1, b_2, b_3, b_5, b_6\}$ respectively. Firstly, the searching range is narrowed from $I\left(=\{i|i=1,2,\cdots,20\}\right)$ down to

Table 1. Fuzzy relationship between causes and symptoms.

a_i \ b_j	b_1	b_2	b_3	b_4	b_5	b_6
a_1	A		A	A	B	
a_2	B					
a_3	B					
a_4	C					
a_5	C					
a_6	D					
a_7			A			
a_8		B			A	A
a_9		C				D
a_{10}	A	D				D
a_{11}	A		A	A	B	
a_{12}			A			
a_{13}			B			
a_{14}			C			
a_{15}		E		B		D
a_{16}			E	B		C
a_{17}					A	A
a_{18}	A		A		B	
a_{19}						A
a_{20}						C

$$I_1 \left(= \left\{ i \mid \underset{j \in J_2}{V} R_{ij} < \text{rather} \quad \text{rather} \quad \text{true}, \underset{j \in J_1}{V} R_{ij} > \text{unknown} \right\} \right)$$
and
$$\left(i.e., I_1 = \left\{ i \mid \underset{j \in J_2}{V} R_{ij} < 0.2, \underset{j \in J_1}{V} R_{ij} > 0 \right\} \right)$$

$$I_2 \left(= \left\{ i \mid \underset{j \in J_2}{V} R_{ij} < \text{rather} \quad \text{true}, \underset{j \in J_1}{V} R_{ij} > \text{unknown} \right\} \right)$$

$$\left(i.e., I_2 = \left\{ i \mid \underset{j \in J_2}{V} R_{ij} < 0.4, \underset{j \in J_1}{V} R_{ij} > 0 \right\} \right).$$

There is no breakdown cause a_i, which lives up to the I_1 and I_2 conditions (Lin et al., 1995). Thus the situation $(i.e., I_1 = I_2 = \phi)$ is found. Next, the searching range is more broadened up to

$$I_3 \left(= \left\{ i \mid \underset{j \in J_2}{V} R_{ij} < \text{true}, \underset{j \in J_1}{V} R_{ij} > \text{unknown} \right\} \right) \left(i.e., I_3 = \left\{ i \mid \underset{j \in J_2}{V} R_{ij} < 0.6, \underset{j \in J_1}{V} R_{ij} > 0 \right\} \right)$$

to investigate the possible breakdown causes. There is a suspected one (*i.e.*, a_{15}), which regarded as "probable", found under the searching range $I_3 \, (\neq \phi)$ after checking fuzzy relation matrix shown in **Table 1** based on the above-set $J_1 \left(= \{b_4\} \right)$ and $J_2 \left(= \{b_1, b_2, b_3, b_5, b_6\} \right)$. Following the suggestion of the "probable" breakdown cause a_{15} (*i.e.*, mal-positioned tension device) from the system, the operator can immediately check it up. It is found nothing wrong with a_{15} after the operator's inspection. Excluding the "probable" breakdown cause a_{15}, the system provides the operator with five suspected breakdown causes shown as follows.

SUGGEST again CHECK	
$a_1 - b_1, b_3, \lvert b_4 \rvert, b_5$	$\left(L_1 = 3.8, J_1 = \{y_4\} \right)$
$a_{11} - b_1, b_3, \lvert b_4 \rvert, b_5$	$\left(L_{11} = 3.8, J_1 = \{y_4\} \right)$
$a_{16} - b_3, \lvert b_4 \rvert, b_6$	$\left(L_{16} = 1.6, J_1 = \{y_4\} \right)$
$a_{15} - b_2, \lvert b_4 \rvert, b_6$	$\left(L_{15} = 1.4, J_1 = \{y_4\} \right)$

where the symptoms with lines to both sides denote the already-recognized ones. The operator re-inspects the product defects in relation to the suspected causes and their related symptoms suggested by the system, and he/she find that there is another two more "stick-out on the edge of cone" (*i.e.,* b_2) and "too much happening in yarn's cut-off" (*i.e.,* b_6). Therefore he can re-input b_2, b_4 and b_6 into the system to proceed with the further diagnosis. According to the observed symptoms, the positive and negative symptom are obtained as $J_1 = \{b_2, b_4, b_6\}$ and $J_2 = \{b_1, b_3, b_5\}$ respectively. Firstly, the searching range is set to

$$I_1 \left(= \left\{ i \Big| \underset{j \in J_2}{V} R_{ij} < \text{rather} \quad \text{rather} \quad \text{true}, \underset{j \in J_1}{V} R_{ij} > \text{unknown} \right\} \right)$$ to investigate the po-

ssible break down causes. The found diagnostic result can be regarded as the actual "cause". There are five suspected breakdowns (*i.e.,* a_9, a_{10}, a_{15}, a_{19}, a_{20}) found based on the searching range $I_1 (\neq \phi)$ after checking fuzzy relation matrix shown in **Table 1** based on the above-set $J_1 \left(= \{b_2, b_4, b_6\} \right)$ and $J_2 \left(= \{b_1, b_3, b_5\} \right)$. The number of possible breakdown causes are effectively reduced from 20 (*i.e.,* a_1, a_2,···, a_{20}) down to 5 (*i.e.,* a_9, a_{10}, a_{15}, a_{19}, a_{20}). The obtained vectors, *i.e.,* A and R, are as follows.

$$\underline{A} = \left(a_9, a_{10}, a_{15}, a_{19}, a_{20} \right), \qquad R = \begin{pmatrix} 0.6. & 0 & 0.4 \\ 0.4 & 0 & 0.4 \\ 0.2 & 0.8 & 0.4 \\ 0 & 0 & 1 \\ 0 & 0 & 0.6 \end{pmatrix}$$

Let the obtained relation matrix R has the following form.

		b_2	b_4	b_6
	a_9	0.6	0	0.4
	a_{10}	0.4	0	0.4
$R=$	a_{15}	0.2	0.8	0.4
	a_{19}	0	0	1.0
	a_{20}	0	0	0.6

　　As the result of product examination the inspector find out there are three defects (*i.e.,* symptoms) occurred, *i.e.,* $b_2 = 1$, $b_4 = 1$, $b_6 = 1$. As mentioned above, there is no solution for $b = a \wedge r$ if the magnitude of r is less than b. Therefore the values of b_2, b_4, and b_6 are adjusted to the maximum values of the respective columns in R matrix and shown as follows.

$$b_2 = \max r_{i2} = 0.6, \quad b_4 = \max r_{i4} = 0.8, \quad b_6 = \max r_{i6} = 1.0,$$

where $i = 9, 10, 15, 19$, and 20.

Once the vectors, *i.e.*, **_R_** and **_B_**, are obtained, we can proceed with the 3-step method mentioned in Section 3 to search for the upper and low boundaries.

Firstly, following the three steps mentioned in Section 4, we encode the unknown occurring possibility of breakdown causes (*i.e.*, a_9, a_{10}, a_{15}, a_{19}, and a_{20}) by using a binary coding method. The bit-size of each of them is set to 7 bits in this study. Thus a chromosome illustrated in **Figure 4** can be formed as a 35 ($=5 \times 7$)-bit string. The search ranges of variable a_9, a_{10}, a_{15}, a_{19}, and a_{20} are set to be the same as [0, 1] (*i.e.*, $\left[d_i^l, d_i^u \right]$, $i = 9, 10, 15, 19$, and 20). Through proceeding with the search mechanism of GA based on Equations (7) and (9), we can find a solution, whose fitness approaches to 1, as the optimal one. Fitness function simulation runs with the crossover, mutation, and reproduction operations under conditions of crossover probability, mutation probability, random seed, and initial population being set to 0.3, 0.033, 0.8 and 30 respectively. **Figure 6** shows the simulation graph for the best fitness and average fitness of the 50 generations. It shows that after 46th generation the solution is not improved. Therefore, we choose vector (0.60, 0.00, 0.99, 0.98, 0.25), which is generated from the 50th generation and has fitness = 0.9998 as the optimal solution. Therefore a null solution $a_i^{(0)}$ is found and shown as follows.

$$a_9^{(0)} = 0.60, \ a_{10}^{(0)} = 0.00, \ a_{15}^{(0)} = 0.99, \ a_{19}^{(0)} = 0.98, \ a_{20}^{(0)} = 0.25$$

Secondly, by means of the null solution, we can search for the upper and low boundaries. **Table 2** and **Table 3** illustrate the searched results for the upper and low ones respectively. When search the upper boundaries, the search ranges of variable a_9, a_{10}, a_{15}, a_{19}, and a_{20} are set different to each other as [0.60, 1], [0, 1], [0.99, 1] [0.98, 1] and [0.25, 1] (*i.e.*,

$$\left[d_9^{l(0)}, d_9^{u(0)} \right], \left[d_{10}^{l(0)}, d_{10}^{u(0)} \right], \left[d_{15}^{l(0)}, d_{15}^{u(0)} \right], \left[d_{19}^{l(0)}, d_{19}^{u(0)} \right] \text{ and } \left[d_{20}^{l(0)}, d_{20}^{u(0)} \right]).$$

Through proceeding with the search mechanism of GA, we can find a solution, whose fitness approaches to 1, as the optimal one. An optimal solution after generations of GA search can be obtained as follows.

$$a_9^{(1)} = 0.66, \ a_{10}^{(1)} = 0.80, \ a_{15}^{(1)} = 0.99, \ a_{19}^{(1)} = 0.99, \ a_{20}^{(1)} = 0.43$$

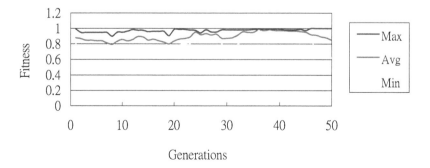

Figure 6. Simulation results.

By narrowing down the search range step by step, the upper boundaries of a_9^u, a_{10}^u, a_{15}^u, a_{19}^u and a_{20}^u can be acquired. **Table 2** shows the searched results after five iterations. Finally, the obtained values of a_9, a_{10}, a_{15}, a_{19}, and a_{20} remains the same (*i.e.*, $a_i^{(6)} = a_i^{(5)}$), the search is stopped.

When search the low boundaries, the search ranges of variable a_9, a_{10}, a_{15}, a_{19} and a_{20} are set different to each other as [0, 0.60], [0, 0], [0, 0.99], [0, 0.98], and [0, 0.25] (*i.e.*, $\left[d_i^{l(0)}, d_i^{u(0)} \right]$, $i = 9, 10, 15, 19, 20$). Through proceeding with the search mechanism of GA, we can find a solution, whose fitness approaches to 1, as the optimal one. An optimal solution after generations of GA search can be obtained as follows.

$$a_9^{(1')} = 0.46, \ a_{10}^{(1')} = 0.00, \ a_{15}^{(1')} = 0.78, \ a_{19}^{(1')} = 0.70, \ a_{20}^{(1')} = 0.11$$

By narrowing down the search range step by step, the low boundaries of a_9^l, a_{10}^l, a_{15}^l, a_{19}^l, and a_{20}^l can be acquired. **Table 3** shows the searched results after five iterations. Finally, the obtained values of a_9, a_{10}, a_{15}, a_{19}, and a_{20} remains the same (*i.e.*, $a_i^{(6')} = a_i^{(5')}$), the search is stopped.

Table 2 and **Table 3** shows that the solution to fuzzy logical equation can be expressed in the form of intervals

$$a_9 = [0,1], \ a_{10} \in [0,1], \ a_{15} \in [0.36,1], \ a_{19} \in [0.44,1], \ a_{20} \in [0,1].$$

The obtained solution allows making a diagnosis conclusion. The cause of the observed defects should be considered as a_{19} (*i.e.*, mal-positioned de-knotter), because of which has a higher solution boundary than the other four. Excluding

Table 2. Genetic search for upper boundaries of the intervals.

N	a_9	a_{10}	a_{15}	a_{19}	a_{20}	
0	0.60	0.00	0.99	0.98	0.25	increasing
1	0.66	0.80	0.99	0.99	0.43	
2	0.87	0.93	1.00	1.00	0.66	
3	0.90	0.97	1.00	1.00	0.93	
4	0.92	0.99	1.00	1.00	0.95	
5	1.00	1.00	1.00	1.00	1.00	
6	1.00	1.00	1.00	1.00	1.00	

Table 3. Genetic search for low boundaries of the intervals.

N	a_9	a_{10}	a_{15}	a_{19}	a_{20}	
0	0.60	0.00	0.99	0.98	0.25	decreasing
1'	0.46	0.00	0.78	0.70	0.11	
2'	0.35	0.00	0.61	0.58	0.01	
3'	0.12	0.00	0.48	0.56	0.00	
4'	0.03	0.00	0.44	0.52	0.00	
5'	0.00	0.00	0.36	0.44	0.00	
6'	0.00	0.00	0.36	0.44	0.00	

the obtained solution, system supports five $a_i s$ of greater L_i value as the suspected breakdown causes for further diagnosis. They are illustrated as follows.

SUGGEST again CHECK	
$a_1 - b_1, b_3, |b_4|, b_5$	$\left(L_1 = 3.8, J_1 = \{y_2, y_4, y_6\}\right)$
$a_{11} - b_1, b_3, |b_4|, b_5$	$\left(L_{11} = 3.8, J_1 = \{y_2, y_4, y_6\}\right)$
$a_8 - |b_2|, b_5, |b_6|$	$\left(L_8 = 2.8, J_1 = \{y_2, y_4, y_6\}\right)$
$a_{17} - b_5, |b_6|$	$\left(L_{17} = 2.0, J_1 = \{y_2, y_4, y_6\}\right)$
$a_{10} - b_1, |b_2|, |b_6|$	$\left(L_{10} = 1.8, J_1 = \{y_2, y_4, y_6\}\right)$

where the symptoms with lines to both sides denote the already-recognized ones.

Through the assistance of the diagnosis system, the operator can obtain three derived suspected breakdown causes a_9, a_{10}, a_{15}, a_{19} and a_{20}, which have a reliability of "*cause*" because the searching range is I_1, to help him/her in troubleshooting and eliminating the breakdown. In this experimental case, after the technician for maintenance in the mill proceeding with the troubleshooting, the exact breakdown cause is confirmed to be a_{19} (*i.e.*, mal-positioned de-knotter). From the diagnostic case illustrated as above, the accuracy of the implementation of this system is approvable. Even when the diagnostic result is not the exact breakdown cause, nevertheless, the system will still provide the operator with some suspected ones for further check. This system can thus achieve the demand of providing with a solution in any circumstance during diagnosing in the real world.

6. Conclusion

The determination on the breakdown causes becomes more effective and efficient by adopting a GA-based diagnosis procedure proposed in the study. It was constructed that using the fuzzy set theory, which does not simply perform the routine calculations like those developed by the conventional programming algorithm, can be more flexible and effective to find the solution to fuzzy logical equation by genetic algorithm. The developed diagnosis model is of the nature of human capability in recognition and evaluation of uncertain linguistic description. Through the assistance of the developed diagnosis model, even a new inspector, who lacks in the expertise and experience in the spinning engineering field, can still easily find out the breakdown causes occurred during manufacturing process and then eliminate them. Furthermore, it is expected that the developed diagnosis model can be applied to other industries for the troubleshooting of machines or facilities as long as the relation matrix for the application in specific field is provided.

References

[1]   Yager, R.R. and Zadeh, L.A. (1992) An Introduction to Fuzzy Logic Applications in

Intelligent Systems. Kluwer Academic Publishers, Boston.
https://doi.org/10.1007/978-1-4615-3640-6

[2]   Kosko, B. (1992) Neural Networks and Fuzzy Systems. Prentice Hall, NJ.

[3]   Zadeh, L. and Kacprzyk, J. (1992) Fuzzy Logic for the Management of Uncertainty.
John Wiley & Sons, Inc., NY.

[4]   Xu, G., Luo, Z., Li, M. and Chen, P. (2001) Mechanical Failure Diagnosis in Unsteady Operating Conditions. *Chinese Journal of Mechanical Engineering*, **37**, 104-
107. https://doi.org/10.3901/JME.2001.12.104

[5]   Chen, P., Taniguchi, M. and Toyota, T. (2003) Intelligent Diagnosis Method of
Multi-Fault State for Plant Machinery Using Wavelet Analysis, Genetic Programming and Possibility Theory. *IEEE International Conference on Robotics and Automation*, **1**, 610-615.

[6]   Hsu, H.M. and Chen, Y.K. (2001) A Fuzzy Reasoning Based Diagnosis System for X
Control Charts. *Journal of Intelligent Manufacturing*, **12**, 57-64.
https://doi.org/10.1023/A:1008903614042

[7]   Welstead, S.T. (1994) Neural Network and Fuzzy Logic Applications in C/C++.
John Wiley & Sons, Inc, NY.

[8]   Liu, H.W. and Wang, G.J. (2007) Multi-Criteria Decision-Making Methods Based
on Intuitionistic Fuzzy Sets. *European Journal of Operational Research*, **179**, 220-
233. https://doi.org/10.1016/j.ejor.2006.04.009

[9]   Pappis, C.P. and Sugeno, M. (1985) Fuzzy Relational Equations and the Inverse
Problem. *Fuzzy Sets System*, **15**, 79-90.
https://doi.org/10.1016/0165-0114(85)90036-3

[10]   Sanchez, E. (1976) Resolution of Composite Fuzzy Equation. *Information and Control*, **30**, 38-48. https://doi.org/10.1016/S0019-9958(76)90446-0

[11]   Torra, V. (2010) Hesitant Fuzzy Sets. *International Journal of Intelligent Systems*,
25, 529-539. https://doi.org/10.1002/int.20418

[12]   Data, S., Samantra, C., Mahapatra, S.S., Mondal, G., Chakraborty, P.S. and Majum-
dar, G. (2013) Selection of Internet Assessment Vendor Using TOPSIS Method in
Fuzzy Environment. *International Journal of Business Performance and Supply
Chain Modelling*, **5**, 1-27. https://doi.org/10.1504/IJBPSCM.2013.051645

[13]   Abdullab, L. and Zulkifli, N. (2015) Integration of Fuzzy AHP and Interval Type-2
Fuzzy DEMATEL: An Application to Human Resource Management. *Expert Systems with Applications*, **42**, 4397-4409. https://doi.org/10.1016/j.eswa.2015.01.021

[14]   Goldberg, D.E. (1989) Genetic Algorithms in Search, Optimization & Machine
Learning. Addison-Wesley Publish Co., NY.

[15]   Zadeh, L.A. (1965) Fuzzy Sets. *Information and Control*, **8**, 338-353.
https://doi.org/10.1016/S0019-9958(65)90241-X

[16]   Chen, S.M., Lee, I.W., Liu, H.C. and Yang, S.W. (2012) Multi-Attribute Decision
Making Based on Interval-Valued Intuitionistic Fuzzy Value. *Expert Systems with
Applications*, **39**, 10343-10351. https://doi.org/10.1016/j.eswa.2012.01.027

[17]   Derika, K., Khodaverdi, R., Olfat, L. and Jatarian, A. (2013) Integrated Fuzzy Multi
Criteria Decision Making Method and Multi-Objective Programming Approach for
Supplier Selection and Order Allocation in a Green Supply Chain. *Journal of
Cleaner and Production*, **47**, 355-367. https://doi.org/10.1016/j.jclepro.2013.02.010

[18]   Murayama, Y. and Ziya, S. (1990) Applying Fuzzy Theory to Breakdown Diagnosis.
System and Control, **24**, 719-725.

[19]   Zimmermann, H.-J. (1991) Fuzzy Set Theory—and Its Application. 2nd Edition,

Kluwer Academic Publishers, Boston, MA.
https://doi.org/10.1007/978-94-015-7949-0

[20] Gen, M. and Cheng, R. (1997) Genetic Algorithms & Engineering Design. John Wiley & Sons, Inc., NY.

[21] Lin, J.J., Tsai, I.S. and Lin, C.H. (1995) An Application of Expert System and Fuzzy Logic to Intelligent Diagnosis System. *Textile Research Journal*, **65**, 697-709.
https://doi.org/10.1177/004051759506501201

[22] Lin, C.A., *et al.* (1990) Report on Causes and Effects of Textile Defects Occurred during Weaving and Spinning. Association of Textile Industry.

[23] Ormerod, A. (1983) Modern Preparation and Weaving Machinery. Butterworth & Co. Ltd., UK.

2

Ordinal Semi On-Line Scheduling for Jobs with Arbitrary Release Times on Identical Parallel Machines

2

Sai Ji[1], Rongheng Li[1*], Yunxia Zhou[2]

[1]Key Laboratory of High Performance Computing and Stochastic Information Processing, Department of Mathematics, Hunan Normal University, Changsha, China
[2]Department of Computer, Hunan Normal University, Changsha, China
Email: *lirongheng@hunnu.edu.cn

Abstract

In this paper, we investigate the problem of semi-on-line scheduling n jobs on m identical parallel machines under the assumption that the ordering of the jobs by processing time is known and the jobs have arbitrary release times. Our aim is to minimize the maximum completion time. An ordinal algorithm is investigated and its worst case ratio is analyzed.

Keywords

Schedule, Algorithm, Worst Case Ratio, Parallel Machines

1. Introduction

The problem of minimizing the maximum completion time for scheduling n jobs on m identical parallel machines (which is denoted by $P_m / \cdot / C_{\max}$) have attracted the interests of many researchers since it was proposed by Graham in 1969 [1]. The problem is defined as follows: Given a job set $L = \{J_1, J_2, \cdots, J_n\}$ of n jobs and an identical parallel machine set $\{M_1, M_2, \cdots, M_m\}$, where job J_j has non-negative processing time p_j, assign the jobs onto the machines so as to minimize the maximum completion of the m machines.

A scheduling problem is called off-line if we have complete information about the job data before constructing a schedule. In contrast, the scheduling problem is called online if the jobs appear one by one and it requires scheduling the arriving job irrevocably on a machine without knowledge of the future jobs. The processing time of next job becomes available only after the current job is scheduled. Graham [1] proposed the List Scheduling (LS) algorithm to minimize the maximum completion time for online scheduling n jobs on m identical parallel machines.

Li and Huang [2] generalized Graham's classical on-line scheduling problem to m identical machines. They describe the requests of all jobs in terms of order. For an order of the job J_j, the scheduler is informed of a 2-tuple (r_j, p_j), where r_j and p_j represent the release time and the processing time of the job J_j, respectively. The orders of request have no release time but appear online one by one at the very beginning time of the system. In this online situation, the jobs' release times are assumed to be arbitrary. If all jobs' release times are zero, then the problem in Li and Huang [2] becomes the same as the Graham's classical on-line scheduling problem.

For the classical online problem on the identical parallel machine system, we know that no algorithm can be better than algorithm LS when the number of machines is less than 4. In many applications, partial information about jobs can be made available in advance. This motivates us to study semi-online scheduling problems when different types of partial information become available [3]. He and Zhang [4], and He and Dosa [5] consider the system when the lengths of all jobs are known in $[1, r]$ with $r \geq 1$. See Cheng et al. [6]; Li and Huang [7]; Seiden et al. [8]; Li et al. [9] for more recent results on semi-online scheduling.

Liu et al. [10] firstly considered ordinal semi-online problem in which it is assumed that the values of the processing times p_j are unknown, but that the order of the jobs by non-increasing processing time is known, i.e., $p_1 \geq p_2 \geq \cdots \geq p_n$. The problem can be denoted as $P_m / \text{ordinal} / C_{\max}$. They proposed an algorithm with worst case performance ratio not greater than $1 + \dfrac{m-1}{m + \left\lceil \dfrac{m}{2} \right\rceil}$. Later $Q_2 / \text{ordinal} / C_{\max}$ is considered by Tan and He [11] and $P_3 / \text{ordinal} / C_{\max}$ is considered by He and Tan [12].

In this paper, we assume that we are given m identical parallel machines $\{M_1, M_2, \cdots, M_m\}$ and an ordinal job list $L = \{J_1, J_2, \cdots, J_n\}$ with arbitrary release times, i.e., each J_j has a release time r_j and a processing size of p_j satisfying $p_1 \geq p_2 \geq \cdots \geq p_n$. Our aim is to minimize the maximum completion time. We denote this problem as $P_m / (\text{ordinal}, r_j) / C_{\max}$.

The rest of the paper is organized as follows. In Section 2, some definitions and the algorithm P are given. In Section 3, we analyze the algorithm P and show its the upper bound of the worst case ratio. In Section 4, we give some concluding remarks.

2. Some Definitions and the Algorithm P

In this section we will give some definitions and an algorithm P.

Definition 1. Let algorithm A be a heuristic algorithm of scheduling job list L. $C_{\max}^A(L)$ and $C_{\max}^{OPT}(L)$ denote the makespan of algorithm A and an optimal off-line algorithm, respectively. We define

$$R(m, A) = \sup_{L} \frac{C_{max}^A(L)}{C_{max}^{OPT}(L)}$$

as the worst case performance ratio of algorithm A.

Definition 2. Suppose that J_j is the current job with information (r_j, p_j), *i.e.*, release time r_j and size of p_j, to be scheduled on machine M_i. We say that machine M_i has an idle time interval for job J_j, if there exists a time interval $[T_1, T_2]$ satisfying the following two conditions:

1) Machine M_i is idle in interval $[T_1, T_2]$ and a job with release time T_2 has been assigned to machine M_i to start at time T_2.

2) $T_2 - \max[T_1, r_j] \geq p_j$.

It is obvious that if machine M_i has an idle time interval for job J_j then we can assign J_j to machine M_i in the idle interval.

The algorithm P:

Let $L = \{J_1, J_2, \cdots, J_n\}$ be a job list of problem $P_m / (\text{ordinal}, r_i) / C_{max}$. We assign jobs of L one by one on machine $M_i (i = 1, 2, \cdots, m)$ according to the following rules:

If $1 \leq i \leq \left\lfloor \dfrac{m}{2} \right\rfloor$ holds, we assign the following jobs on machine M_i:

$$\{J_i\} \cup \left\{ J_{2m+1-i+k\left(m+\left\lceil \frac{m}{2} \right\rceil\right)} \mid k \geq 0 \right\}.$$

If $1 + \left\lfloor \dfrac{m}{2} \right\rfloor \leq i \leq m$ holds, we assign the following jobs on machine M_i:

$$\{J_i\} \cup \left\{ J_{2m+1-i+k\left(m+\left\lceil \frac{m}{2} \right\rceil\right)} \mid k \geq 0 \right\} \cup \left\{ J_{3m+1-i+k\left(m+\left\lceil \frac{m}{2} \right\rceil\right)} \mid k \geq 0 \right\}.$$

Assignment example for $m = 5$:

$$
\begin{array}{llllll}
M_1: & J_1 & J_{10} & J_{18} & & \cdots \\
M_2: & J_2 & J_9 & J_{17} & & \cdots \\
M_3: & J_3 & J_8 & J_{13} & J_{16} & J_{21} & \cdots \\
M_4: & J_4 & J_7 & J_{12} & J_{15} & J_{20} & \cdots \\
M_5: & J_5 & J_6 & J_{11} & J_{14} & J_{19} & \cdots
\end{array}
$$

Note: The above assignment just means the order of the job's assigning, not mean the order of job's processing because of the release times of the jobs. For example on machine M_1, if $r_1 = 6, p_1 = 8, r_{10} = 6, p_{10} = 6$, then J_{10} begin to be processed at time zero and J_1 begin to be processed at 6 even though J_1 is assigned before J_{10} because J_1 appears before J_{10}.

The following symbols will be used in the analysis of this paper later on:

1) $P_1^n = \sum_{j=1}^n p_j$, $P_k^n = \sum_{j=k}^n p_j$.

2) U_i: the total sum of the idle time on machine M_i in the schedule P.

3) C_i: The completion time of machine M_i in the schedule P. It is equal to

the total sum of the processing time of the jobs assigned on machine M_i and the idle time of machine M_i in the schedule P. It is easy to see that $C_{\max}^P(L) = \max\{C_1, C_2, \cdots, C_m\}$ holds.

1) $[h]_i$: the index of the h-th job assigned on machine M_i in the schedule P.

2) $\lceil x \rceil$: It represents the smallest integer not less than x.

3) $\lfloor x \rfloor$: It represents the largest integer not bigger than x.

3. Main Results

The following simple inequality will be referred to later on:

$$C_{\max}^{OPT}(L) \geq \max\left\{\frac{\sum_{j=1}^n p_j}{m}, r_j + p_j, j = 1, 2, \cdots, n, U_i + p_i, i = 1, 2, \cdots, m\right\}$$

Furthermore it is easy to get

$$C_{\max}^{OPT}(L) \geq U_i, i = 1, 2, \cdots, m$$

Lemma 1: For any job list $L = \{J_1, J_2, \cdots, J_n\}$ from problem $P_m / (\text{ordinal}, r_i) / C_{\max}$, suppose that h jobs are assigned on machine M_i by algorithm P. If $h \geq 2$ and $[h]_i - [1]_i = [h]_i - i \geq \dfrac{h-1}{x}$ hold, then we have

$$C_i \leq x P_{i+1}^n + U_i + p_i.$$

Proof: It is easy to see that $\forall h \geq 2, x \geq \dfrac{h-1}{[h]_i - i}$ holds. Firstly we prove the following statement by induction for h:

$$x P_{i+1}^{[h]_i} \geq P_{[2]_i} + \cdots + P_{[h]_i} + \left[x\left([h]_i - [1]_i\right) - (h-1)\right] P_{[h]_i} \tag{1}$$

For $h = 2$ we have

$$x P_{i+1}^{[2]_i} = x\left(P_{[1]_i+1} + \cdots + P_{[2]_i}\right) \geq x\left[\left([2]_i - [1]_i\right) P_{[2]_i}\right]$$
$$= P_{[2]_i} + \left[x\left([2]_i - [1]_i\right) - (2-1)\right] P_{[2]_i}$$

That means the statement is true for $h = 2$. Now suppose (1) holds for $h = k$, i.e.,

$$x P_{i+1}^{[k]_i} \geq P_{[2]_i} + P_{[3]_i} + \cdots + P_{[k]_i} + \left[x\left([k]_i - [1]_i\right) - (k-1)\right] P_{[k]_i}.$$

Then for $h = k+1$ we have

$$x P_{i+1}^{[k+1]_i} \geq P_{[2]_i} + P_{[3]_i} + \cdots + P_{[k]_i} + \left[x\left([k]_i - [1]_i\right) - (k-1)\right] P_{[k]_i}$$
$$+ x\left(P_{[k]_i+1} + P_{[k]_i+2} + \cdots + P_{[k+1]_i}\right)$$
$$\geq P_{[2]_i} + P_{[3]_i} + \cdots + P_{[k]_i} + \left[x\left([k]_i - [1]_i\right) - (k-1)\right] P_{[k]_i}$$
$$+ \left[x\left([k+1]_i - [k]_i\right)\right] P_{[k+1]_i}$$
$$\geq P_{[2]_i} + P_{[3]_i} + \cdots + P_{[k]_i} + \left[x\left([k]_i - [1]_i\right) - (k-1)\right] P_{[k+1]_i}$$

$$+\left[x\left(\left[k+1\right]_i-\left[k\right]_i\right)\right]p_{\left[k+1\right]_i}$$

$$=p_{\left[2\right]_i}+p_{\left[3\right]_i}+\cdots+p_{\left[k+1\right]_i}+\left[x\left(\left[k+1\right]_i-\left[1\right]_i\right)-\left(k+1-1\right)\right]p_{\left[k+1\right]_i}$$

By (1) we have

$$xP_{i+1}^n+U_i\geq xP_{i+1}^{\left[h\right]_i}+U_i\geq p_{\left[2\right]_i}+p_{\left[3\right]_i}+\cdots+p_{\left[h\right]_i}$$

$$+\left[x\left(\left[h\right]_i-\left[1\right]_i\right)-\left(h-1\right)\right]p_{\left[k\right]_i}+U_i$$

$$\geq p_{\left[2\right]_i}+p_{\left[3\right]_i}+\cdots+p_{\left[h\right]_i}+U_i=C_i-p_i$$

where the last equality results from $\left[1\right]_i=i$ by the rules of algorithm P. The claim is proved.

Lemma 2: For any job list $L=\left\{J_1,J_2,\cdots,J_n\right\}$ from problem $P_m/\left(ordinal,r_i\right)/C_{\max}$, we have

$$C_i\leq\begin{cases}\dfrac{2p_{i+1}^n}{3\left(m-i+1\right)}+U_i+p_i & 1\leq i\leq m;\ m\text{ is even}\\[3mm]\dfrac{2p_{i+1}^n}{3\left(m-i+1\right)+1}+U_i+p_i & 1\leq i\leq\dfrac{m-1}{2};\ m\text{ is odd}\\[3mm]\dfrac{4p_{i+1}^n}{3m+1}+U_i+p_i & \dfrac{m+1}{2}\leq i\leq m;\ m\text{ is odd}\end{cases}$$

Proof: Case 1: m is even and $1\leq i\leq m$.

Case 1.1: $1\leq i\leq\dfrac{m}{2}$ and $h=k+2$.

By the rules of P we have

$$\frac{h-1}{\left[h\right]_i-i}=\frac{k+2-1}{2m+1-2i+\dfrac{3km}{2}}=\frac{2k+2}{4m-4i+2+3km}$$

$$=\frac{2\left(k+1\right)}{3\left(k+1\right)\left(m-i+1\right)+3k\left(i-1\right)+m-i-1}$$

$$\leq\frac{2\left(k+1\right)}{3\left(k+1\right)\left(m-i+1\right)}=\frac{2}{3\left(m-i+1\right)}$$

Case 1.2: $\dfrac{m}{2}<i\leq m$ and $h=2k+1$.

$$\frac{h-1}{\left[h\right]_i-1}=\frac{2k}{2m+1-2i+\dfrac{3km}{2}}$$

$$=\frac{2k}{3k\left(m-i+1\right)+3k\left(i-1-\dfrac{m}{2}\right)+2\left(m-i\right)+1}$$

$$\leq\frac{2}{3\left(m-i+1\right)}$$

Case 1.3: $\dfrac{m}{2}<i\leq m$ and $h=2k+2$

$$\frac{h-1}{[h]_i-1}=\frac{2k+1}{3m+1-2i+\dfrac{3km}{2}}$$

$$=\frac{2\left(k+\dfrac{1}{2}\right)}{3\left(k+\dfrac{1}{2}\right)(m-i+1)+3k\left(i-1-\dfrac{m}{2}\right)+\dfrac{3m-i-1}{2}}$$

$$\leq\frac{2}{3(m-i+1)}$$

Let $x=\dfrac{2}{3(m-i+1)}$, by Lemma 1 when m is even and $1\leq i\leq m$ we have

$$C_i\leq\frac{2P_{i+1}^n}{3(m-i+1)}+U_i+p_i$$

Case 2: m is odd. $1\leq i\leq\dfrac{m-1}{2}$ and $h=k+2$ hold.

$$\frac{h-1}{[h]_i-1}=\frac{k+2-1}{2m+1-2i+\dfrac{k(3m+1)}{2}}$$

$$=\frac{2(k+1)}{3(k+1)(m-i+1)+(k+1)+3k(i-1)+m-i-2}$$

$$\leq\frac{2(k+1)}{3(k+1)(m-i+1)+(k+1)+3k(i-1)+i+1-2}$$

$$\leq\frac{2(k+1)}{3(k+1)(m-i+1)+(k+1)}$$

$$\leq\frac{2}{3(m-i+1)+1}$$

Let $x=\dfrac{2}{3(m-i+1)+1}$, by Lemma 1, when m is odd and $1\leq i\leq\dfrac{m-1}{2}$ we have

$$C_i\leq\frac{2P_{i+1}^n}{3(m-i+1)+1}+U_i+p_i$$

Case 3: m is odd and $\dfrac{m+1}{2}\leq i\leq m$

Case 3.1: $h=2k+1$

$$\frac{h-1}{[h]_i-i}=\frac{2k}{2m+1-2i+\dfrac{k(3m+1)}{2}}\leq\frac{4}{3m+1}$$

Case 3.2: $h=2k+2$

$$\frac{h-1}{\lceil h\rceil_i-i}=\frac{2k+1}{3m+1-2i+\dfrac{k(3m+2)}{2}}$$

$$= \frac{4\left(k+\dfrac{1}{2}\right)}{\left(k+\dfrac{1}{2}\right)(3m+1)+\dfrac{3}{2}+\dfrac{9m}{2}-4i}$$

$$\leq \frac{4}{3m+1}$$

Let $x=\dfrac{4}{3m+1}$, when m is odd and $\dfrac{m+1}{2}\leq i\leq m$ we have

$$C_i \leq \frac{4P_{i+1}^n}{3m+1}+U_i+p_i$$

Hence the Lemma is proved.

Theorem 3 For any job list $L=\{J_1,J_2,\cdots,J_n\}$ from problem $P_m/(\text{ordinal},r_i)/C_{\max}$ we have:

$$R(m,P)\leq 2+\frac{m-1}{m+\left\lceil\dfrac{m}{2}\right\rceil}$$

Proof: Case 1: If m is even and $1\leq i\leq m$ holds, by Lemma 2 we have

$$C_i \leq p_i+\frac{2P_{i+1}^n}{3(m-i+1)}+U_i$$

$$=p_i-\frac{2P_1^i}{3(m-i+1)}+\frac{2P_1^n}{3(m-i+1)}+U_i$$

$$=\frac{2}{3(m-i+1)}\left(\frac{3(m-i+1)}{2}p_i-P_1^i\right)+\frac{2P_1^n}{3(m-i+1)}+U_i$$

$$\leq \frac{3m-5i+3}{3(m-i+1)}p_i+\frac{2m}{3(m-i+1)}\times\frac{P_1^n}{m}+U_i$$

$$\leq \frac{8m-8i+6}{3(m-i+1)}\max\left\{p_i,\frac{P_1^n}{m},U_i\right\}$$

$$\leq \frac{8m-8i+6}{3(m-i+1)}C_{\max}^{OPT}(L)$$

$$\leq \frac{8m-2}{3m}C_{\max}^{OPT}(L)$$

where the last inequality results from the fact that $\dfrac{8m-8x+6}{3(m-x+1)}$ is a decreasing function of x in interval $x\in[1,m]$

Case 2: m is odd and $1\leq i\leq \dfrac{m-1}{2}$

By Lemma 2 we have

$$C_i \leq p_i+\frac{2P_{i+1}^n}{3(m-i+1)+1}+U_i$$

$$=p_i-\frac{2P_1^i}{3(m-i+1)+1}+\frac{2P_1^n}{3(m-i+1)+1}+U_i$$

$$= \frac{2}{3(m-i+1)+1} \left(\frac{3(m-i+1)+1}{2} p_i - P_1^i \right) + \frac{2P_1^n}{3(m-i+1)+1} + U_i$$

$$\leq \frac{3m-5i+4}{3(m-i+1)+1} p_i + \frac{2m}{3(m-i+1)+1} \times \frac{P_1^n}{m} + U_i$$

$$\leq \frac{8m-8i+8}{3(m-i+1)+1} \max \left\{ p_i, \frac{P_1^n}{m}, U_i \right\}$$

$$\leq \frac{8m-8i+8}{3(m-i+1)+1} C_{max}^{OPT}(L)$$

$$\leq \frac{8m}{3m+1} C_{max}^{OPT}(L)$$

where the last inequality results from the fact that $\dfrac{8m-8x+6}{3(m-x+1)+1}$ is a decreasing function of x in interval $x \in [1, m]$.

Case 3: m is odd and $\dfrac{m+1}{2} \leq i \leq m$

By Lemma 2 we have

$$C_i \leq p_i + \frac{4}{3m+1} P_{i+1}^n + U_i$$

$$= p_i + \frac{4}{3m+1} \left(P_1^n - P_1^i \right) + U_i$$

$$= \frac{4}{3m+1} \left[\frac{(3m+1) p_i}{4} - (p_1 + p_2 + \cdots + p_i) \right] + \frac{4}{3m+1} P_1^n + U_i$$

$$\leq \frac{4}{3m+1} \left[\frac{(3m+1) p_i}{4} - i p_i \right] + \frac{4}{3m+1} P_1^n + U_i$$

$$= \frac{3m-4i+1}{3m+1} p_i + \frac{4}{3m+1} P_1^n + U_i$$

$$\leq \frac{10m-4i+2}{3m+1} \max \left\{ p_i, \frac{P_1^n}{m}, U_i \right\}$$

$$\leq \frac{10m-4i+2}{3m+1} C_{max}^{OPT}(L)$$

$$\leq \frac{8m}{3m+1} C_{max}^{OPT}(L)$$

By the above conclusions, when m is even we have $C_i \leq \dfrac{8m-2}{3m} C_{max}^{OPT}(L)$

hold for $i = 1, 2, \cdots, m$. Hence we get

$$\frac{C_{max}^P(L)}{C_{max}^{OPT}(L)} \leq \frac{\frac{8m-2}{3m} C_{max}^{OPT}(L)}{C_{max}^{OPT}(L)} = \frac{8m-2}{3m} = 2 + \frac{m-1}{m + \left\lceil \dfrac{m}{2} \right\rceil}$$

When m is odd then $C_i \leq \dfrac{8m}{3m+1} C_{max}^{OPT}(L)$ hold for $i = 1, 2, \cdots, m$. Hence we get

$$\frac{C_{\max}^{P}(L)}{C_{\max}^{OPT}(L)} \leq \frac{\frac{8m}{3m+1}C_{\max}^{OPT}(L)}{C_{\max}^{OPT}(L)} = \frac{8m}{3m+1} = 2 + \frac{m-1}{m+\left\lceil \frac{m}{2} \right\rceil}$$

Thus we get

$$R(m,P) = \sup_{L} \frac{C_{\max}^{P}(L)}{C_{\max}^{OPT}(L)} \leq 2 + \frac{m-1}{m+\left\lceil \frac{m}{2} \right\rceil}$$

Hence the theorem is proved.

4. Concluding Remarks

In this paper, we consider the semi-online scheduling problem $P_m / (\text{ordinal}, r_i) / C_{\max}$ in which the job list has non-increasing processing times and arbitrary release times. An algorithm is investigated and it is shown that its worse case performance ratio is bounded by $2 + (m-1) \big/ \left(m + \left\lceil \frac{m}{2} \right\rceil \right)$ for all values of m. For this problem, to investigate better algorithms or give lower bound and upper bound would be worth doing. There are many other scheduling problems where ordinal algorithms could be developed. The investigations to find good algorithms for these problems would be also of interest to the scheduling community.

Acknowledgements

This work was partly supported by the Chinese National Natural Science Foundation Grant (No.11471110) and the Foundation Grant of Education Department of Hunan (No. 16A126).

References

[1]   Graham, R.L. (1969) Bounds on Multiprocessing Timing Anomalies. *SIAM Journal on Applied Mathematics*, **17**, 416-429. https://doi.org/10.1137/0117039

[2]   Li, R.H. and Huang, H.C. (2004) On-Line Scheduling for Jobs with Arbitrary Release Times. *Computing*, **73**, 79-97. https://doi.org/10.1007/s00607-004-0067-1

[3]   Kellerer, H., Kotov, V., Speranza, M.G. and Tuza, Z. (1997) Semi On-Line Algorithms for the Partition Problem. *Operations Research Letters*, **21**, 235-242. https://doi.org/10.1016/S0167-6377(98)00005-4

[4]   He, Y. and Zhang, G. (1999) Semi On-Line Scheduling on Two Identical Machines. *Computing*, **62**, 179-187. https://doi.org/10.1007/s006070050020

[5]   He, Y. and Dósa, G. (2005) Semi-Online Scheduling Jobs with Tightly-Grouped Processing Times on Three Identical Machines. *Discrete Applied Mathematics*, **150**, 140-159. https://doi.org/10.1016/j.dam.2004.12.005

[6]   Cheng, T.C.E., Kellerer, H. and Kotov, V. (2012) Algorithms Better Than LPT for Semi-Online Scheduling with Decreasing Processing Times. *Operations Research Letters*, **40**, 349-352. https://doi.org/10.1016/j.orl.2012.05.009

[7]   Li, R.H. and Huang, H.C. (2007) List Scheduling for Jobs with Arbitrary Release

Times and Similar Lengths. *Journal of Scheduling*, **10**, 365-373.
https://doi.org/10.1007/s10951-007-0042-8

[8] Seiden, S., Sgall, J. and Woeginger, G.J. (20000 Semi-Online Scheduling with De-
     creasing Job Sizes. *Operations Research Letters*, **27**, 215-227.

[9] Li, R.H., Cheng, X.Y. and Zhou, Y.X. (2014) On-Line Scheduling for Jobs with
     Non-Decreasing Release Times and Similar Lengths on Parallel Machines. *Optimi-
     zation-A Journal of Mathematical Programming and Operations Research*, **63**,
     867-882.

[10] Liu, W.P., Sidney, J.B. and Vliet, A. (1996) Ordinal Algorithm for Parallel Machine
     Scheduling. *Operations Research Letters*, **18**, 223-232.
     https://doi.org/10.1016/0167-6377(95)00058-5

[11] Tan, Z.Y. and He, Y. (2001) Semi Online Scheduling with Ordinal Data on Two
     Uniform Machines. *Operations Research Letters*, **28**, 221-231.
     https://doi.org/10.1016/S0167-6377(01)00071-2

[12] He, Y. and Tan, Z.Y. (2002) Ordinal-Online Scheduling for Maximizing the Mini-
     mum Machine Completion Time. *Journal of Combinatorial Optimization*, **6**,
     199-206. https://doi.org/10.1023/A:1013855712183

3

Maze Navigation via Genetic Optimization

David J. Webb[1], Wissam M. Alobaidi[2*], Eric Sandgren[2*]

[1]Axalta Coating Systems, Front Royal, Virginia, USA
[2]Systems Engineering Department, Donaghey College of Engineering & Information Technology, University of Arkansas at Little Rock, Little Rock, Arkansas, USA
Email: *wmalobaidi@ualr.edu, *exsandgren@ualr.edu

Abstract

One of the most interesting applications of genetic algorithms falls into the area of decision support. Decision support problems involve a series of decisions, each of which is influenced by all decisions made prior to that point. This class of problems occurs often in enterprise management, particularly in the area of scheduling or resource allocation. In order to demonstrate the formulation of this class of problems, a series of maze problems will be presented. The complexity of the mazes is intensified as each new maze is introduced. Two solving scenarios are introduced and comparison results are provided. The first scenario incorporated the traditional genetic algorithm procedure for the intended purpose of acquiring a solution based upon a purely evolutionary approach. The second scenario utilized the genetic algorithm in conjunction with embedded domain specific knowledge in the form of decision rules. The implementation of domain specific knowledge is intended to enhance solution convergence time and improve the overall quality of offspring produced which significantly increases the probability of acquiring a more accurate and consistent solution. Results are provided below for all mazes considered. These results include the traditional genetic algorithm final result and the genetic algorithm optimization approach with embedded rules result. Both results were incorporated for comparison purposes. Overall, the incorporation of domain specific knowledge outperformed the traditional genetic algorithm in both performance and computation time. Specifically, the traditional genetic algorithm failed to adequately find an acceptable solution for each example presented and prematurely converged on average within 54% of their specified generations. Additionally, the most complex maze generated an optimal path directional sequence (i.e. N, S, E, W) via a traditional genetic algorithm which possessed only 50% of the required allowable path sequences for maze completion. The incorporation of embedded rules enabled the genetic algorithm to locate the optimum path for all examples considered within 5% of the traditional genetic algorithm computation time.

Keywords

Maze Navigation, Genetic Optimization

1. Introduction

Decision support has developed into a broad spectrum of applications encompassing optimization through a variety of methods including genetic algorithms [1]. The traditional genetic algorithm is an evolutionary approach where problem characteristics are encoded to initially form random chromosome strings where strings are paired and the exchange of essential data is passed to create offspring. This offspring is evaluated against an objective function and potential optimization constraints which determine the success of the derived offspring. Additional key factors in the genetic algorithm evolutionary process include penalty factors which minimize the occurrence of poor offspring and mutation which randomly alters the encoded string to produce designs potentially unattainable within a small population size. Extensive background and theory regarding the fundamental methodology of the genetic algorithm can be found in [2] and [3].

The aim of this research is to illustrate the use of domain specific knowledge to enhance the genetic algorithm search through the minimization of computation time for solution convergence. Domain specific knowledge has been introduced into the genetic algorithm in the form of a two-phase rule approach to enhance both topological and structural optimization problems as demonstrated by Webb, *et al.* [4] and [5].

This study determines the appropriate path sequence to effectively negotiate a series of mazes within this prescribed research. Similarly to this optimization initiative, the use of domain specific knowledge was demonstrated by Alobaidi, *et al.* [6] to determine the optimal travel path sequences for the Traveling Salesman problem through the use of a rule based genetic optimization algorithm. Overall, the incorporation of a rule based enhancement to the genetic algorithm can be introduced within a variety of methods which includes a phased based rule encoding scheme as proposed by Sandgren *et al.* [7]. Phase one mimics the formulation of a traditional genetic algorithm string; however the second phase utilizes rule based chromosome strings to determine what domain specific knowledge or rule executes to ultimately improve the outcome of phase one. This research exposes embedded rules within the traditional genetic algorithm to further illustrate an alternative means for utilizing domain specific knowledge while enhancing the traditional genetic algorithm process.

2. Traditional Genetic Optimization Approach

Traditional genetic optimization or scenario one began with a series of encoded strings which represents the framework of a maze under investigation. These encoded strings allow the genetic algorithm to determine whenever a move is selected (*i.e.* N, E, S, W) that the move is a legitimate move within the maze. A maze essentially is a predefined amount of space where a grid or lattice is formed which represents a series of rows and columns of square blocks. Each block formed within the lattice represents a "cell". The surrounding walls of user specified cells are removed and the formation of a maze becomes apparent. The strings within this input file are four characters long which represent the directions of north, east, south and west respectively. Each character within the string can either represent the values of "0" or "1" to appropriately define each cell. A value of "0" for the first character within the first row indicates that there is a north wall within the first cell of the grid. Conversely, a value of "1" for the first character within the first row indicates an absence of a north wall within the first cell of the lattice. Each cell is labeled throughout the maze where the first block or entrance of the maze is designated by (1, 1), meaning row one, column one, and is located at the lower left corner as illustrated by the example in **Figure 1**. The exit or last cell for the maze illustrated in **Figure 1** is numerically identified by (10, 10) which is the upper right corner of the maze. Strings within the initial maze input file are read in left to right and row by row beginning with the first cell block. All mazes investigated began with the starting cell of (1, 1) and exited at the last cell of the grid. These constant start and end locations were imposed since this generated the longest and most difficult search solution possible for the genetic algorithm. The objective was to locate the travel route which connected the start cell with the end cell. The function of the genetic algorithm was to generate an initial travel sequence string based upon travel directions of north, east, south, and west. The amount of characters which composed of a maximum travel sequence was equal to the number of cells generated by the implementation of a grid. Each character within the travel sequence is assigned a numeric value within a range of four possible values. **Table 1** provides the possible values for which a character within the travel sequence string could potentially represent. Additionally, **Table 2** illustrates the genetic algorithm parameters

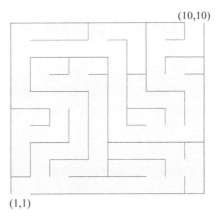

Figure 1. 10×10 grid maze.

Table 1. Character representation values for travel sequence string.

Character Value	Representation
1	North
2	East
3	South
4	West

Table 2. Genetic input parameters.

GENETIC INPUT PARAMETERS
Population Size = Maze Grid Size * 10
Probability of Mutation = 0.02
Number of Generations = (5 * Maze Grid Size) + Number of Best Generation Members to Pass to the Next Generation
Penalty Factor = 10
Multiplier of Penalty Factor = 2
Number of Best Generation Members to Pass to the Next Generation = 2
Number of Generations Between Penalty Factor Updates = 10

utilized in the problem formulation for all mazes considered.

A random population of travel sequences is generated and evaluated by the objective function as illustrated in Equation (1). If deemed a legitimate move within the maze, the objective function calculates the total distance of each travel sequence, however the final result is path and distance weighted as illustrated in Equation (2), for the directional moves within the travel sequence are theoretically legitimate, but actual distances may not be calculated in the event N-S or E-W moves are introduced into the travel sequence. Once evaluated by the objective function, the best travel sequences are selected and placed within a mating pool, where travel sequences are randomly paired and genetic chromosome cross over commences. Chromosome cross over is the process of mating two parent travel sequence strings by the random selection of a numbered character shared by both strings. Once a shared character between both strings is selected, each chromosome string exchanges characteristics the right of the selected gene until the end of both chromosome strings has been reached. Subsequent to genetic cross over, each offspring produced is evaluated by the objective function, where directional moves within the new travel sequence are only implemented if legitimate within the maze. Illegitimate moves within travel sequences are simply ignored by the objective function and the travel sequence string is reduced in total length. This process continues until a predetermined number of generations of offspring have been produced. Mutation, or the random alteration of genes of a parent travel sequence string within the mating pool occurs, however the probability is minimal. Mutation introduces randomness, which provides the design or decision chromosomes with characteristics normally unattainable subsequent to a number of generated offspring. Upon the completion of a user specified number of generations, the genetic algorithm has potentially created a travel sequence string which encompasses the total or partial path which unites both start and end cells.

Objective Function:

$$f(x) = \sqrt{\left(\left(x_{\text{actual}} - x_{\text{final}} \right)^2 + \left(y_{\text{actual}} - y_{\text{final}} \right)^2 \right)} \tag{1}$$

Weighted objective function $f(x)_{\text{Weighted}}$

$$f(x)_{\text{Weighted}} = W1 - W2 * \left(\sqrt{\left(\left(x_{\text{actual}} - x_{\text{final}} \right) + \left(y_{\text{actual}} - y_{\text{final}} \right)^2 \right)} - W3 * \left(npath - C \right) \right)$$
$$\tag{2}$$

where, $npath =$ total number of paths each cell move possesses that culminates the defined path.

x_{actual}, y_{actual}, x_{final}, & y_{final} are parameters which represent the start and end point locations of travel sequences for each maze considered which determine overall travel distance

$W1$, $W2$, & $W3$ are relevant weighting factors to balance out the outcome of the objective function with the number of moves required utilizing constant factor C. The use of a weighted objective function accounts for directional moves within the travel sequence; however actual distance values may not be calculated in the event N-S or E-W moves are introduced into the travel sequence

3. Genetic Optimization via Embedded Rules

Domain specific knowledge in the form of rules were embedded within scenario one. These rules are governed by each travel sequence and the travel sequence is controlled by the genetic algorithm.

The cells which compose of the maze are initially predefined by how many exits each cell possesses and if the cell possesses only one exit, information is provided to which direction the available exit is located (*i.e.* N, E, S or W). When a cell is located within the travel sequence and only one exit is available, the genetic code is provided with what direction out the cell possesses. With this information, a wall is created to block off the cell, creating a block, so that no future travel sequences may enter. All cells are updated with the creation of this new wall and the process continues whenever a travel sequence encounters a one exit cell. This prescribed embedded rule is attributed by prior knowledge acquired from Williams [8]. Additionally, when the objective function evaluates each move within a specific travel sequence, redundant moves are removed such as N-S and E-W, so that every move accepted creates an actual distance.

The implementation of rules within the objective function subroutine which eliminate redundant moves before being drawn is controlled by the genetic code, since the travel sequence is governed by the genetic algorithm and rules are applied as travel sequences are introduced to the embedded rules. This also holds true for walls created when travel sequences encounter a cell with only one exit. The rule for the implementation of a wall is only executed if the genetic code generates a travel sequence which leads to a cell with only one exit. Computation time for solving all mazes considered was minimal with the inclusion of embedded rules.

4. Results

Three mazes were investigated and solved by the use of both a traditional genetic algorithm and a genetic algorithm with embedded rules. Each maze scenario presented was programmed in Visual Basic [9]. Genetic algorithm parameters utilized in the formulation of the provided results are illustrated in **Table 3**. The mazes constructed were 10 × 10, 20 × 20, and 50 × 50 cell mazes, which demonstrated a gradual progression in maze complexity as each maze was examined and solved. Overall, the genetic algorithm which incorporated embedded rules was the most effective optimization approach. The injection of domain specific knowledge into a genetic algorithm significantly enhanced computation time and the quality of genetic offspring produced. Genetic results for both optimization approaches initially appear at the end of the second generation, for both optimization techniques generated new offspring travel sequence strings immediately following the construction of the initial random population. The generation of new offspring subsequent to the creation of an initial random population was implemented to immediately reduce any extraneous travel sequence strings from the random population to potentially improve genetic offspring and computation time. Lastly, graphical representations of objective function versus generation were constructed for each maze solving procedure considered.

Function evaluations considered are derived via Equation (3) below

$$\text{Function Evaluations} = \text{Population}_{\text{Size}} * \text{Generation}_{\text{Size}} \qquad (3)$$

5. Example One: 10 × 10 Cell Maze

Below illustrated in **Figure 2** is the initial 10 × 10 cell maze before the commencement of genetic optimization. Notice that the complexity of the maze is fairly straightforward, but results below confirm that a conventional genetic algorithm was unable to locate an acceptable solution.

5.1. Traditional Genetic Algorithm Result (Scenario One)

The traditional genetic algorithm result is shown below in **Figure 3**. Upon the

Table 3. Maze genetic parameters.

Maze Grid Size	Population Size	Generation Size	Function Evaluations
10 × 10	100	52	5200
20 × 20	200	102	20,400
50 × 50	500	252	126,000

Figure 2. 10 × 10 cell maze.

Figure 3. Genetic algorithm result.

completion of fifty two generations and an initial population size of one hundred, the genetic algorithm was unable to locate an acceptable solution. Population and generation sizes must be largely increased to potentially locate the maze solution. The objective function versus generation graph provided in **Figure 4** revealed an overall steady increase in objective function until generation forty five and remained constant throughout the remainder of the fifty two specified generations. An increase in these genetic input parameters would significantly hinder computation time, and would further reinforce the necessity to refine the genetic algorithm procedure. Theoretically, once a considerable number of generations of offspring have been produced an acceptable solution would be achieved. However, genetic input parameters were increased on several occasions, but an acceptable solution was still not acquired.

5.2. Genetic Algorithm with Embedded Rules Result (Scenario Two)

Below illustrated in **Figure 5** is the final result of the 10 × 10 cell maze which was solved by the use of a genetic algorithm with embedded domain specific

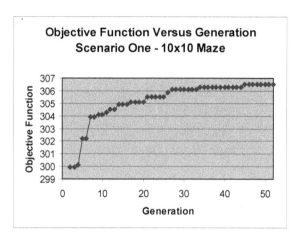

Figure 4. Objective function versus generation.

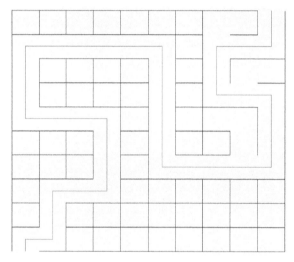

Figure 5. Embedded rules final result.

knowledge. Genetic input parameters were identical to the traditional genetic optimization result illustrated in **Figure 3**. An examination of **Figure 5** revealed that not all travel paths were blocked, which clearly indicated for even the least complex of mazes that the embedded rules are travel sequence dependent, where each travel sequence is controlled by the genetic algorithm. Furthermore, the objective function versus generation graph illustrated in **Figure 6** revealed that a solution was found upon the conclusion of the second generation of offspring produced. In comparison to **Figure 4**, the traditional genetic optimization approach spawned fifty two generations of offspring, yet was incapable of generating an acceptable solution. Clearly this approach is the optimal method for solving this class of problems.

6. Example Two: 20 × 20 Cell Maze

Figure 7 represents the 20 × 20 cell maze before genetic optimization has commenced. In comparison to the previously illustrated 10 × 10 maze, the complexity has significantly increased, which requires larger genetic input parameters for

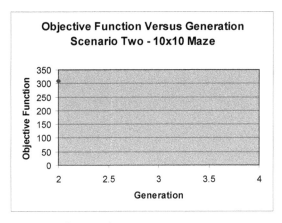

Figure 6. Objective function versus generation.

Figure 7. 20 × 20 cell maze.

the traditional genetic algorithm technique, for the genetic algorithm is a global search method based upon an evolutionary approach.

6.1. Traditional Genetic Algorithm Result (Scenario One)

Illustrated within **Figure 8** is the traditional genetic algorithm result. Genetic input parameters consisted of a population size of two hundred with one hundred-two generations. Notice that an acceptable solution was unable to be located upon the conclusion of one hundred-two generations. Population and generation genetic input parameters were manipulated on several instances but, an acceptable solution remained unachievable.

An examination of **Figure 9** revealed a steady increase in objective function over a period of eighty generations, however inactivity was apparent throughout the remaining twenty two generations.

6.2. Genetic Algorithm with Embedded Rules Result (Scenario Two)

The illustration within **Figure 10** represents the final result which utilized the

Figure 8. Genetic algorithm result.

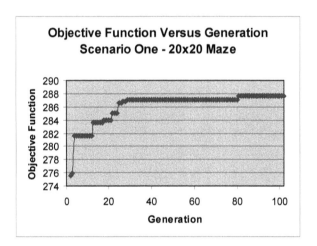

Figure 9. Objective function versus generation.

Figure 10. Embedded rules final result.

genetic algorithm with an embedded rules approach applied to the 20×20 cell maze. Notice that all routes were not blocked, for the genetic algorithm found the optimal path without traveling to every available location, which further reinforced that the rules embedded are executed based upon travel sequences controlled by the genetic algorithm. **Figure 11** revealed that a solution was found within the second generation of offspring produced. A comparison with the result illustrated in **Figure 8** showed that the traditional genetic algorithm solution generated a final result which was incomplete, and furthermore failed to locate the correct travel path concluding one hundred-two generations of offspring. Failure to locate the correct travel path upon the conclusion of the conventional genetic algorithm method further reinforces the necessity of a rule based scenario to enhance the traditional genetic algorithm. Potentially large phase two population and generation sizes would be considered to further refine this conventional genetic algorithm result, for a vast variety of rule sequences must be generated to correct the inadequately generated travel path.

7. Example Three: 50 × 50 Cell Maze

The final maze investigated consisted of a 50×50 cell maze [10]. This maze incorporated the highest level of complexity among the mazes previously examined. Twenty five hundred cell blocks were manipulated in the formation of the maze illustrated below in **Figure 12**. The ability to utilize domain specific knowledge within a genetic algorithm to enhance solution time and the quality of offspring generated, while demonstrating that an acceptable solution can be located at this level of complexity, settles any disputes with regard to the need for rules within a genetic algorithm.

7.1. Traditional Genetic Algorithm Result (Scenario One)

The traditional genetic algorithm approach was unable to locate an acceptable solution shown in **Figure 13** however unlike the 20×20 cell maze traditional

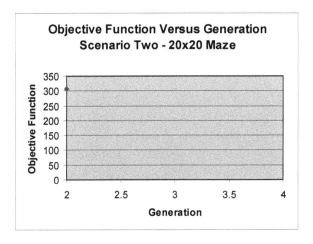

Figure 11. Objective function versus generation.

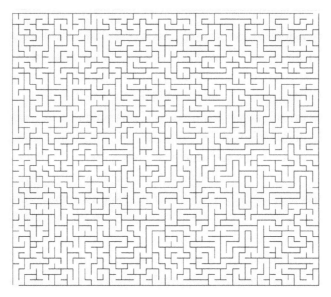

Figure 12. 50 × 50 cell maze.

Figure 13. Genetic algorithm result.

genetic algorithm result; the genetic algorithm was able to locate a portion of the optimal path. Genetic input parameters consisted of a population size of five hundred and a generation size of two hundred fifty-two. Since an acceptable portion of the path was located, an increase in genetic input parameters would potentially improve the probability of locating a more acceptable solution in comparison to the previous 20 × 20 and 10 × 10 maze results. Surprisingly, the conventional genetic algorithm procedure failed to locate the complete travel path for each maze considered.

An examination of **Figure 14** shows a steady but minimal increase in objective function over a period of one hundred eighty-seven generations, yet remained inactive throughout the remaining sixty five generations.

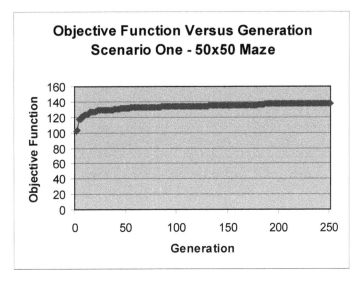

Figure 14. Objective function versus generation.

7.2. Genetic Algorithm with Embedded Rules Result (Scenario Two)

The genetic algorithm which incorporated embedded rules was utilized to solve the 50 × 50 cell maze. Genetic input parameters remained identical to its counterpart. This optimization approach effectively solved the maze illustrated in **Figure 15**. Similar to previous results, this optimization approach successfully located the maze exit without traveling to every possible location within the maze, but only by travel sequences created by the genetic algorithm. The objective function versus generation graph within **Figure 16** revealed that the final solution was located upon the completion of four generations of offspring. A comparison with **Figure 14** clearly indicates that the incorporation of embedded rules significantly decreases computation time and enhances the quality of genetic offspring produced, since only four generations of offspring were required to achieve a solution, where two hundred fifty-two generations were completed using a traditional genetic algorithm approach, yet a complete solution remained unattainable.

8. Concluding Remarks

The implementation of embedded rules within a genetic algorithm based upon domain specific knowledge significantly decreases computation time and enhances the quality of offspring produced during each generation. A complete and accurate solution was located for all mazes investigated which employed the use of domain specific knowledge within a conventional genetic algorithm. The traditional genetic algorithm approach failed to solve each maze provided, while subjected up to extensively larger generations than its counterpart approach. Lastly, the genetic algorithm with embedded rules required only 5% of the solution time for all mazes considered in comparison to the traditional genetic algorithm

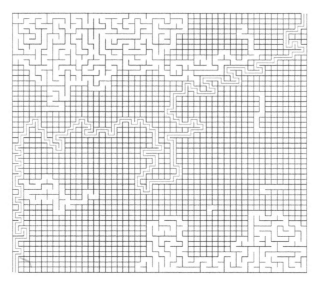

Figure 15. Embedded rules result.

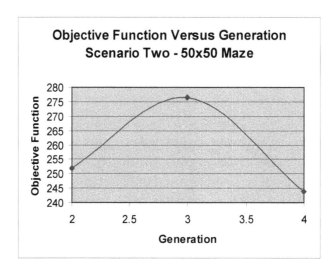

Figure 16. Objective function versus generation.

to locate an acceptable solution which effectively solved each maze.

References

[1]   Alobaidi, W., Sandgren, E. and Alkuam, E. (2017) Decision Support through Intelligent Agent Based Simulation and Multiple Goal Based Evolutionary Optimization. *Intelligent Information Management*, **9**, 97-113. https://doi.org/10.4236/iim.2017.93005

[2]   Goldberg, D.E. (1989) Genetic Algorithms in Search, Optimization and Machine Learning. Addison-Wesley, Reading, MA.

[3]   Gen, M. and Cheng, R. (1997) Genetic Algorithms & Engineering Design. John Wiley & Sons, Inc., New York.

[4]   Webb, D., Liu, Q., Alobaidi, W. and Sandgren, E. (2017) Topological Design via a Rule Based Genetic Optimization Algorithm. *American Journal of Computational Mathematics*, **7**, 291-320. https://doi.org/10.4236/ajcm.2017.73023

[5]   Webb, D., Alobaidi, W. and Sandgren, E. (2017) Structural Design via Genetic Op-
      timization. *Modern Mechanical Engineering*, **7**, 73-90.
      https://doi.org/10.4236/mme.2017.73006

[6]   Alobaidi, W., Webb, D. and Sandgren, E. (2017) A Rule Based Evolutionary Opti-
      mization Approach for the Traveling Salesman Problem. *Intelligent Information
      Management*, **9**, 115-132. https://doi.org/10.4236/iim.2017.94006

[7]   Sandgren, E., Webb, D. and Pedersen, J.B. (n.d.) A Rule Based Evolutionary Algo-
      rithm for Intelligent Decision Support.

[8]   Williams, S. (2004) Maze Solving. http://www.undu.com/Articles/000229a.html

[9]   Microsoft Corporation (1998) Microsoft Visual Basic Version 6.0.

[10] Mazes (2004). http://www.mazes.org.uk/

4

Predicting Optimal Trading Actions using a Genetic Algorithm and Ensemble Method

Kazuma Kuroda

Data Marketing Laboratory, Tokyo, Japan
Email: mokuzenshingo@me.com

Abstract

Machine learning has been applied to the foreign exchange market for algorithmic trading. However, the selection of trading algorithms is a difficult problem. In this work, an approach that combines trading agents is designed. In the proposed approach, an artificial neural network is used to predict the optimum actions of each agent for USD/JPY currency pairs. The agents are trained using a genetic algorithm and are then combined using an ensemble method. We compare the performance of the combined agent to the average performance of many agents. Simulation results show that the total return is better when the combined agent is used.

Keywords

Artificial Intelligence, Ensemble Learning, Genetic Algorithms, Neural Networks, FOREX

1. Introduction

The Foreign Exchange Market (FOREX) has become complex due to the introduction of floating exchange rates and the expansion of global trading markets. Due to this complexity, predicting future prices and designing trading algorithms have been considered as challenging problems. Recently, researchers have started to design trading algorithms.

Artificial neural networks (ANN) are often used in prediction tasks and system modeling. ANNs use nonlinear functions; thus, they are robust in complex and dynamic environments such as the FOREX [1] [2]. Generally, ANNs are trained using the back-propagation algorithm. However, the back-propagation algorithm may become stuck in a local minimum. Therefore, previous studies [3] [4] have used genetic algorithms (GA) to avoid this problem because such algorithms can search global optimum solutions.

GAs are heuristic algorithms based on Darwinian evolution and are frequently used to find optimum solutions. In the case of a trading algorithm, GAs have been used to determine the optimum trading model parameters, such as the connection weights of the ANN, feature selection, and the settlement width (difference between the closing price of the position and the price at the time of settlement) [5] [6]. In this context, a GA can provide a variety of agents with different trading strategies.

Here, the problem lies with the selection of the agent. Although the best agent with training data is obtained, the results are often incorrect with test data. A previous study [3] demonstrated that the average performance of different agents outperformed the best agent in the training data. However, from an asset efficiency perspective, this approach is impractical because it must hold many trading positions.

Ensemble methods combine the outputs of base models using a majority vote mechanism to create a single output [7]. Many studies have demonstrated that ensemble methods show superior performance for a variety of problems, such as image classification [8] and facial recognition [9].

In this study, we employed an ensemble method to combine trading agents. In the proposed method, we begin by constructing multiple agents. Here, an ANN and conditional equations are used in the agents' decision mechanisms. A GA is used to train the connection weights of the networks, the period used to calculate technical indicators, and the settlement width. Next, we combine the output of the trained agents using a majority vote mechanism. We performed tests to determine whether the combined agent outperforms the average performance of many agents.

The remainder of this paper is organized as follows. A detailed description of the algorithm used to predict optimum trading actions is given in Section 2, and Section 3 discusses the performance of the proposed approach. Conclusions are given in Section 4.

2. Algorithm to Predict Optimum Actions

The procedure to obtain the combined agent is divided into two steps. The first step is construction of the base models, and the second step is combining the outputs of the base models. In this section, we describe these processes in detail.

2.1. Construction of Base Models

Trading agents are constructed by the training architecture shown in **Figure 1**. Here, each agent comprises two modules, *i.e.*, signal and strategy modules. The signal module uses price data as input and generates a signal (Long, Short, or Do-nothing) evaluated market condition as output, which we refer to as the *market signal*. The strategy module determines the trading action from the *market signal*, the trading position, and past prices. The GA calculates the fitness

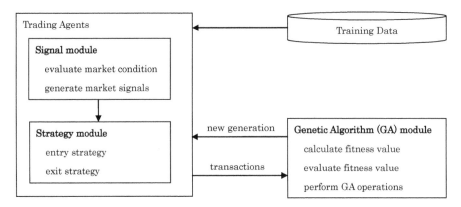

Figure 1. Architecture to train trading agents.

according to the trading action of the agent and evolves the agents using this fitness value.

1) Signal Module

The ANN is used to evaluate market conditions and generate the *market signal*, and the network comprises four input neurons. The inputs to these neurons are three technical indicators and bias. The networks contain six hidden units, where the activation function of all hidden units is a sigmoid function. The output neurons of the networks consist of three, each neurons corresponding to the *market signal*. The GA optimizes the connection weights from the input layer to the output layer.

The following three technical indicators, which are calculated from the price data, are used as input to the networks. In addition, the GA optimizes the period used to calculate the technical indicators. The relative strength indicator (RSI) is used to determine when the market is over-bought or over-sold [10] and is given by the following equation:

$$\text{RSI} = 100 - (100/1 + \text{RS}),$$

where RS is the average gain over *n* hours divided by the average loss over *n* hours. The average directional index (ADX) describes when a market is trending without considering trend direction [11]. Note that an increasing ADX value represents the trend strength. To quantify the trend strength, we use diffADX, which is given by the following equation:

$$\text{diffADX}_t = \text{ADX}_t - \text{ADX}_{t-1},$$

where diffADX_t is the trend strength for time step t and ADX_t is the ADX for time step t. The directional movement index comprises two lines, *i.e.*, plus directional movement (DM+) and minus directional movement (DM−), and defines the trend direction [11]. DM+ represents an upward trend direction, and DM− represents a downward trend direction. For simplicity, we use uniDMI, which is given as follows:

$$\text{uniDMI}_t = \text{DM}+_t - \text{DM}-_t,$$

where uniDMI_t is the trend direction for time step t, $\text{DM}+_t$ is the DM+ for time step t, and DM$-_t$ is the DM$-$ for time step t.

2) Strategy Module

The strategy module determines the trading action according to the following rules. Note that the trading action of time step t is determined by the data point of time step $t - 1$. If an agent does not hold a trading position, then the agent takes a position according to the *market signal*. If an agent holds a long position, then the trading action is determined using the following rules:

$$\text{Close-Out} = \text{currentHigh} > \text{positionClose} + \omega_1 \times \text{Volatility};$$

$$\text{currentLow} < \text{positionClose} - \omega_2 \times \text{Volatility};$$

$$\text{The } market \ signal \text{ is Short}$$

$$\text{Do-Nothing} = \text{otherwise}$$

where current High and current Low are the high and low prices among the data points, respectively, position Close is the closing price of the position, and Volatility is the standard deviation of the closing price over the last seven hours. ω_1 and ω_2 are parameters used to optimize the settlement width. If an agent holds a short position, then the trading action is determined using the following rules:

$$\text{Close-Out} = \text{currentLow} < \text{positionClose} - \omega_3 \times \text{Volatility};$$

$$\text{currentHigh} > \text{positionClose} + \omega_4 \times \text{Volatility};$$

$$\text{The } market \ signal \text{ is Long}$$

$$\text{Do-Nothing} = \text{otherwise}$$

where ω_3 and ω_4 are parameters used to optimize the settlement width.

3) Genetic Algorithm

The GA evaluates the fitness and evolves the trading agents according to the fitness value. Here, the fitness is the total return calculated using raw prices. As mentioned previously, the GA evolves the connection weights of the ANN, the period used to calculate technical indicators, and the settlement width. The evolutionary process is as follows.

1) Randomly initialize a population of agents.

2) Provide training data to each agent and obtain the trading action for each time step.

3) Trade according to the trading action and observe the returns of each time step.

4) Calculate the fitness from the returns of each time step at the end of the training data.

5) Evaluate each agent in the population according to their fitness and select parents for new agents.

6) Create new agents based on the selected parents using crossover and mutation operators.

7) If the termination condition is satisfied, this process is terminated; otherwise, return to step 2.

2.2. Combined Base Models

The outputs of the trained agents are combined by majority vote to create a single output. For each time step, the trained agents generate trading actions on the new data point and the closing price of the position as input. Then, the most frequently output trading actions are taken as the output of the combined agent.

3. Experiment and Results

In this section, we apply the proposed ensemble approach to USD/JPY currency pairs to test whether the combined agent outperforms the average performance of many agents. Here, the return is JPY-based. The training algorithm was run 500 times on the training data, and the resulting best agents for each generation were added to the agent pool. We used a population with 500 individuals over 500 generations. Then, to address the overtraining problem, the result obtained by applying validation data to the agent in the agent pool was used to select the generation to be tested. We obtained 500 agents as a result. Those agents were then used to compare the performance of the combined agent and the average of the agents on the test data.

3.1. Data Collection

The agents were trained, validated, and tested using USD/JPY hourly data. Each data point included the opening and closing price and the high and low price for each hour interval. The original training data consisted of 30115 samples for the period 03/01/2010 9:00 pm to 31/12/2014 9:00 pm. Training was performed with the training data, which was the original training data inverted and added [12]. The validation data comprised 6097 samples for the period 01/01/2015 9:00 pm to 31/12/2015 10:00 pm. The test data comprised 9263 samples for the period 04/01/2016 12:00 am to 01/07/2017 1:00 am.

3.2. Results

The results of training and validation for each generation are shown in **Figure 2**. As can be seen, a peak was reached near 200 generations for both the training and validation data. In addition, the results were stable after 200 generations. After 200 generations, the best generation was generation 437 on the validation data, and this generation was chosen for testing.

The statistics of the tested agents are summarized in **Table 1**, and the cumulative returns are shown in **Figure 3**. In **Table 1**, the Total Return column is the sum of all returns of agents, the Win rate column is the percentage of transactions with positive returns, and the Trades column is the number of closed positions. The results show that the performance of the ensemble approach is superior to the approach using the average performance of many agents.

4. Conclusion

We have designed the ensemble approach that combines trading agents. In the

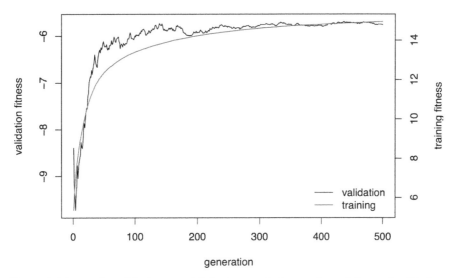

Figure 2. Mean value of the best models in the population on the training and validation data per year.

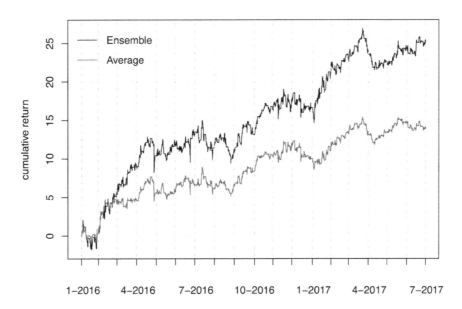

Figure 3. Comparison of cumulative return between the combined agent (Ensemble) and the average of agents (Average).

Table 1. Statistics of tested agents (Ensemble: results of combined agents; Average: mean value of tested agents).

	Total return	Win rate	Trades
Ensemble	25.0	54.7%	2331
Average	13.8	54.1%	1880

proposed method, an ANN is used to predict the optimum actions of trading agents for USD/JPY currency pairs. These agents are trained using a GA and then are combined using an ensemble method. We performed tests to determine whether the combined agent outperforms the average performance of many agents. The results show that the total return is better when the ensemble method is used. In addition, the ensemble approach takes only a single position; thus, it is more asset efficient than approaches that use the average performance of many agents. In conclusion, the proposed ensemble approach works as an alternative to using the average performance of many agents.

References

[1] Kamruzzaman, J. and Sarker, R. (2004) ANN-Based Forecasting of Foreign Currency Exchange Rates. *Neural Information Processing*, **3**, 49-58.

[2] Vincenzo, P., Vitoantonio, B. and Michele, A. (2011) An Artificial Neural Network Model to Forecast Exchange Rates. *Journal of Intelligent Learning Systems and Applications*, **3**, 57-69. https://doi.org/10.4236/jilsa.2011.32008

[3] Yaman, A., Stephen, L. and Izidor, G. (2014) Evolutionary Algorithm Based Approach for Modeling Autonomously Trading Agents. *Intelligent Information Management*, **6**, 45-54. https://doi.org/10.4236/iim.2014.62007

[4] Kenneth, O.S. and Risto, M. (2004) Competitive Coevolution through Evolutionary Complexification. *Journal of Artificial Intelligence Research*, **21**, 63-100.

[5] Hirabayashi, A., Claus, A. and Iba, H. (2009) Optimization of the Trading Rule in Foreign Exchange Using Genetic Algorithm. *GECCO* '09 *Proceedings of the 11th Annual Conference on Genetic and Evolutionary Computation*, Montreal, 8-12 July 2009, 1529-1536. https://doi.org/10.1145/1569901.1570106

[6] Ibrahim, A.E.M. (2014) Evolutionary Approach to Forex Expert Advisor Generation. *Intelligent Information Management*, **6**, 129-141. https://doi.org/10.4236/iim.2014.63014

[7] Witten, I. and Frank, E. (2005) Data Mining: Practical Machine Learning Tools and Techniques. 2nd Edition, Morgan Kaufmann, San Francisco.

[8] Silwattananusarn, T., Kanarkard, W. and Tuamsuk, K. (2016) Enhanced Classification Accuracy for Cardiotocogram Data with Ensemble Feature Selection and Classifier Ensemble. *Journal of Computer and Communications*, **4**, 20-35. https://doi.org/10.4236/jcc.2016.44003

[9] El Khiyari, H. and Wechsler, H. (2016) Face Recognition across Time Lapse Using Convolutional Neural Networks. *Journal of Information Security*, **7**, 141-151. https://doi.org/10.4236/jis.2016.73010

[10] Murphy, Jr. J.E. (1994) Stock Market Probability: Using Statistics to Predict and Optimize Investment Outcomes. Revised Edition, Irwin.

[11] Sheimo, M.D. (1998) Cashing in on the Dow: Using Dow Theory to Trade and Determine Trends in Today's Markets. CRC Press, Boca Raton.

[12] Badarch, T., Shu, L. and Iba, H. (2011) A Trading Method in FX Using Evolutionary Algorithms: Extensions Based on Reverse Trend and Settlement Timing. *GECCO* '11 *Proceedings of the 13th Annual Conference Companion on Genetic and Evolutionary Computation*, Dublin, 12-16 July 2011, 139-140.

5

Business Process Analysis and Simulation: The Contact Center of a Public Health and Social Information Office

Antonio Di Leva[1], Emilio Sulis[1], Manuela Vinai[2]

[1]Department of Informatics, University of Torino, Torino, Italy
[2]QRS SocCoop—Consorzio Sociale Il Filo da Tessere, Biella, Italy
Email: dileva|sulis@di.unito.it, vinai@qrsonline.it

Abstract

This article proposes a framework, called BP-M* which includes: 1) a methodology to analyze, engineer, restructure and implement business processes, and 2) a process model that extends the process diagram with the specification of resources that execute the process activities, allocation policies, schedules, times of activities, management of queues in input to the activities and workloads so that the same model can be simulated by a discrete event simulator. The BP-M* framework has been applied to a real case study, a public Contact Center which provides different typologies of answers to users' requests. The simulation allows to study different system operating scenarios ("What-If" analysis) providing useful information for analysts to evaluate restructuring actions.

Keywords

Business Process Management, Public Health and Social Services Administration, Contact Center analysis, Discrete Event Simulation

1. Introduction

In the context of Business Process Management (BPM) [1], a large attention has been given to events, activities and decisions dealing with the processes of an organization.

Several techniques have been developed in the analysis of the actual (As-Is) situation of organization's processes, as well as in the re-engineering phase that leads to restructured (To-Be) processes. Among the existing techniques, computer-based Discrete Event Simulation (DES) [2] is one of the most used analysis approach.

Several research areas have already used simulation techniques, *i.e.*, Computational Social Science [3], Geography [4] or Sociology [5]. Although different simulation techniques have been involved in business processes, their application in the field of BPM has not yet been developed as it deserves [6]. Nevertheless, planning, management and decision-making would greatly benefit from the analysis of the outcomes of simulated scenarios. Simulation results allow to detect inefficiencies, bottlenecks, constraints, and risks as well as to estimate the performance of the system when process modifications, as new strategies or an increase of the workload, have to be applied.

Nowadays, the public sector is increasingly required to provide better services at lower cost. In this article, we deal with the Contact Center of a public social and welfare center. Our work includes the following three points of interest:

1) Framework: a general and repeatable methodological framework has been developed and applied to real cases. It includes both traditional analysis techniques (such as SIPOC diagrams) and recent techniques such as "What-If" analysis by scenario simulation.

2) Real Data: the simulation model was developed based on a careful statistical analysis of real data for the process under consideration.

3) Performance indicators: the proposed approach allows treating simultaneously several different process indicators, such as cycle times, resource utilization, queues (bottlenecks), costs and so on.

In the following section, we introduce a review of related works on BPM and simulations studies, including some applications (Section 2). Section 3 describes the methodological framework, while Section 4 details the construction of the As-Is model for the case study used in this article. Section 5 describes the definition of the scenarios used to specify possible evolutions of the As-Is model and their analysis using a discrete event simulator. Finally, we draw some concluding remarks in Section 6.

2. Related Works

The analysis of business processes usually refers to methods, techniques, and software used to support the management of an organization [1]. Recently, a large attention involves the procedures concerning design, control, and analysis of operational tasks regarding humans, documents, organizations, or applications [1].

The adoption of computer-based simulations to business process analysis and modeling was first applied in industrial re-engineering [7] [8]. In the public sector, some studies modeled public policies [9], services [10], public administration processes [11], political decision-making [12], as well as care processes in the medical field [13].

Simulations was also applied to call centers, which focus on phone-calls [14] [15], and to contact centers, dealing with more complex cases of user requests

[16].

In addition to statistical approaches (*i.e.*, staff-planning [17], resources optimization [18], queueing modeling [19]), Discrete Event Simulations emerged as an alternative method to model contact center [17] and, more recently, also Agent-Based modeling techniques have been applied [20] [21].

In recent works, computer-based Decision Support Systems provided effective and efficient workforce planning and performance reporting in call centers [22]. In a similar study, a flexible business process modeling, simulation and re- engineering (BPMSR) approach was presented [23]. Scenario analysis (or "What-If" analysis) has been applied to explore different options for restructuring an existing process [24] before any change is effectively made.

3. The BP-M* Framework

This section introduces our methodological framework that is based on the BP-M* Methodology and the BP-M* Process Model.

3.1. The BP-M* Methodology

The BP-M* Methodology has been briefly described in [25] and consists of four phases:

1) Context Analysis: the context analysis phase aims to fix the overall strategic scenario of the enterprise and to determine the organizational components that will be investigated.

2) Functional Analysis and Process Engineering: the initial purpose of this phase is the determination of the activities that are carried out in the corporate functions involved in the process and of the causal relationships existing among them. The process is then reconstructed starting from external input/output events and/or objects: this gives the Process Diagram (sometimes referred to as a process map or flowchart). The process model must therefore be validated with stakeholders involved in the process, using animation and simulation of its specification, obtaining the so called As-Is model. This model provides managers and engineers with a careful specification of the enterprise as it stands, out of which they can make: a) a good assessment of its status and b) an accurate estimation of available capabilities.

3) Process Diagnosis and Reorganization: the purpose of this phase is to trace back from the problems highlighted in the previous phase to possible solutions to be taken in order to restructure the As-Is model generating in this way the new To-Be version.

4) Information System and Workflow Implementation: when the To-Be model has been approved, it has to be transmitted to engineers for implementation. In the BP-M* methodology, two implementation aspects are considered: 1) the specification of the Information System environment, and 2) the specification of the Workflow execution environment.

Because the aim of this paper is the analysis of a real process, we will deal primarily with Phase 2 of the BP-M* methodology, other phases will not be discussed.

In the following, we describe the specification model used in the methodology.

3.2. The BP-M* Process Model

In the BP-M* approach, process activities do their job by working on **transactions**. A transaction is an object that flows through the process and represents such things as an order form in an order entry process, a patient which follows a surgical procedure, or a component in a manufacturing line.

The BP-M* Process Model integrates the process diagram with a description of how each activity deals with a transaction, how much time it takes and what are the necessary resources. The basic elements of the model are:

- **Activities**. Activities take time to deal with a transaction and one of the primary objectives of a process modeling and simulation approach is to measure times and costs related to the process. In the BP-M*Process Model it is possible to define the period of time (duration) that each activity takes to deal with a transaction and to assign costs both to activities and to the resources used at the activities.

- **Resources**. A resource is a person, machinery or an organizational asset used to process a transaction. In the BP-M* Process Model you can specify the amount of resources available, the behavior of resources, work schedules, and the allocation of resources to activities. When multiple transactions are processed, activities can contend for resources.

- **Times and Costs**. The most common objectives of the process modeling and simulation tasks are to measure the time a process takes to be executed and to determine process and transaction costs. In a simulation, time is usually measured as the time required for a transaction to flow through a process, from an initial event to a final event which is usually referred to as cycle time. A cycle time typically includes the time required for each activity to deal with a transaction, and the time a transaction spends waiting in a queue to enter an activity or waiting for a necessary resource to become available. During a simulation, costs are accumulated and reported by transaction, by activity, and by resource.

Time and cost are closely related and you may find yourself trading one off for the other. For example, if you want to reduce processing time, you may add additional resources, but this may have the effect of increasing processing cost. On the other hand, you may reduce cost by reducing resources, but this may increase processing time. One of the great benefits of process simulation is to easily make this trade-offs and determine their impacts.

The new concepts that have been introduced to better characterize the process will be illustrated best during the analysis of the following case study.

4. The SPUN Case Study

Our case study is related to a public Contact Center (CC), called SPUN, which furnishes health and social information to citizens of an urban area of about 50,000 inhabitants in the northern Italy (the name SPUN is the acronym of Italian words "Sportello Unico", which means Central Information desk). The existing wide spectrum of social and health agencies available to citizens provides many and very different benefits to peoples' well-being, such as services, subsidies, incentives, facilitation or discounts. Sometimes, it is difficult for users to correctly address their needs, often involving different agencies at the same time.

The needs of users can range from very simple cases (such as the opening hours of a certain service) to more complex cases involving different public agencies, as well as the knowledge of rights and laws that are often difficult to access by people.

After several interviews with manager and operators of the office (Phase 1 of the BP-M* methodology), we documented the core aspects of the process in a SIPOC diagram. A SIPOC (Suppliers, Inputs, Process, Outputs and Customers) diagram is a high-level overview of a process that is used in different approaches to process improvement, such as the Six Sigma methodology [26]. In our case, the SIPOC diagram is detailed in **Figure** 1.

Suppliers are the users of the service, posing as input a request by calling the CC desk. Once the request is received, operators have to establish its type. For simple cases [41%], they directly answer to the call. In complex cases [59%], operators must obtain the necessary information by consulting manuals or other external agencies. The answer to the user's request is the output object of the process that will be provided to the user who made the request. We analyzed real data about the functioning of the service in last five years. In particular, to be closer on today's functioning, we focused on data about the type of contacts and the type of requests for the year 2016.

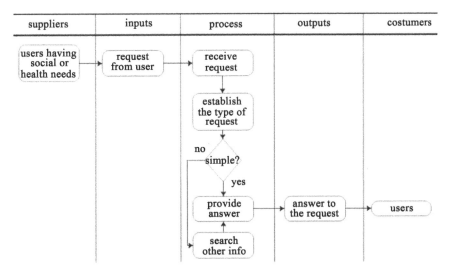

Figure 1. SIPOC diagram of the SPUN contact center.

First the type of contacts mostly concern phone calls from citizens, but contacts by operators of other organizations and agencies are also relevant. The direct access to the SPUN office by citizens is another important way to ask information, while the e-mail requests are of little importance, even if we notice an interesting increment in the last two years (see **Table 1**).

The argument of requests regards in majority Home care and Economic benefits, and this parameter is important because it is linked to the time that the operator spends to respond. For example, **Table 2** shows the arguments of the requests and the average time used by the operator to communicate and explain the answer.

This type of generic analysis provides a first insight for managers on the operation of the Contact Center service.

According to the Phase 2 of the BP-M* methodology, activities, events and decision points of the CC process, and the causal relationships that exist among them were analyzed. Using the Business Process Modeling and Notation (BPMN) language [27] the CC process diagram is illustrated in **Figure 2**. The diagram has been designed with the iGrafx Process 2015 [28] tool that supports the latest version of the BPMN language (BPMN2.0).

Table 1. Typology of contacts in the year 2016: number N of requests and percentage.

Contacts	N. of requests	%
Phone calls	1301	46.8
Direct access	702	25.3
Email	22	0.8
Other organizations	754	27.0
Total	2779	100

Table 2. Arguments of requests, count, percentage and average estimated duration (minutes).

Arguments of requests	Count	%	Duration
Economic benefits	639	23.0	15
Home care	636	22.9	20
Social information	502	18.1	5
Healt information	307	11.0	5
Residential care	292	10.5	15
Disability	149	5.4	20
Support	119	4.3	20
Work and training	67	2.4	10
Housing	68	2.4	5
Total	2779	100	

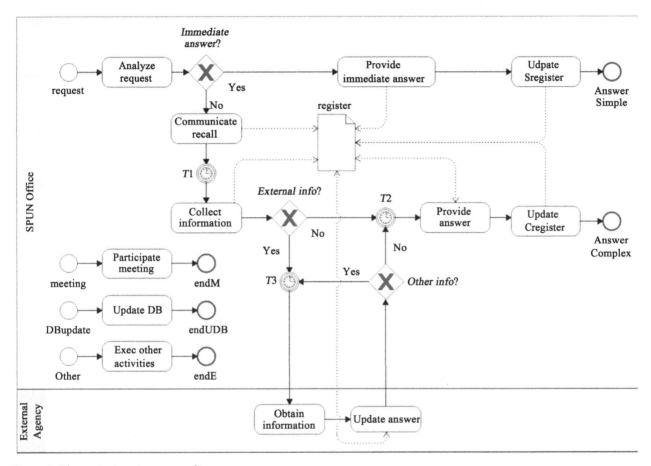

Figure 2. The contact center process diagram.

The diagram includes:

- Four concurrent **processes**, the *CC* process and three *Back-office* processes.
- Each process has an **initial event** (respectively, *request, meeting, DB update* and *Other*) and a **final event** (respectively, *answer, end M, end UDB* and *end E*).
- Two **lanes**, *SPUN Office* and *External Agency*, which contain **activities** (rectangles with rounded corners) and **gateways** (diamonds).
- Three **timer events**, T1, T2 and T3, representing a delay when operators take over the processing of the request as soon as possible.
- An **artifact**, *register*, which represents a set of tables containing data on (simple and complex) requests and answers.

    Process activities can be described as follows.

- *Analyze request.* In this task the operator must decide whether the request is simple (the answer is known) or complex.
- *Provide immediate answer.* When the answer is known, it must be provided to the client and then the operator updates the table of simple answers (*Update Sregister* activity).
- *Communicate recall.* When the operator is not able to give an immediate response, the customer must be informed that there will be a recall until full in-

formation has not been recovered.

- *Collect information.* The operator searches for the correct answer in the previous answers table and has to decide whether other organizations must be consulted.
- *Provide answer.* When the answer is complete, it must be provided to the client and then the operator updates the table of complex answers (*Update Cregister* activity).
- *Obtain information.* If the CC tables do not contain the required information, the operator will try to obtain the answer asking to other organizations or public agencies, and then update the answer table (*Update answer* activity).

The analysis of historical CC data has also allowed us to quantify the decision points (or gateways) of the process. In particular, the following gateways have been identified:

- *Immediate answer?* Simple requests are immediately solved (and follow the Yes [41%] branch), while difficult ones (No [59%] branch) have to be processed in a more detailed manner.
- *External info?* Several requests can be solved only by information existing in the CC internal tables (No [33%] branch), the other have to be solved with (at least) one external consultation (Yes [67%] branch).
- *Other info?* A small percentage of requests require the consultation of more agencies (Yes [10%] branch), the other requests (No [90%] branch) do not require further investigation.

Back-office activities: Operators are engaged in other activities not directly related to customers, such as periodic updates of the database (*Update DB*) as well as meetings with stakeholders (*Participate meetings*) or the participation in other activities of the SPUN center (*Exec other activities*).

These activities can be represented as concurrent processes that operate in parallel to the main one and use the same resources.

5. Simulation and What-If Analysis

The simulation environment for the BP-M* Process Model is based on the iGrafx Process2015 tool which is very suitable for process mapping and simulation modeling in business process management projects. It not only allows to specify the process diagram, but also the extensions for the BPMN language required in the BP-M* Process Model can be taken into account, as the definition of resources, their allocation policy, the duration of activities and so on (see Section 3.2).

5.1. As-Is Model Development

The statistical analysis of the CC context provided quantitative information for the assessment of the execution time for the various activities of the process. Oftentimes the duration of an activity depends essentially on the type of request that arrives at the Contact Center; this raises the need to distinguish different types of request and can be done by introducing some attributes for the transaction which represents the incoming request.

An **attribute** is a variable used to communicate information and manage the flow of transactions through a process. Some common uses of attributes are:

- Setting the duration of an activity based on the value of a transaction attribute.
- Controlling the flow of a specific transaction through a decision output.

In our case study, we specified four attributes: *contact, argument, agency,* and *needs*. For instance, according to **Table 1**, the attribute contact (which can take the values: phone, direct, email and org) refers to the different ways in which requests arrive at the Contact Center desk, including: 1) by phone calls [phone: 46.8%], 2) from people who present themselves directly to the office [direct: 25.3%], 3) by e-mail [email: 0.8%] and 4) from other organizations [org: 27.1%].

The data on the type of request is used by iGrafx Process2015 to introduce the transactions during the simulation of the CC process. In particular, the generator which corresponds to the initial event *request* introduces 11 transactions per day distributed in a random manner in the intervals defined by the timetable of **Figure 3**. For instance, three requests arrive between 9.00 am and 10.30 am, and so on.

For each transaction, the distribution function *setTypeOfContact* returns a value for the attribute *contact*. For example, the intervals in **Figure 4** specify that 46.8% of the time the function returns the value phone and so on.

The function *setTimeOfContact* (see **Figure 5**) is used to set the average duration of the activity *Analyze request* by mapping the set (phone, direct, email, org) into a set of time values.

Table 3 shows for each activity the temporal distribution that was used in the simulation.

Set Timetable

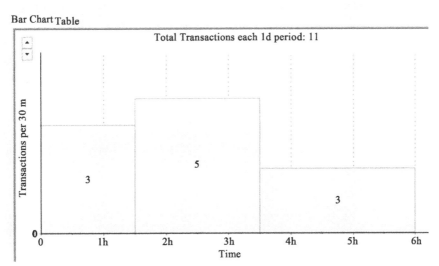

Figure 3. The dialog box to define the transaction distribution.

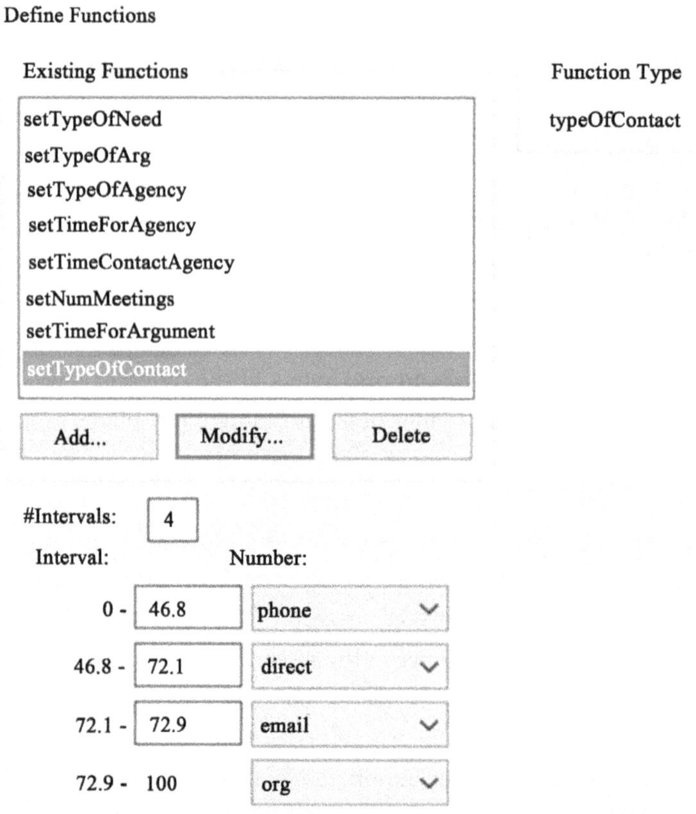

Define Functions

Existing Functions   Function Type

setTypeOfNeed   typeOfContact
setTypeOfArg
setTypeOfAgency
setTimeForAgency
setTimeContactAgency
setNumMeetings
setTimeForArgument
setTypeOfContact

Add...   Modify...   Delete

#Intervals: [4]

Interval: Number:

0 -   [46.8]   phone   ∨

46.8 - [72.1]   direct   ∨

72.1 - [72.9]   email   ∨

72.9 - 100   org   ∨

Figure 4. The dialog box to define the *setTypeOfContact* distribution function.

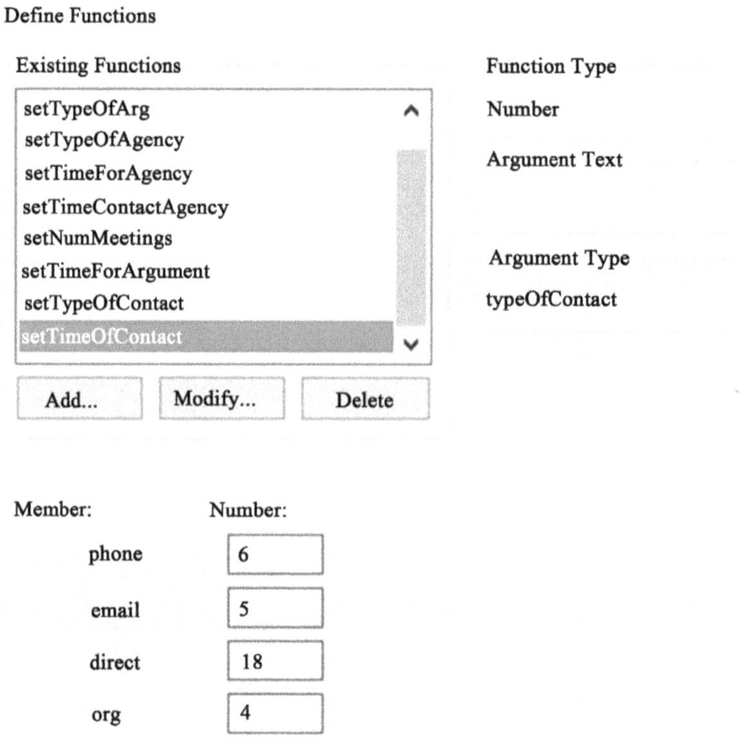

Define Functions

Existing Functions   Function Type

setTypeOfArg   ∧   Number
setTypeOfAgency
setTimeForAgency   Argument Text
setTimeContactAgency
setNumMeetings
setTimeForArgument   Argument Type
setTypeOfContact
setTimeOfContact   ∨   typeOfContact

Add...   Modify...   Delete

Member: Number:

phone   [6]

email   [5]

direct   [18]

org   [4]

Figure 5. The dialog box to define the *setTimeOfContact* function.

Table 3. Duration of activities (minutes).

Activity	Duration
Analyze request	*setTimeOfContact*
Communicate recall	Dist(1:3)
Collect information	TriangleDist(10;25;15)
Provide immediate answer	*setTimeForAnswer*
Update register	TriangleDist(1;3;1,5)
Provide answer	TriangleDist(5;15;10)
Obtain information	*setTimeForAgency*
Update answer	TriangleDist(3;10;7)
Participate meetings	TriangleDist(1;30;10)
Update DB	TriangleDist(5;15;7)
Exec other activities	TriangleDist(15;60;25)

In **Table 3**, TriangleDist(m;M;md) stands for a triangular distribution in the range minimum (m), maximum (M), and median value (md). Dist(m:M) stands for a uniform distribution in range from minimum (m) to maximum (M) value.

Figure 6 shows the dialog box to specify a resource. The figure explains the definition of number of resources, costs and overtime policy for the two operators that work together to respond to customer requests. The schedule is the working hours (between 9 am and 3 pm) of the SPUN office (and of the operators), and is described in another dialog box.

Figure 7 illustrates the specification of the duration (*Task* clause) of the activity *Collect information* by a triangular distribution TriangleDist(10;25;15). In the *Resources* clause, it is possible to specify the resources needed to perform the activity. For the SPUN case, all activities are performed by a single operator, except for the activity *Participate meetings* that requires both operators.

5.2. As-Is Model Validation

Once the As-Is model is completed with the description of resources and their use in the activities, generators of transactions to be entered during the simulation, and the time required by the activities, it is necessary to validate the model in order to check that it represents the system as it is and with all the aspects needed to build up new scenarios to increase the service level of the system.

The validation step can be easily performed if the process specification language is executable. In this case, it is possible to simulate the process and verify the validity of the model by comparing the values obtained from the simulation, for a set of indicators, with the same values measured on the real process.

In our tests, 150 weeks (about 3 years) of work of the Contact Center have been taken into account. The validation analysis has covered the average *cycle time* for the different activities of the process, resulting from the sum of the av-

Define Resources

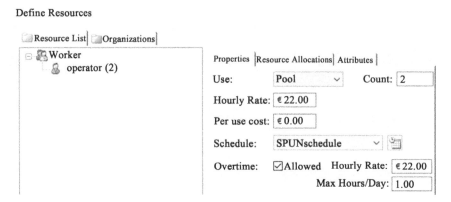

Figure 6. The dialog box to define resources.

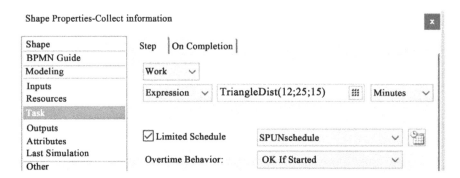

Figure 7. The dialog box to define the duration of the *Collect information* activity.

erage *working time* (the time spent by the operators during the execution of the activity) and the average *waiting time* (includes time waiting for resources necessary to the activity and the time in which the resources are inactive, for example, are outside working hours).

Table 4 shows the simulation results for the activities of the CC process. In the table, the G type for the *Analyze request* activity indicates that this activity is always performed, while the S or C type indicates that the corresponding activities are carried out only for simple (S) or complex (C) tasks.

The results shown in **Table 4** were presented to managers and operators in the contact center who judged reasonable these simulated times based on their experience and an assessment with real data (controlled over a short period, about 3 months, of work).

The comparison between simulated and actual times concludes the validation step for the As-Is model which is then ready for the analysis of possible different scenarios.

5.3. What-If Analysis

A scenario can be defined as a description of a possible future situation. Scenarios are not meant to be a complete description of the future, but rather to consider the basic elements of a possible future and to draw the attention of analysts to the key factors that can help to effectively improve the process.

Table 4. Average times (minutes) for the activities of the CC process.

Type	Activity	N.	Avg. Cycle	Avg. Work	Avg. Wait
G	Analyze request	8250	12.06	8.50	3.56
S	Provide immediate answer	3373	13.89	13.89	0.00
S	Update Sregister	3373	5.78	2.32	3.46
C	Collect information	4877	20.62	16.70	3.93
C	Communicate recall	4877	1.99	1.99	0.00
C	Obtain information	3593	67.87	17.83	50.04
C	Update answer	3593	18.09	6.65	11.44
C	Provide answer	4877	46.62	9.99	36.62
C	Update Cregister	4877	27.24	4.68	22.56

Scenarios will be compared on the basis of a significant set of indicators. Literature is full of indicators on contact centers [29], typically focused on the quantitative aspects of the service. In particular, in agreement with the Contact Center management three groups of indicators were taken into account:

1) Service Level (SL). A common way to define Service Level is by looking at the fraction of requests answered within a defined time frame (usually called the Acceptable Waiting Time-AWT). A typical value is that 80% of all calls has to be answered in 20 seconds [30], but for the SPUN case is not important to be fast, but to respond completely and correctly. According to the manager, a particularly interesting indicator is the service level for complex requests. In this case, a 12-working-hours AWT is considered acceptable (higher delays are not), so the SL indicator will be evaluated as the percentage of complex requests handled before the AWT, over the total number of complex requests. According to management, values higher than 80% are considered satisfactory.

2) Resource Utilization (RU) measures the average percent of time operators are actively occupied on a request.

3) Cost Per Contact (CpC). In our case, only the cost of operators has been taken into account because the Contact Center desk is housed in a public center and then other costs (infrastructure, energy, rents and so on) were not considered relevant by the management.

In the BP-M* approach the specification of the scenarios to be analyzed is very simple if they can be defined as changes to be made to the As-Is model parameters. According to the managers, four different types of scenarios have been considered for our case study, which will then be compared with the baseline scenario provided by the As-Is model of the CC process (Base scenario):

1) **Workload (S1)**: two increments (20% and 40%) of the workload will be considered, from 11 requests per day to 13 requests (S1.1) and 15 requests (S1.2).

2) **Mixing of requests (S2)**: two different mixing will be considered, S2.1 (60% simple, 40% complex) and S2.2 (25% simple, 75% complex).

3) **Opening hours (S3)**: in the first sub-scenario (S3.1) the opening time is limited in the morning (between 9 am and 1 pm) from Monday to Friday, with the same workload of 11 requests per day (reduction in service opening time). In the second sub-scenario (S3.2) the service opening time is also extended to Saturdays (between 9 am and 1 pm) but the workload remains roughly the same as the Base scenario (9 requests for 6 days are expected).

4) **Composite scenario (S4)**: different types of change can be applied simultaneously. For example, we can assign to simple requests a higher priority than the one reserved for complex requests (priority change) and introduce tools to improve response times. In fact, we plan to install an integrated information system and the assisted search of the answers should improve response times, lowered by at least 20%.

Each scenario has been simulated on the basis of 150 weeks and the results are shown in **Table 5**. Note that:

a) **SL**: for what concerns the Service Level, only complex requests have been considered because simple ones did not present any particular problems.

b) **RU**: for what concerns the Resource Utilization, account has been taken for all the activities carried out by operators (including back-office activities).

c) **CpC**: for what concerns the costs per contact, they are considered separately for simple (**CpCS**) and complex requests (**CpCC**) as their values are significantly different. Costs are reported in euros.

Let us start on the Service Level SL, which is focused on complex requests (they have a stronger impact on the process as a whole).

As shown in **Table 5**, the reduction in opening time (S3.1 and S3.2) greatly influences the delay in answering to complex requests: the service level drops to about 50%, which means that about half of requests exceeds the acceptable waiting time. At the same time, resources become overweighed (resource utilization RU increases up to about 90% in both S3.1 and S3.2 scenarios). Even the increase in complex requests (Scenario S1.2) produces the same result. In both cases, the level of service is not satisfactory.

Focusing on costs, only scenario S4 shows a significant reduction in cost per contact (about 5% for complex requests and 10% for simple ones). This means that the costs for the organization are roughly proportional to the number of contacts and, for example, costs related to scenario S1.2 (40% increase in contacts) have been considered hard to deal with by management.

Table 5. Resource utilization, service level and costs per contact (simple and complex).

	Base	S1.1	S1.2	S2.1	S2.2	S3.1	S3.2	S4
SL	87.8%	84.5%	76.7%	87.9%	87.0%	54.3%	43.8%	88.7%
RU	66.1%	74.3%	84.5%	55.4%	70.0%	89.3%	87.2%	59.6%
CpCS	8.94	8.95	8.94	8.88	9.03	8.65	8.80	8.10
CpCC	20.73	20.88	20.80	20.89	20.83	20.92	20.99	19.60

The simulation results of the various scenarios were considered very interesting by the service manager and are currently being studied to determine whether or not it is possible, and how, to improve the organization of the contact center.

6. Conclusions

In this paper, we described a model-based approach, the BP-M* framework, to design and reason about the organization's business environment, with a focus on Key Performance Indicators.

The BP-M* framework includes a methodology to model, validate and analyze business processes, and an extended process model that allows the simulation of the actual (As-Is) process. A "What-If" analysis of scenarios which describe possible evolutions of the actual process has been introduced and in this way analyst scan get useful suggestions for deciding on the most appropriate restructuring actions to improve the process efficiency (To-Be model).

The possibilities offered by the BP-M* framework have been illustrated through the complex case study SPUN, which describes the behavior of a public Contact Center that answers to different typologies of users' requests. The SPUN case has demonstrated that it is possible to build an accurate model of the process being tested, able to be validated and analyzed by a powerful discrete event simulator.

The simulation allows to easily study a number of possible operational scenarios ("What-If" analysis), thus providing the analysts with useful information to evaluate the restructuring actions on the CC process. In the near future, the phases of the BP-M* methodology that have not been discussed in this article will be considered and illustrated with the help of the SPUN case study.

Acknowledgements

We are grateful for collaboration to managers and operators of the SPUN Contact Center of the Consorzio Sociale "Il Filo da Tessere". SPUN is a project financed by two Italian public institutions, ASL BI and Cissabo.

References

[1] Dumas, M., La Rosa, M., Mendling, J. and Reijers, H.A. (2013) Fundamentals of Business Process Management. Springer, Berlin.
https://doi.org/10.1007/978-3-642-33143-5

[2] Fishman, G. (2013) Discrete-Event Simulation: Modeling, Programming, and Analysis. Springer Science & Business Media, Berlin.

[3] Lazer, D., Pentland, A.S., Adamic, L., *et al.* (2009) Life in the Network: The Coming Age of Computational Social Science. *Science*, **323**, 721-723.
https://doi.org/10.1126/science.1167742

[4] O'Sullivan, D. and Perry, G.L. (2013) Spatial Simulation: Exploring Pattern and Process. John Wiley & Sons, Hoboken. https://doi.org/10.1002/9781118527085

[5] Gilbert, N. and Troitzsch, K. (2005) Simulation for the Social Scientist. McGraw-

Hill Education (UK), New York.

[6]   Van der Aalst, W.M., Nakatumba, J., Rozinat, A. and Russell, N. (2010) Business Process Simulation. In: vom Brocke, J. and Rosemann, M., Eds., *Handbook on Business Process Management* 1, Springer, Berlin, 313-338. https://doi.org/10.1007/978-3-642-00416-2_15

[7]   Scheer, A.W. and Nuttgens, M. (2000) Aris Architecture and Reference Models for Business Process Management. In: Van der Aalst, W.M., *et al.*, Eds., *Business Process Management*, LNCS 1806, Springer, Berlin, 376-389. https://doi.org/10.1007/3-540-45594-9_24

[8]   Reijers, H.A. (2003) Design and Control of Workflow Processes: Business Process Management for the Service Industry. Springer-Verlag, Berlin. https://doi.org/10.1007/3-540-36615-6

[9]   Lempert, R. (2002) Agent-Based Modeling as Organizational and Public Policy Simulators. *Proceedings of the National Academy of Sciences*, **99**, 7195-7196. https://doi.org/10.1073/pnas.072079399

[10]   Gulledge Jr., T.R. and Sommer, R.A. (2002) Business Process Management: Public Sector Implications. *Business Process Management Journal*, **8**, 364-376. https://doi.org/10.1108/14637150210435017

[11]   Kovacic, A. and Pecek, B. (2007) Use of Simulation in a Public Administration Process. *Simulation*, **83**, 851-861. https://doi.org/10.1177/0037549707087249

[12]   Rouchier, J. and Thoyer, S. (2006) Votes and Lobbying in the European Decision-Making Process: Application to the European Regulation on GMO Release. *Journal of Artificial Societies and Social Simulation*, **9**, No. 3.

[13]   Di Leva, A. and Sulis, E. (2017) Process Analysis for a Hospital Emergency Department. *International Journal of Economics and Management Systems*, **2**, 34-41.

[14]   Gans, N., Koole, G. and Mandelbaum, A. (2003) Telephone Call Centers: Tutorial, Review and Research Prospects. *Manufacturing & Service Operations Management*, **5**, 79-141. https://doi.org/10.1287/msom.5.2.79.16071

[15]   Min, H. and Yu, V. (2008) Reengineering Call Centre Operations Using Simulation. International Journal of Services Technology and Management, **9**, 71-78.

[16]   Kosiba, E., Newhard, D. and Papadopoulos, N. (2006) System and Method for Generating Forecasts and Analysis of Contact Center Behavior for Planning Purposes. US Patent No. 7103562.

[17]   Seetharaman, K., Fama, J. and Hamilton, E. (2011) Methods for Long-Range Contact Center Statistical Planning Utilizing Discrete Event Simulation, US Patent No. 8015042 B2.

[18]   L'Ecuyer, P. (2006) Modeling and Optimization Problems in Contact Centers. *Proceedings of the Third International Conference on Quantitative Evaluation of Systems*, Washington DC, 11-14 September 2006, 145-154.

[19]   Koole, G. and Mandelbaum, A. (2002) Queueing Models of Call Centers: An Introduction. *Annals of Operations Research*, **113**, 41-59. https://doi.org/10.1023/A:1020949626017

[20]   Borshchev, A. and Filippov, A. (2004) From System Dynamics and Discrete Event to Practical Agent Based Modeling: Reasons, Techniques, Tools. *Proceedings of the 22nd International Conference of the System Dynamics Society*, 25-29 July 2004, Oxford.

[21]   Lewis, B.G., Herbert, R.D., Summons, P.F. and Chivers, W. (2007) Agent-Based

Simulation of a Multi-Queue Emergency Services Call Centre to Evaluate Resource Allocation. *MODSIM* 2007, *International Congress on Modelling and Simulation, Modelling and Simulation Society of Australia and New Zealand*, Christchurch, 10 -13 December 2007, 11-17.

[22] Sencer, A. and Ozel, B.B. (2013) A Simulation-Based Decision Support System for Workforce Management in Call Centers. *Simulation*, **89**, 481-497. https://doi.org/10.1177/0037549712470169

[23] Doomun, R. and Jungum, N.V. (2008) Business Process Modelling, Simulation and Reengineering: Call Centres. *Business Process Management Journal*, **14**, 838-848.

[24] Lam, K. and Lau, R. (2004) A Simulation Approach to Restructuring Call Centers. *Business Process Management Journal*, **10**, 481-494. https://doi.org/10.1108/14637150410548119

[25] Di Leva, A. and Femiano, S. (2011) The BP-M* Methodology for Process Analysis in the Health Sector. *Intelligent Information Management*, **3**, 56-63. https://doi.org/10.4236/iim.2011.32007

[26] McCarthy, B.M. and Stauer, R. (2001) Enhancing Six Sigma through Simulation with iGrafx Process for Six Sigma. *Proceedings of the 33rd Conference on Winter Simulation*, Arlington, 9-12 December 2001, 1241-1247. https://doi.org/10.1109/WSC.2001.977440

[27] BPMN (2014) Business Process Model and Notation. http://www.omg.org/spec/BPMN/2.0.2/

[28] iGrafx Process (2015) iGrafx Process Automation User Guide. http://www.igrafx.com

[29] Mehrotra, V. and Fama, J. (2003) Call Center Simulation Modeling: Methods, Challenges and Opportunities. *Proceedings of the 35th Winter Simulation Conference*, New Orleans, 7-10 December 2003, 135-143.

[30] Robinson, G. and Morley, C. (2006) Call Centre Management: Responsibilities and Performance. *International Journal of Service Industry Management*, **17**, 284-300. https://doi.org/10.1108/09564230610667122

Decision Support through Intelligent Agent based Simulation and Multiple Goal based Evolutionary Optimization

Wissam Alobaidi[1]*, Eric Sandgren[1]*, Entidhar Alkuam[2]

[1]Systems Engineering Department, Donaghey College of Engineering & Information Technology, University of Arkansas at Little Rock, Little Rock, USA
[2]Department of Physics and Astronomy, College of Arts, Letters, and Sciences, University of Arkansas at Little Rock, Little Rock, USA
Email: *wmalobaidi@ualr.edu, *exsandgren@ualr.edu

Abstract

Agent based simulation has successfully been applied to model complex organizational behavior and to improve or optimize aspects of organizational performance. Agents, with intelligence supported through the application of a genetic algorithm are proposed as a means of optimizing the performance of the system being modeled. Local decisions made by agents and other system variables are placed in the genetic encoding. This allows local agents to positively impact high level system performance. A simple, but non trivial, peg game is utilized to introduce the concept. A multiple objective bin packing problem is then solved to demonstrate the potential of the approach in meeting a number of high level goals. The methodology allows not only for a systems level optimization, but also provides data which can be analyzed to determine what constitutes effective agent behavior.

Keywords

Decision Support, Multiple Goal, Agent Based, Genetic Optimization, Bin Packing

1. Introduction

Over the past ten years, there has been an increasing interest in agent based modeling and simulation. Summaries of application to manufacturing, planning and scheduling are given by Shen *et al.* [1], Marik [2] and Yoo [3]. An agent refers to a software segment that performs a specific task. This task may be simple or complex and the agent may be intelligent or not. An intelligent agent refers to one that has some form of reasoning and learning capability. The agent taxonomy allows for a model to be developed for systems that involve complex behavior. When the model is integrated with a global optimization algorithm, the ability to improve performance at both a local and systems level becomes possible. Often, the decisions which are made by a local agent are based on experiential data which may have a very local context. System complexity often makes it extremely difficult to look forward in time or to consider global rather than local objectives. This leads to inefficiencies, which if avoided, could improve the operational efficiency of the system. In industry segments involving logistics and manufacturing, this efficiency gain may make the difference between operating at a profit or loss. As the fixed cost of operation increases (energy, labor and raw materials), the only way to remain profitable is through increasing operational efficiency. An evolutionary optimization algorithm may be utilized to assist the local decision making capability of the agents to achieve this system goal. This combination represents an innovative idea and holds the promise of a significant gain in productivity over a wide range of industries.

The strengths and weaknesses of agent based modeling coupled to mathematical optimization for a situation involving multiple objective distributed resource allocation in a dynamic environment are reviewed by Davidsson *et al.* [4]. Narzisi *et al.* [5] optimized an agent based model for emergency response planning where the optimization was performed by an evolutionary algorithm. Optimization applied to parameter tuning of the agents has been performed with both a single objective by Calvez [6] and multiple objectives by Rogers [7]. Specific instances of the utilization of agent based simulation in conjunction with various optimization approaches have been presented by Deshpande [8] and Gjerdrum *et al.* [9] for manufacturing scheduling, Sirikipanichkul [10] for freight hub location, Neagu [11] for transport logistics and by Botterud [12] for expansion in electricity markets. It is clear from the wealth of research activity in the application of agent based modeling and simulation that the approach offers a valid means for addressing complex, real world problems. The difficulty in most applications involves how to best utilize optimization as a means of improving the performance of the system being modeled. Intelligence at the local and global level is difficult to implement through experience or rule based approaches. The value of coupling of a genetic optimizer directly to the individual agents is investigated herein.

Agents are often introduced as elements which model the behavior of humans performing a specific task. Many such tasks represent highly skilled positions such as a scheduler for a line of a manufacturing plant or a loader for a freight hub. For operations involving complex reasoning, it is difficult to develop consistent performance under varying day to day conditions. This is particularly true when such reasoning must include local and global objectives. The ability to share the intelligence between an agent's knowledge base and an optimization algorithm helps to insure that all goals are factored into the solution and the entire solution space is investigated. The results from such an optimization in practice can help improve the behavior of a local agent over time and some of the intelligence supplied through the optimization can be incorporated into the logic employed by the agent. This allows a framework to be built for a specific application class for which the performance can be continuously improved over time.

The particular implementation considered in this study will involve simple agents performing tasks that involve a certain level of reasoning. The agent in each system is coupled to an evolutionary or genetic optimization algorithm. The optimization algorithm utilizes a goal programming formulation in order to address multiple objectives. Two examples are presented which allow for the approach to be developed and demonstrated. The first example involves the solution of a simple, but non-trivial, peg game where the agent must make all move decisions with a global goal of solving the game. The second example involves a multiple objective bin packing problem with the agent being responsible for packing a rectangular trailer with a prescribed set of shipments or loads. Both examples involve only a single agent, but the approach is scalable to include any number of agents. The approach leads to a distributed rule based decision support environment that can be applied to complex problems encountered over a wide range of industries. The contribution of this work is in the demonstration of how a combination of evolutionary optimization methods and agent based simulation can solve decision support problems.

2. An Evolutionary Goal Programming Approach

For a decision support system implementation utilizing intelligent agents, the agents must be capable of making a sequence of decisions at the local level which determine not only local but global system behavior and performance. The impact of each individual decision is influenced by all previous decisions and all future decisions are impacted as well. The traditional nonlinear mathematical programming formulation for this problem class is defined as:

$$\text{Maximize} f(x); x = \left[x_1, x_2, x_3, \cdots, x_n\right]^{\mathrm{T}} \tag{1}$$

Subject to

$$g_j(x) \geq 0; j = 1, 2, \cdots, J \tag{2}$$

$$h_k(x) = 0; k = 1, 2, \cdots, K \tag{3}$$

and

$$x_i^{low} < x_i < x_i^{high} \tag{4}$$

In this formulation, $f(x)$ represents a measure of global performance which is to be maximized. This measure may be linear or nonlinear and related to efficiency, profit or any calculable quantity. The design or decision vector, x, is composed of all decision possibilities that each agent must make at the local level. Additional design variables may be included to allow for evaluation of non-agent based decision related factors. The design variables may be continuous, integer or discrete and may be defined on a range as by Equation (4), or as a set of discrete or integer valued choices. The number of assigned decision values may vary for each individual decision variable and the design variable vector includes the local decisions for all local agents. Equations (2) and (3) define constraints which establish the feasible search space. The greater or less than constraint given by Equation (2), allows for a constraint which can be over satisfied, while the equality constraint given by Equation (3) specifies a constraint which must be exactly satisfied.

The mathematical formulation presented above is useful for the solution of a wide range of problems. Difficulties arise, however, when multiple objectives are desired as well as soft constraints. Soft constraint represent conditions which are desirable but are allowed to be violated if beneficial trade-offs may be made among the values of the other objectives. A goal formulation may be applied to the decision support problem to easily include these additional aspects. A goal programming formulation for the broad class of decision support problems may be expressed as follows:

$$\text{Maximize} f\left(x\right) = \sum_{i=1}^{I} W_{kj} P_k \left\{d_i^+ + d_i^-\right\} \tag{5}$$

for $k = 1, 2, \cdots, K$

$$j = 1, 2, \cdots, J$$

where the d_i^+ and d_i^- are positive valued variables and represent the under and over achievement of goals which may be specified by one of the following goal constraint equation forms:

$$G_j\left(x\right) + d_i^- = b_i \tag{6}$$

$$G_j\left(x\right) - d_i^+ = b_i \tag{7}$$

and

$$G_j\left(x\right) - d_i^- + d_i^+ = b_i \tag{8}$$

From a comparison to a linear programming formulation, the d_i^- and d_i^+ deviational variables may be thought of as a form of slack variables. With this analogy, the first two goal constraints may be seen to be less than or equal to and greater than or equal to forms. The third form essentially represents a hard equality constraint, which allows for absolute requirements to be met. In a goal formulation, only the deviational variables appear in the objective function as represented by Equation (5). Each deviational variable, however, is a function of the decision variables. The specific form of the objective function allows for weighting factors, W_{kj}, and for goal priorities P_k for each goal. There is no limit to the total number of goals allowed. An evolutionary optimization algorithm may be implemented to address either the formulation given by Equations (1)-(4) or for that given by Equations (5)-(8). The general flow of the algorithm is presented in **Figure 1**.

3. The Peg Game: A Simple Example

The implementation of an optimization controlled, agent based decision support

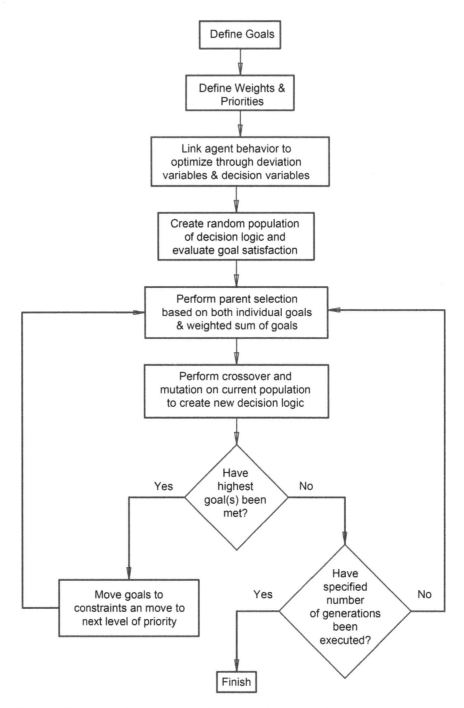

Figure 1. Flowchart of evolutionary goal programming approach.

application is best demonstrated through the consideration of a simple, but non-trivial, example. The example utilized here involves a peg game which has a simple measure of success, but no clear-cut strategy to implement in a given game situation. The game consists of fifteen uniformly spaced holes on a game board that is configured as an equilateral triangle. The game layout is presented in **Figure 1**. The holes on the game board are filled with pegs which can be removed according to the rules of the game. The game begins as the user removes one peg from the board and then continues by jumping pegs as allowed by the current configuration. A peg may be jumped only if a peg is directly adjacent to it and the opposite position is vacant. Once a peg has been jumped, that peg is removed from the game board and the process continues. The game terminates when all possible moves have been made. If a single peg remains, the game is considered to be won. As with most decision support problems, the current game condition at any point in the solution process is determined by all previous moves. At each step in the game, however, an appropriate move may be determined by an agent whose intelligence is derived from an evolutionary optimization algorithm.

The agent, which is implemented in the game simulation, must make the decisions which control the operation of the game. At each game state, the agent is responsible for selecting which peg to move among all possible pegs that can move. This is a convenient, low level implementation of agent based modeling where the agent only has the tasks of identifying possible moves and selecting one at each game state. The mathematical description of the optimization problem would be difficult without the agent based simulation. This is because the determination of possible moves, the selection of a move at each game state and even the number of moves required to complete an individual game simulation vary from simulation to simulation. The mathematical formulation for this particular implementation may be expressed as follows:

$$\text{Minimize } f(x) = \text{Number of pegs remaining at stage } p \qquad (9)$$

where

$$x = \left[x_1, x_2, x_3, \cdots, x_{14}\right]^{\mathrm{T}} \qquad (10)$$

And

$$x_1 = \text{first peg removed to start the game}; x_1 \in \{1, 2, 3, \cdots, 15\} \qquad (11)$$

x_n = peg movement option from list of possible moves at game simulation step n,
$$n = 1, 2, 3, \cdots, 14; x_n \in \{1, 2, \cdots, n_{\text{moves}}\} \qquad (12)$$

and n_{moves} is defined as the maximum moves available at any game state and p is defined as the game state where no more moves are available. Note the design variables in the encoding are integer in nature and are only known as the simulation progresses from game state to game state. Since the only goal is to minimize the number of pegs remaining after all moves have been made, the formulation given by Equations (9)-(12) is equivalent to the formulation given by Equations (1)-(4). The agent utilization, coupled with an evolutionary optimization algorithm allows for a straightforward implementation of the intelligent decision support structure.

With most agent implementations, intelligence can be introduced to guide the decision making of the agent. The difficulty with this approach is that the impact of local decisions made at each game state are difficult to relate to the final game execution result. This situation is common in a wide range of applications where local decisions, made with local information may lead the enterprise far from the global or system optima. Specific examples include trailer packing for a LTL operation, truck fleet routing, pick-up and deliveries, home care medical staff scheduling and routing, and many others. The efficacy of local decision making can be improved through the coupling to an evolutionary optimization algorithm which is capable of making local decisions in a global, multiple goal objective context. A post optimal analysis can be executed to extract key characteristics of sound local decisions that led to the optimal global solution. This information can be utilized to improve the local intelligence of the agent. Over time the decisions at the local level can be split between the agent acting independently and the genetic algorithm enforcing decisions.

An evolutionary or genetic algorithm is well suited to deal with the general agent based decision support problem. It can easily handle integer valued variables as well as a variable number of moves, or game steps in this case, for each simulation or objective function evaluation. Another positive feature of the algorithm is that it can handle solution spaces with many local minima which is common in decision support applications. Coupled with a goal programming formulation, multiple objectives can be handled which is another common trait of this problem class. The optimization begins with randomly selected decisions for the agent at each move and continually refines the decisions until a single peg remains at the end of a game simulation. These decisions constitute the optimal decisions for the game playing agent. The decisions can then be evaluated for global characteristics that could possibly be built into the stand alone agent intelligence in future implementations.

The procedure described above was implemented for the fifteen peg game and a solution was generated within thirty generations with a population of two hundred decision strategies for the game agent in each generation. In order to track the solution, the holes on the game board are numbered and this numbering scheme is shown in **Figures 2-4** document the final decision strategy utilized by the agent in a move by move fashion.

The post optimal analysis for this example is difficult due to the elementary nature of the decision options. However, it can be noted that the optimal decision strategy did seem to be centered around both keeping the number of choices at each step as large as possible and to maintain some semblance of grouping

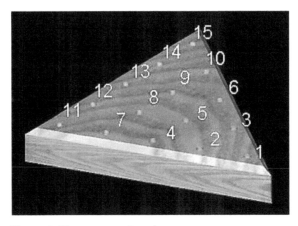

Figure 2. The peg game board.

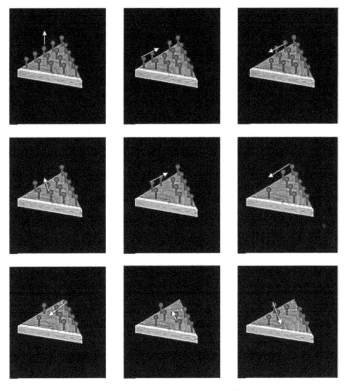

Figure 3. First 9 moves for the 15 peg game solution.

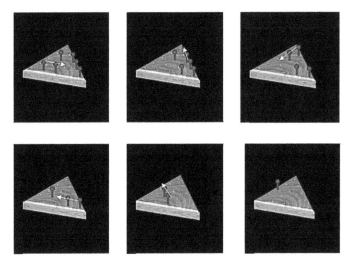

Figure 4. Final 6 moves for the 15 peg game solution.

of the pegs at each game step. Both of these characteristics are aligned with the anticipated solution strategy for the peg game. As the applications become more complex, this simple correlation between decision strategy and results is not expected, but useful information may be gathered as a number of scenarios are executed.

4. Multi-Objective Bin Packing: A More Challenging Example

The bin packing problem fits in well with the decision support framework where agents are utilized with partial intelligence supplied by an evolutionary optimization algorithm. Both the two and three dimensional bin packing have been studied extensively, and remains as NP hard problems. Solution approaches have been generated through simulated annealing by Rao [13] as well as through the application of genetic algorithms [14] [15] [16] [17]. None of these solution approaches considered a multi-objective solution. An agent based approach was proposed by Lau [18], and heuristic approaches by Epstein [19] and Lim [20] provide insight to potential agent based logic and behavior. In a multi-objective form, the problem formulation can be utilized to address critically important aspects of the transportation industry. The operation of a less than full load (LTL) business involves the packing of semi-trailers with individual shipments which are then transported through a series of hubs. At each hub, shipments are generally unloaded from one trailer and reloaded in another. Upon reaching the final hub destination, the shipment is delivered locally through a separate operation termed pick-up and delivery. One of the highest skill labor jobs is the loader as the efficiency of the business is highly dependent on the placement of each shipment in the trailer as well as the load fill of the trailer before leaving the hub. The loader in this example will be represented by an agent. The genetic optimization algorithm will provide global decision making ability to the loading agent. The traditional bin packing solution would focus on trailer fill, but in this example other factors or goals are considered as well. Among these factors are placement of top-loads, priority loads, front loading common hub destination shipments and the center of gravity of the trailer after loading.

The maximum fill condition is astraightforward one. Trailer fill refers to the amount of total volume in the trailer filled by shipments. Any unfilled space represents lost efficiency, as the trailer will execute the appointed route whether or not it is completely filled. As trailer fill increases, it potentially reduces the number of trailers required to transfer all shipments through the hub network to their final destinations. The only caveat is that the trailer may weigh out, rather than cube out. The term cube out refers to filling the trailer volume to capacity, while the term weigh out refers to the total loaded weight of the shipments being equal to the maximum allowed, even though there may be unused volume. LTL shipments may be pallet based or individual items, and as a general rule, most are rectangular in shape. Top load shipments are those that are fragile and cannot have any other shipments placed on top of them. These loads will generally be placed at the very top of the trailer. Priority loads are those shipments which must progress through the hub network as quickly as possible. An additional charge is associated with priority shipments and this charge is only justified if the shipment arrives when promised. In order to facilitate a reduction in time for priority loads, they are ideally placed near the rear of the trailer so they may be unloaded and reloaded as soon as a hub is reached.

Front loading is a term which is used when a number of shipments with the same hub destination following the current one, or the same final destination are loaded in the front of the trailer. This allows the trailer to be unloaded, leaving these shipments untouched as the inbound trailer becomes the outbound trailer to the next destination. Each reduction in handling for a shipment reduces the risk of damage as well as a savings in time and labor. Finally, the center of gravity of a loaded trailer is important. If the center of gravity is too high or not centered in width or toward the front in length, a bad handling condition may occur. The possibility of a roll over as a corner is traversed at speed is also a possibility. Each condition added beyond the traditional maximum fill adds complexity to the optimization problem solution. On the other hand, significant value is added to the transportation firm. A single trailer example is considered here in order to demonstrate the approach. The extension to all trailers in service at an LTL is certainly possible, particularly with the parallel nature of the process.

In order to model the agent based trailer loading example, the trailer is subdivided into a series of small rectangular solids. The size of each rectangular solid may be decreased in order to increase the accuracy along with the associated level of computational complexity for solving the problem. In this example a grid of 4 × 5 rectangular solids is introduced at each of 12 individual sections along the length of the trailer as shown in **Figure 5**. This subdivision results in a total of 240 individual loading volumes. With this simplification, a set of loads or shipments may be placed in the trailer by the loading logic resident in the local loading agent. To take the example a step further, consider the set of shipments listed in **Table 1**. Each of the individual 23 shipments has dimensions, weight, next hub destination, priority and an indication of the shipment being a top load only load. The next hub destination (7 total) represents the hub the shipment is to be sent to after processing at the current hub destination for the trailer. The priority (1, 2 or 3), is an indication of a shipment which must be processed as quickly as possible as it is a premium shipment. The shipments with a priority of one are the highest priority shipments. In this example, the total volume of all shipments is equal to the total trailer volume.

The goals utilized in the formulation for this example are as follows: The total volume fill should be as great as possible. All top loads should have no load placed on top of them. The high priority loads should be located in the rear of the trailer and shipments with the same next destination should be consolidated as a head load in the front of the trailer. Finally, the center of gravity should be as low as possible, as near to the center of the trailer width as possible and as far forward in the trailer as possible. The goal programming formulation for this

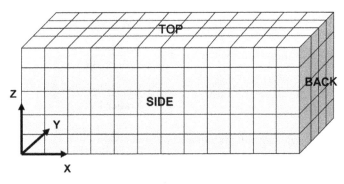

Figure 5. Trailer volume division.

Table 1. Shipment data for example problem.

Load	Hub Destination	Weight	Priority	Top Load	Dimensions (x/y/z)
1	2	10.0	2	No	4/3/2
2	3	8.5	3	No	4/5/2
3	3	7.5	2	No	4/2/2
4	4	5.0	1	No	2/2/2
5	2	5.0	1	No	2/2/2
6	2	8.0	2	No	2/2/2
7	3	5.0	2	No	2/2/2
8	4	2.0	2	Yes	1/1/1
9	2	2.0	3	Yes	1/1/1
10	5	2.0	3	No	1/1/2
11	6	2.0	3	No	1/1/2
12	7	2.0	2	Yes	1/1/2
13	2	3.0	2	No	2/2/4
14	5	3.0	3	No	2/2/3
15	8	3.0	2	No	2/3/1
16	9	5.0	1	Yes	2/1/2
17	7	2.0	2	Yes	2/1/1
18	3	4.0	2	No	2/3/4
19	5	2.0	2	Yes	2/2/2
20	6	2.0	2	Yes	2/2/2
21	3	9.0	2	No	2/5/2
22	4	3.0	2	No	2/4/2
23	8	3.0	2	Yes	2/1/2

problem statement is as follows:

$$\text{Maximize } f(x) = W_1 d_1^+ + W_2 d_2^+ + W_3 d_3^+ + W_4 d_4^+ + W_5 d_5^+$$
$$+ W_6 d_6^+ + W_7 \left(d_7^+ + d_8^- \right) + W_8 d_9^+ \tag{13}$$

$$G_1(x) + d_1^- = 0.95; \text{ where } G_1(x) = \frac{\text{Trailer Fill}}{\text{Total Trailer Volume}} \tag{14}$$

$$G_2(x) - d_2^+ = 0; \text{ where } G_2(x) = \text{Number of Covered Top Loads} \tag{15}$$

$$G_3(x) - d_3^+ = 0; \text{ where } G_3(x) = \text{Inaccessible Priority 1 Shipments} \tag{16}$$

$$G_4(x) - d_4^+ = 0; \text{ where } G_4(x) = \text{Priority Shipments in Front Half Of Trailer} \tag{17}$$

$$G_5(x) + d_5^- = 0.25; \text{ where } G_5(x) = \frac{\text{Front Load Fill}}{\text{Trailer Volume}} \tag{18}$$

$$G_6(x) - d_6^+ = 0.33; \text{ where } G_6(x) = \frac{CG_z \text{ Location}}{\text{Trailer Height}} \tag{19}$$

$$G_7(x) - d_7^+ + d_8^- = 0.50; \text{ where } G_7(x) = \frac{CG_y \text{ Location}}{\text{Trailer Width}} \tag{20}$$

$$G_8(x) - d_9^+ = 0.50; \text{ where } G_8(x) = \frac{CG_z \text{ Location}}{\text{Trailer Length}} \tag{21}$$

The above formulation may look complex, but it is actually a straightforward statement of the goals of the trailer loading problem. The first goal constraint states that the loaded percentage of the trailer should be at least 95 percent. Any shortfall is represented by the underachievement deviational variable d_1^+ which appears in the objective function to be minimized. No penalty is associated with a fill greater than 95 percent as expected. The underachievement variable appears in the objective function with a weight W_1 which allows it to have a high priority (W_1 large or a smaller priority) (W_1 smaller or equal to other goal weights). The second goal constraint states that no top loads may be covered or the underachievement variable d_2^+ will negatively impact the objective function by the number of covered top-loads multiplied by weighting factor W_2. Using a similar interpretation, the third goal constraint states that all priority one loads must be immediately accessible on opening the trailer. The fourth goal constraint requires priority level two shipments to be located in the real half of the trailer. The fifth goal constraint requires a front load fill with a common next hub destination to be at least 25 percent of the total volume. The sixth, seventh and eighth goal constraints require the CG location to be lower than or equal to 1/3 the trailer height, as close to the 1/2 the width (trailer center) as possible and closer to the front of the trailer than the rear. Any deviation from the desired goal constraint specifications results in a contribution to the objective function which penalizes that particular loading placement. It is extremely likely that no loading placement will satisfy all goals. However, the algorithm will do what it can to minimize underachievement of critical goals. The relative magnitude of the weighting factors may be adjusted to see what trade-offs are available among the various goal satisfaction levels. A priority based formulation may also be implemented which requires higher priority to be completely satisfied before lower priority goals may be considered.

The formulation represented by Equations (13)-(21) was coded and a solution was attempted with an evolutionary optimization algorithm. In order to execute the packing through an encoding which assists the loading agent implemented, the encoding structure was defined as follows:

$$x = \left[x_{1a}, x_{1b}, x_{1c}, x_{2a}, x_{2b}, x_{2c}, \cdots, x_{23a}, x_{23b}, x_{23c} \right] \tag{22}$$

The values which determine the placement of each individual shipment are ordered in triple valued groups. The first value of the three groups determines the loading order. The second group determines whether the shipment is placed starting from the right or left side of the trailer. The third determines the rotation (90 degrees) of the shipment before loading. The three tiered value structure is repeated for each shipment to be loaded in the trailer. The agent transforms the encoding values into a sequence of operations, as defined by the encoding, which determines the location of each shipment and the finished loaded configuration of the trailer. In order to place some of the intelligence at the agent, top loads were not allowed to have a load placed on top after they are placed. Also the agent logic prevents any two shipments from occupying the same volume which is a difficulty with some bin packing algorithms.

The solution located by the intelligent agent based optimization is shown in **Figures 6-10**. Each figure gives a top, side and rear view of the loaded trailer as specified by the optimal solution located through the application of the goal programming formulation. The position of all loads may not be able to be discerned in all figures, but the key shipment placements are visible. **Figure 6** simply presents the placement of each of the 23 individual shipments. The point of note here is that the trailer fill was 100 percent which actually overachieved the first goal constraint level. **Figure 7** documents the fact that all top load shipments are located at the top of the trailer and have no loads placed on top of them. Once again, this was guaranteed by the intelligent agent placing the shipments. **Figure 8** documents the fact that all priority one loads are immediately accessible once the trailer doors are opened and that while all medium priority

2	2	20	20	8	9	17	15	21	21	10	10
2	2	20	20	11	11	17	15	21	21	16	16
2	2	19	19	6	6	7	7	23	23	16	16
2	2	19	19	6	6	7	7	23	23	12	12

2	2	19	19	6	6	7	7	23	23	12	12
2	2	19	19	6	6	7	7	22	22	4	4
2	2	18	18	1	1	1	1	22	22	4	4
2	2	18	18	1	1	1	1	22	22	3	3
2	2	18	18	1	1	1	1	22	22	3	3

12	16	16	10
4	4	5	5
4	4	5	5
3	3	3	3
3	3	3	3

Side View   **Back View**

Figure 6. Shipment placement for optimal solution.

2	2	20	20	8	9	17	15	21	21	10	10
2	2	20	20	11	11	17	15	21	21	16	16
2	2	19	19	6	6	7	7	23	23	16	16
2	2	19	19	6	6	7	7	23	23	12	12

2	2	19	19	6	6	7	7	23	23	12	12
2	2	19	19	6	6	7	7	22	22	4	4
2	2	18	18	1	1	1	1	22	22	4	4
2	2	18	18	1	1	1	1	22	22	3	3
2	2	18	18	1	1	1	1	22	22	3	3

12	16	16	10
4	4	5	5
4	4	5	5
3	3	3	3
3	3	3	3

Figure 7. Top load placement for optimal solution.

2	2	20	20	8	9	17	15	21	21	10	10
2	2	20	20	11	11	17	15	21	21	16	16
2	2	19	19	6	6	7	7	23	23	16	16
2	2	19	19	6	6	7	7	23	23	12	12

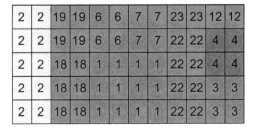

2	2	19	19	6	6	7	7	23	23	12	12
2	2	19	19	6	6	7	7	22	22	4	4
2	2	18	18	1	1	1	1	22	22	4	4
2	2	18	18	1	1	1	1	22	22	3	3
2	2	18	18	1	1	1	1	22	22	3	3

12	16	16	10
4	4	5	5
4	4	5	5
3	3	3	3
3	3	3	3

Figure 8. Priority shipment placement for optimal solution.

2	2	20	20	8	9	17	15	21	21	10	10
2	2	20	20	11	11	17	15	21	21	16	16
2	2	19	19	6	6	7	7	23	23	16	16
2	2	19	19	6	6	7	7	23	23	12	12

2	2	19	19	6	6	7	7	23	23	12	12
2	2	19	19	6	6	7	7	22	22	4	4
2	2	18	18	1	1	1	1	22	22	4	4
2	2	18	18	1	1	1	1	22	22	3	3
2	2	18	18	1	1	1	1	22	22	3	3

12	16	16	10
4	4	5	5
4	4	5	5
3	3	3	3
3	3	3	3

Figure 9. Front load shipment loading for optimal solution.

2	2	20	20	8	9	17	15	21	21	10	10
2	2	20	20	11	11	17	15	21	21	16	16
2	2	19	19	6	6	7	7	23	23	16	16
2	2	19	19	6	6	7	7	23	23	12	12

2	2	19	19	6	6	7	7	23	23	12	12
2	2	19	19	6	6	7	7	22	22	4	4
2	2	18	18	1	1	1	1	22	22	4	4
2	2	18	18	1	1	1	1	22	22	3	3
2	2	18	18	1	1	1	1	22	22	3	3

12	16	16	10
4	4	5	5
4	4	5	5
3	3	3	3
3	3	3	3

Figure 10. Center of gravity location for optimal solution.

loads are not in the rear half of the trailer. Most are packed as well as they could be. **Figure 9** shows the frontload to represent a total of 52 individual volume elements (all to the hub represented by the color blue) which represents 21.6 percent of the total fill. Finally, the CG location is documented in **Figure 9**. The top and back views show the CG is located in the center of the trailer with respect to width, and is approximately one third of the height of the trailer. The CG location along the length of the trailer is slightly beyond the half-way point.

The solution depicted by **Figures 6-10** demonstrate the effectiveness of the overall solution approach. The only goals unmet include the medium priority placement which could not be completely met due to the number and volume of these shipments. The front fill goal was slightly under the desired level and the CG location was slightly farther back than desired. The overall packing, however, was amazingly effective in meeting the goals of the shipping company. A traditionally accepted solution for the bin packing problem would be a 100 percent fill, but the solution offered here not only provides the fill, but also meets a host of other importance performance criteria. A trade-off may be made between the intelligence implemented at the agent itself and how much intelligence is provided to the agent through the genetic optimization algorithm. This balance may be adjusted over time as the methodology is adjusted for a specific application. Extension to multiple trailer loading is a straightforward process. A post optimal analysis of the result simply points out the need to form a head-load, carefully place the priority and top loads and balance the distribution of the weight of the various shipments. A traditional human loader, or even an intelligent agent implementation would have difficulty trading off the various objectives or goals without some computational support.

5. Summary and Conclusions

The use of a genetic or evolutionary algorithm to provide intelligent decision making for an agent was demonstrated for both a single objective and multiple-objective problems. The ability to deal with complex, high level goals or objectives has been documented. The use of a goal programming formulation provided a straightforward means of addressing goals which translate directly into an increase in operational efficiency. The solution generated for both the peg game and trailer loading examples demonstrate the potential of the methodology. The coupling of a genetic algorithm and an agent based framework for modeling opens a wide range of applications for systems level optimization. This is significant as most optimization approaches to decision support look at local improvements. They seldom considers the multiple, competing objectives which are present in virtually every "real world" application.

The peg game represents a simple but non-trivial application of the approach. It typifies a decision support problem as the ultimate success in solving the game is a result of each and every move made by the agent. At each move, the agent must consider a range of options, and the current positioning of the pegs is a result of all previous moves. In order to solve the problem, the optimizer must provide the agent with the appropriate logic to generate the solution. A simple random approach, without any strategy will not solve the game in any reasonable time. Being able to generate the solution with a small population and within a relatively few number of generations is an indication of the promise of the approach in a broader context. The solution of the trailer loading problem with consideration of goals including not only fill but head-load percentage, shipment priority, top-load location and center of gravity location documents the potential in solving real world applications which are currently handled in a sub-optimal way through human intervention. The result is a direct reflection on the potential impact in not only operational efficiency of a hub, but on the safety of the loaded trailer. It also demonstrates that the evolutionary optimization algorithm can support an agent which has a large number of competing goals or objectives.

The use of a goal programming formulation allows for straightforward problem formulation, and the evolutionary optimization allows a global search to be conducted in a complex decision space. A post optimal analysis allows for local decision logic to be improved over time as well as distributing the intelligence between the agent and the optimizer. The ability of addressing multiple goals while solving a NP hard problem represents a significant achievement. Extensions to other decision support problems such as logistics and scheduling are currently being investigated.

References

[1]   Shen, W., Hao, Q., Yoon, H.J. and Noorie, D.H. (2006) Applications of Agent-Based Systems in Intelligent Manufacturing: An Updated Review. *Advanced Engineering Informatics*, **20**, 415-431.

[2]   Marik, V. and McFarlane, D. (2005) Industrial Adoption of Agent-Based Technologies. *IEEE Intelligent Systems*, **20**, 27-35. https://doi.org/10.1109/MIS.2005.11

[3]   Yoo, M.J. (2002) An Industrial Application of Agents for Dynamic Planning and Scheduling. *Proceedings of the 1st International Joint Conference on Autonomous Agents and Multiagent Systems: Part 1*, Bologna, 15-19 July 2002, 264-271. https://doi.org/10.1145/544741.544804

[4]   Davidsson, P., Persson, J.A. and Holmgren, J. (2007) On the Integration of Agent-Baser and Mathematical Optimization Techniques. In: Nguyen, N.T., Grzech, A., Howlett, R.J. and Jain, L.C., Eds., *Agent and Multi-Agent Systems: Technologies and Applications. KES-AMSTA* 2007. *Lecture Notes in Computer Science*, Vol. 4496, Springer, Berlin, Heidelberg, 1-10. https://doi.org/10.1007/978-3-540-72830-6_1

[5]   Narzisi, G., Mysore, V. and Mishra, B. (2006) Multi-Objective Evolutionary Optimization of Agent-Based Models: An Application to Emergency Response Planning. *IASTED International Conference on Computational Intelligence*, November 2006.

[6]   Calvez, B. and Hutzler, G. (2005) Automatic Tuning of Agent-Based Models Using Genetic Algorithms. In: Sichman, J.S. and Antunes, L., Eds., *Multi-Agent-Based Simulation VI. MABS* 2005. *Lecture Notes in Computer Science*, Vol. 3891, Springer, Berlin, Heidelberg, 41-57.

[7]   Rogers, A. and von Tessin, P. (2004) Multi-Objective Calibration for Agent-Based Models. *5th Workshop on Agent-Based Simulation*.

[8]   Deshpande, S. and Cagan, J. (2004) An Agent Based Optimization Approach to

Manufacturing Process Planning. *Journal of Mechanical Design*, **126**, 46-55.
https://doi.org/10.1115/1.1641186

[9]   Gjerdrum, J., Shah, N. and Papageorgiou, L.G (2001) A Combined Optimization
      and Agent-Based Approach to Supply Chain Modelling and Performance Assess-
      ment. *Production Planning and Control*, **12**, 81-88.
      https://doi.org/10.1080/09537280150204013

[10] Sirikijpanichkul, A., Van Dam, K., Ferreira, L and Lukszo, Z. (2007) Optimizing the
      Location of Intermodal Freight Hubs: An Overview of the Agent Based Modelling
      Approach. *Journal of Transportation Systems Engineering and Information Tech-
      nology*, **7**, 71-81.

[11] Neagu, N., Dorer, K., Greenwood, D. and Calisti, M. (2006) LS/ATN: Reporting on
      a Successful Agent-Based Solution for Transport Logistics Optimization. *IEEE
      Workshop on Distributed Intelligent Systems: Collective Intelligence and Its Appli-
      cations*, Prague, 15-16 June 2006, 213-218. https://doi.org/10.1109/dis.2006.46

[12] Botterud, A., Mahalik, M.R., Veselka, T.D. and Ryu, H.S. (2007) Multi-Agent Simu-
      lation of Generation Expansion in Electricity Markets. *IEEE Power Engineering So-
      ciety General Meeting*, Tampa, FL, 24-28 June 2007, 1-8.

[13] Rao, R.L. and Iyengar, S.S. (1994) A Stochastic Approach to the Bin-Packing Prob-
      lem. *Proceedings of the 1994 ACM Symposium on Applied Computing*, Phoenix,
      Arizona, 6-8 March 1994, 261-265. https://doi.org/10.1145/326619.326742

[14] Rohlfshagen, P. and Bullinaria, J.A. (2007) A Genetic Algorithm with Exon Shuf-
      fling Crossover for Hard Bin Packing Problems. *Proceedings of the 9th Annual
      Conference on Genetic and Evolutionary Computation*, London, 7-11 July 2007,
      1365-1371. https://doi.org/10.1145/1276958.1277213

[15] Pimpawat, C. and Chaiyaratana, N. (2004) Three-Dimensional Container Loading
      Using a Cooperative Co-Evolutionary Genetic Algorithm. *Applied Artificial Intelli-
      gence*, **18**, 581-601. https://doi.org/10.1080/08839510490483260

[16] Corcoran, A.L. and Wainwright, R.L. (1992) A Genetic Algorithm for Packing in
      Three Dimensions. *Proceedings of the 1992 ACM/SIGAPP Symposium on Applied
      Computing*, Kansas City, 1021-1030. https://doi.org/10.1145/130069.130126

[17] Mantean, O. (2007) Genetically Designed Heuristics for the Bin Packing Problem.
      *Proceedings of the 9th Annual Conference Companion on Genetic and Evolutio-
      nary Computation*, London, 7-11 July 2007, 2869-2872.
      https://doi.org/10.1145/1274000.1274088

[18] Lau, H. C. and Wang, H. (2005) A Multi-Agent Approach for Solving Optimization
      Problems Involving Expensive Resources. *Proceedings of the 2005 ACM Sympo-
      sium on Applied Computing*, Santa Fe, New Mexico, 13-17 March 2005, 79-83.
      https://doi.org/10.1145/1066677.1066699

[19] Epstein, L. and Van Stee, R. (2006) This Side Up! *ACM Transactions on Algo-
      rithms*, **2**, 228-243. https://doi.org/10.1145/1150334.1150339

[20] Lim, A. and Zhang, X. (2005) The Container Loading Problem. *Proceedings of the
      2005 ACM Symposium on Applied Computing*, Santa Fe, New Mexico, 13-17
      March 2005, 913-917. https://doi.org/10.1145/1066677.1066888

A Rule based Evolutionary Optimization Approach for the Traveling Salesman Problem

Wissam M. Alobaidi[1*], David J. Webb[2], Eric Sandgren[1*]

[1]Systems Engineering Department, Donaghey College of Engineering & Information Technology, University of Arkansas at Little Rock, Little Rock, AR, USA
[2]Axalta Coating Systems, Front Royal, VA, USA
Email: *wmalobaidi@ualr.edu, *exsandgren@ualr.edu

Abstract

The traveling salesman problem has long been regarded as a challenging application for existing optimization methods as well as a benchmark application for the development of new optimization methods. As with many existing algorithms, a traditional genetic algorithm will have limited success with this problem class, particularly as the problem size increases. A rule based genetic algorithm is proposed and demonstrated on sets of traveling salesman problems of increasing size. The solution character as well as the solution efficiency is compared against a simulated annealing technique as well as a standard genetic algorithm. The rule based genetic algorithm is shown to provide superior performance for all problem sizes considered. Furthermore, a post optimal analysis provides insight into which rules were successfully applied during the solution process which allows for rule modification to further enhance performance.

Keywords

Traveling Salesman, Evolutionary Optimization, Rule Based Search, Heuristic Optimization, Hybrid Genetic Algorithm

1. Introduction

The traveling salesman problem is an example of a NP complete problem where the computational time required to generate an exact solution increases exponentially with the number of cities involved. The objective is to minimize the path length required to visit a specified set of N cities, starting at one city, visiting each city exactly one time and returning to the city from which the path was originated. This problem is known as a combinatorial minimization problem with discrete variables. The discrete nature of the problem arises from the fact that each city may be numbered as an integer selection and a non-integer selection has no significance. The number of possible routes is factorially large, so that the solution may not be generated practically via an exhaustive search. The discrete nature of the problem eliminates the use of gradient nonlinear programming techniques as well as introducing a large number of local minima. The selection of cities without replacement (each city is visited only once) adds another difficulty in generating the solution through the use of a traditional genetic based algorithm. The problem's origin dates back to the early days of linear programming and continues to serve as a benchmark for new solution algorithms. The problem is representative of a large number of practical optimization formulations, including electronic circuit design, scheduling, pick-up and delivery and providing home health care or other services. The size of practical applications can range from tens of cities to tens of thousands of cities. While many algorithms can solve problems involving tens of cities, most have extreme difficulty with problems involving over one hundred cities.

A host of solution algorithms have been developed to address the traveling salesman problem over a time period of more than fifty years starting with the pioneering work of Dantzig [1]. The original work treated the problem as a discrete linear programming problem and was severely limited in the number of cities that could be addressed. Since that time, applications of various branch and bound methods [2] have been applied to handle the discrete nature of the problem. Simulated annealing [3] [4] approaches have been utilized in order to avoid the multitude of local minima contained in the problem. Tabu search [5] and other meta-heuristic approaches have been applied as another means of locating a global solution. Neural networks applications provide one means of implementing a simplistic rule based solution [6]. Ant colony search [7] provides another approach which seeks to mimic natural processes to avoid being trapped at local minima. Various versions of evolutionary optimization [8] [9] have been developed for the particular problem class represented by the traveling salesman problem. An excellent summary of approaches prior to 1983 is provided by Kindervater and Lenstra [10]. Summaries of more modern approaches are common in the literature [11] [12] [13]. The search for a reliable solution technique continues today with recent work by Agarhor *et al.* [14] utilizing an improved genetic algorithm based on the behavior of predatory animals, and the previous work by Kaur and Murugappan [15] who produced a hybrid genetic algorithm which works on combinations of nearest neighboring cities in conjunction with a traditional genetic algorithm. Much progress has been made over the years, but to date generating an optimal solution to the traveling salesman problem remains a difficult task. It remains the topic of considerable interest.

An interesting collective attribute found in most of the approaches is the application of heuristic procedures imbedded in various aspects of the solution process. These procedures are found to work well for certain classes or subsets of the traveling salesman problem, but few algorithmic platforms exist which can implement a wide range of heuristics in an intelligent environment. A rule based, evolutionary approach has the compatibility of supporting a general heuristic environment where the success of each heuristic can be monitored and the overall performance of the algorithm can be improved over time through continued monitoring and refinement of the heuristics implemented.

The goal here is to demonstrate that a rule based genetic algorithm operating with a simplistic rule set can perform as well or better than an expert, which in this case will be represented by an algorithm explicitly designed for this class of problems, the method of simulated annealing. A brief review of the simulated annealing approach and a conventional genetic algorithm will lead into the development of the rule based approach. The three algorithms are then executed on sets of randomly generated traveling salesman problems ranging in size from ten to one hundred cities. Each problem size is represented by ten problems where the location of each city is generated randomly within the defined solution space. All algorithms are tasked with solving the same set of problems. None of the algorithms tested are claimed to be overly efficient, but the results represent the general trend which would be expected in the application of a generic implementation of the particular algorithm class. The results from this comparative study show the initial promise of the rule based approach. To further document the power of the approach, a set of fifteen problems taken from TSBLIB 95 [16] were also tested. This problem set includes problems collected specifically designed to test new solution methods for the traveling salesman problem.

From the work conducted to date, many of the most promising approaches to solving the traveling salesman problem have involved the use of heuristics. The ability to imbed an arbitrary set of heuristics into the framework of a genetic algorithm forms the basis of this research. Rules generated from previous hybrid methods have been combined with new strategies to form an efficient solution algorithm. This algorithm is tested on a wide variety of problems to demonstrate the ability of the approach in generating the global optimum for problems. While it is fairly easy to generate a local solution that is within five to ten percent of the global optimum, it is extremely difficult to generate the global optimum. In all test cases utilized, the global optimum was located. It is also demonstrated that by tracking the success of the various heuristics or rules, the algorithm can undergo continuous modification to increase the performance. This can lead to an automated rule update which would allow for an aspect of learning occurring.

2. Simulated Annealing

Simulated annealing is a global optimization technique which mimics the behavior of cooling metal from a molten to a solid state. At high temperatures, the molecules are free to move freely in the molten metal. As the liquid cools and solidifies, however, the mobility of the molecules is lost. If the process is carefully controlled and the cooling takes place in a relatively slow fashion, a pure crystal-line structure is formed. This structure represents the state of minimum energy. If the cooling is allowed to occur too rapidly, the material ends up in an amorphous state having higher energy in the structure. Most optimization algorithms are greedy in that they attempt to reach the minimum in the least amount of time. This corresponds to the quick quenching of a molten metal and generally results in the location of local minima. Following the analogy of the simulated annealing technique, a non-greedy or global optimization technique can be generated which is ideally suited for the traveling salesman problem.

The simulated annealing method is based on the Boltzmann probability distribution which expresses the probabilistic distribution of energy states for a system in equilibrium. The distribution may be expresses as:

$$\text{Prob}(E) \sim \exp\left(-\frac{E}{KT}\right) \tag{1}$$

In the above equation, T represents the system temperature, E, the system energy and k, the Boltzmann constant which is a physical constant. The equation states that even at a low temperature, there is a probability that the system may be in a high energy state. It is therefore possible to leave a local minimum energy state and find a lower energy state, although it may be necessary to temporarily increase the energy state to accomplish this. In the early 1950s, this principle was incorporated into a numerical optimization algorithm, known as the Metropolis algorithm [17]. From a current objective function value of E_1, a second value, E_2 will be accepted with a probability of

$$P = \exp\left(\frac{-(E_2 - E_1)}{KT}\right) \tag{2}$$

If E_2 is less than E_1, the probability is greater than unity and the new point is accepted. Even if E_2 is greater than E_1, there is a finite possibility of acceptance. This provides a general downhill search, with an occasional uphill move to help increase the likelihood of locating the global minimum. The values of K and T help define a specific algorithm. As the temperature T is reduced, the possibility of accepting a design which is inferior to the current design decreases.

To actually implement a Metropolis algorithm, several elements must be defined. These elements include:

1. A representation of possible system configurations
2. A random generator of new system configurations
3. An objective function to be minimized which can be calculated directly from a system configuration
4. A control parameter, T, and an annealing schedule which specifies how the temperature is lowered during the search process.

Some problem specific experimentation is generally required in order to determine appropriate values of T and the cooling schedule consisting of the number of iterations taken between temperature changes and the amount of a temperature change. An implementation for the traveling salesman problem is straightforward.

Given a series of city location coordinates (x_i, y_i) for a total of N cities, the task becomes one of determining the order of travel from one city to the next while visiting each city exactly once and returning to the originating city by traveling the minimum total distance. The representation of possible system configurations is given by selecting a set of N integers without replacement which represents a possible route for the salesman. New configurations may be generated in a large number of ways. The particular generator used in this study is given in Numerical Recipes [18]. Two types of city rearrangements are considered. The first selects a portion of the route, removes it and replaces the path with the same cities in reverse order. The second rearrangement removes a portion of the path and inserts the removed path in a different location. These rearrangements were suggested by Lin [19]. They are of interest in this study as they are actually rule based modifications which can easily be implemented within the rule based genetic code. The objective function is simply the total distance traveled which in this case will be:

$$F(x) = \sum_{i=1}^{N} \left\{ \left(x_i - x_{i+1} \right)^2 + \left(y_i - y_{i+1} \right)^2 \right\}^{\frac{1}{2}} \tag{3}$$

It is understood that the $N+1$ point is the origination city (city 1). The annealing schedule used is that suggested in the text Numerical Recipes. A starting temperature, T, is selected which is larger than any change in distance normally encountered during a reconfiguration. Each temperature is held constant for 100 N reconfigurations or after 10 N successful reconfigurations, whichever occurs first. The temperature is then decreased by ten percent and the process repeated until no improvement is made during the current iteration.

3. Solution via a Traditional Genetic Algorithm

In order to gauge the difficulty of solution of the traveling salesman problem, a traditional genetic algorithm was also utilized. Some modification was required in the design encoding and crossover operations to guard against the introduction of duplicate cities appearing in a specific design representation. As with the simulated annealing technique, a design representation consists of N unique values, with each value representing a city to visit. The order of the string of values signifies the order of travel which allows the total distance traveled to be calculated via Equation (3). For example a design representation for a ten city problem could be:

X = {1, 4, 7, 3, 5, 9, 2, 6, 10, 8}

Or

X = {7, 4, 2, 10, 3, 9, 1, 5, 8, 6}

Each representation consists of ten unique cities to visit in the order specified. The difficulty for the genetic algorithm is that there is no inherent way of re-

stricting the re-use of cities (*i.e.* selection without replacement). The second issue involves the crossover operation. As an example, let the two design representations listed above be the selected parents for a crossover operation. In addition, let the crossover point be given as the fifth position in the string. Switching
the first and second portions of the design representations at the fifth position
produces the following offspring:

$X_1 = \{1, 4, 7, 3, 5, 9, 1, 5, 8, 6\}$

And

$X_2 = \{7, 4, 2, 10, 3, 9, 2, 6, 10, 8\}$

Notice that even though both parent representations had no duplication of cities, both child representations do have multiple replications. Thus, the child representations do not represent valid travel orders for the problem. There are a
number of possible implementations to avoid this problem. The one selected for
this trial was simply to let each original design encoding to be represented by a
string of integers, each ranging in value from one to N. Duplicate city values are
eliminated during the distance evaluation by simple replacement of the duplicate
values with the nearest (in number) city which has not been used previously in
the design encoding. For example, the order represented by X_1 above would be
evaluated as the string:

$X_1' = \{1, 4, 7, 3, 5, 9, 2, 6, 8, 10\}$

This replacement scheme also eliminates the crossover issue as duplicate values in the design representation are eliminated before evaluating the objective
function. With this modification, the remainder of the genetic algorithm remained as coded for general problem solution.

4. The Rule Based Genetic Code

As opposed to a traditional genetic formulation, a rule based formulation utilizes
an encoding which contains rules which operate on one or more trial orderings
of cities. A single rule, or a combination of multiple rules, may be executed at
any point in the solution process. As the process continues, the trial orderings
improve and a history of which rules or combination of rules were successful in
the search is maintained. This procedure converts the genetic algorithm to a
heuristic approach which is more in line with algorithms which have proven to
be capable of solving the traveling salesman problem. The maintained history
may be utilized to improve the rule set by eliminating rules which had little impact on the process and continually improving the rule which were utilized successfully. A rich set of potential rules is available from the wide variety of heuristic algorithms generated to date. A major advantage of the rule based approach
is that the encoding size utilized in the algorithm need not increase with the size
of the problem being solved.

At an elementary level, the rule based evolutionary process may be defined by
an encoding of a rule set similar to that shown in **Figure 1**. Here, the first element in the encoding string identifies how many rules are to be executed. This

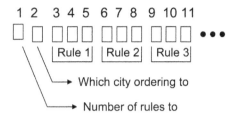

Figure 1. A rule based encoding for the traveling salesman problem.

allows for several rules to be applied to a trial ordering at the same time. The second element in the decision string specifies which current trial ordering of cities to apply the rules to. If only a single trial ordering is maintained, this element may be eliminated. Realizing the fact that there are a multitude of local minima in the search space, it seems wise to operate on a population of trial city orderings. This may increase the solution time, but allows for a population of rules to be applied to a population of trial orderings. Subsequent groups of encoding elements are utilized to define which specific rule or rules to apply with specific information blocks which define precisely how each rule is to be executed. The fact that only three such rule execution blocks are included in the encoding represented in **Figure 1** is not a limitation as the encoding may be expanded as needed or desired. In order to insure consistency in the crossover operation, the length of each rule execution block equal in length.

For the rule based genetic code, five separate rules were implemented. These rules are described as follows:

1. Selecting a group of cities in the design representation, removing them and inserting the group in an alternate location.
2. Selecting the closest neighbors to a specific city and exchanging the position of the nearest neighbors with the current neighbors.
3. Ordering a selected subgroup of cities by relative distance to each other.
4. Selecting a group of cities and reversing the order of the cities in that group.
5. Reordering a sub-group of cities based on roulette wheel selection based on distance.

Rules one and four are simply the rules implemented in the simulated annealing code. Rules two and three are distance re-ordering procedures as is rule five which actually makes use of coding present in the genetic algorithm. Rule five is specifically inserted to allow for a route selection which is not simply the local least distance from city to city to help avoid the arrival at a local minimum. Other rules could have been selected and perhaps would have been more appropriate. The goal here is to simply demonstrate the effectiveness of the concept rather than to develop the ultimate genetic algorithm for the traveling salesman problem.

The encoding of the rules in a design encoding is contained in the generic format listed below:

$$A\,B\,C_1 D_1 E_1 F_1 \quad C_2 D_2 E_2 F_2 \quad C_3 D_3 E_3 F_3 \cdots C_n D_n E_n F_n \qquad (4)$$

The A field represents the number of rules to apply, the B field represents which of the current city orderings to apply the rule set to. The field C_i represents which rule to apply and the fields D_i, E_i and F_i provide specific rule implementation information. The subscript n represents the maximum number of rules to be exercised in one modification of a selected design encoding (7 for this trial). The values for the B string position are integers in the range of one to the number of trial city orderings retained in the search process. The range of values for string position C_i includes the integers from one to the number of possible rules (5 in this example). The values of the remaining string positions are interpreted according to the rule specified by the C_i string position. For this particular implementation, the fields D_i, E_i and F_i represent city location or design string location and as such can have any integer value from 1 to N, the number of cities to visit. The specific interpretation of these values is defined as:

For rule 1:

D_i represents the first city in the selected group for movement in the design string.

E_i represents the number of cities in the selected group for movement.

F_i represents the city after which the selected string is inserted.

For rule 2:

D_i represents the first city in the selected group to re-order by distance.

E_i represents the number of cities to re-order by distance.

F_i is ignored for this rule implementation.

Note: The execution of this rule simply starts at the city specified in the field D_i and selects the closest city from the following cities of number specified in the field E_i and swaps the positions of the cities accordingly. This may be thought of a crude way of locally minimizing the distance of a sub-group of cities.

For rule 3:

D_i represents the city selected from which to locate nearest neighbors to.

E_i represents the number of nearest neighbors to find and swap positions with existing citiy neighbors.

F_i is ignored for this rule implementation.

For rule 4:

D_i represents the starting city for the group of cities to be reversed in order.

E_i represents the number of cities in the group to be re-ordered.

F_i is ignored for this rule implementation.

For rule 5:

D_i represents the first city in the selected group to re-order by distance based on roulette wheel selection.

E_i represents the number of cities to re-order.

F_i represents the position to initiate the random number generator for the roulette wheel spins.

Note: This rule is similar in nature to rule 3, however it allows for the selection of adjacent cities which are not nearest neighbors which is important to avoid being trapped in a local minimum. The value specified by the field F_i is important in that it allows the rule to be executed in the exact way for each future generation.

5. The Test Problem Set

A series of test problems was generated randomly on a ten mile by ten mile rectilinear region. Problem size was varied with ten problems each at sizes of ten, twenty, fifty and one hundred cities. The x and y coordinates for each problem were stored in a data file which was subsequently read in to the various optimization algorithms. A solution for each set of ten problems was generated by simulated annealing, a traditional genetic algorithm and a rule based genetic algorithm. The results were then averaged for each solution method for each grouping of the same number of cities. While the ten city problem set was relatively easily solved, the difficulty increased significantly with the number of cities considered as expected. The algorithm performance results are summarized in **Table 1**.

From the above table several interesting observations can be made. First of all, the traditional genetic algorithm was not well suited for this class of problem. The ten city problem set was solved with the identical average number of path distance evaluations as for the simulated annealing algorithm. As the number of cities increased, however, the traditional genetic algorithm was simply incapable of locating a solution regardless of population size and number of generations allowed. This would indicate that the traditional genetic algorithm would have similar difficulty solving any routing or scheduling problem. The method of simulated annealing worked reliably on small scale problems, but it had difficulty locating the exact optimal solution. As expected, the number of path evaluations increased dramatically with problem size, and with additional experimentation in parameter selection, the results are likely to improve.

The interesting result is that the rule based genetic algorithm outperformed the simulated annealing technique both in the number of path evaluations re-

Table 1. Solution summary for various algorithms on traveling salesman problems of various size.

Number of Cities	Genetic Code	Genetic Code	Simulated Annealing	Simulated Annealing	Rule Based GA	Rule Based GA
	Average Function Evaluations	Times Best Solution Located	Average Function Evaluations	Times Best Solution Located	Average Function Evaluations	Times Best Solution Located
10	10800	10	10800	10	133	10
20	*	0	39600	10	2657	10
50	*	0	121500	4	76009	10
100	*	0	321000	1	228763	10

*indicates solution not achieved with reasonable number of evaluations.

quired as well as the ability to locate the best solution. No significant effort was
made to establish the best operational parameters for the code. It should be
noted that the rule based code utilized an initial population based on randomly
generated paths. It is difficult to compare results between the rules based genetic
algorithm and the simulated annealing algorithm as they arrived at different solutions for many of the test problems. In general the speed of solution may be
traced directly to the number of path evaluations which are plotted in **Figure 2**.

The number of function evaluations required for the rule based genetic algorithm is significantly below that required by the simulated annealing algorithm.
Both algorithms demonstrate a significant increase in required function evaluations as problem size increases which points out the difficulty in solving this
class of problems as the scale increases. Exact numbers of evaluations may vary
with input parameter selection and as such exact comparisons should be made
with caution. It definitely can be stated, however, that the performance of the
rule based genetic algorithm is as good or superior to the simulated annealing
technique and orders of magnitude better than the performance of a traditional
genetic algorithm.

The solution for one of the problems of each size is pictured in the following
Figures 3-6.

From **Figures 3-6**, it can be seen that the solutions generated are reasonable
paths to minimize the distance traveled. It can also be seen how the difficulty of
the problem increases with the number of cities considered.

The results on these randomly generated problem sets demonstrate the potential of a rule based genetic approach. It was the only algorithm of those tested
which was capable of consistently generating global solutions to the test problems. The other algorithms could generate local optimal solutions that were
within a few percent of the global optimal solution. This demonstrates that even

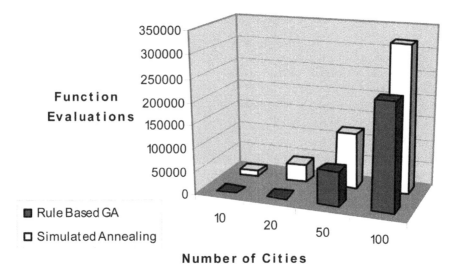

Figure 2. Comparison of number of the average number of function evaluations required
for solution between algorithms.

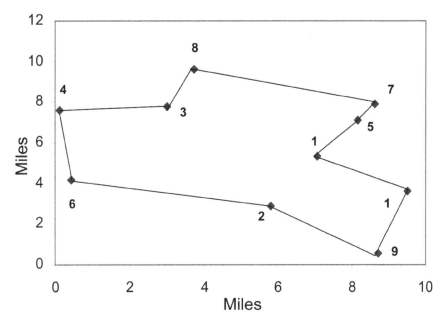

Figure 3. Solution path for a ten city problem.

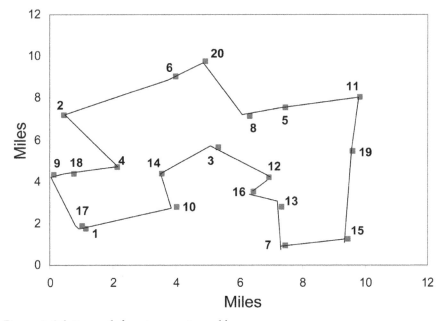

Figure 4. Solution path for a twenty city problem.

though the simulated annealing approach was designed to find global minima, this is not always the case. The other point of note is in the number of function evaluations required to generate the solution. The rule based algorithm was more efficient, although the efficiency dropped off as the problem size increased. Even for the one hundred city test group, however, the number of function evaluations was considerably lower. Thus, the rule based approach was more robust in relation to locating the global solution as well as more efficient in the solution time required.

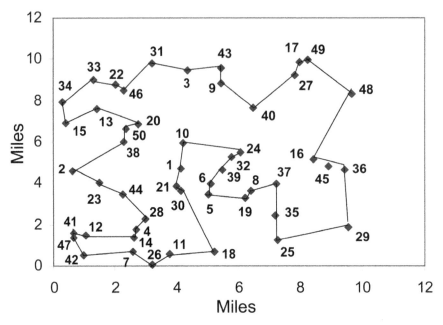

Figure 5. Solution path for a fifty city problem.

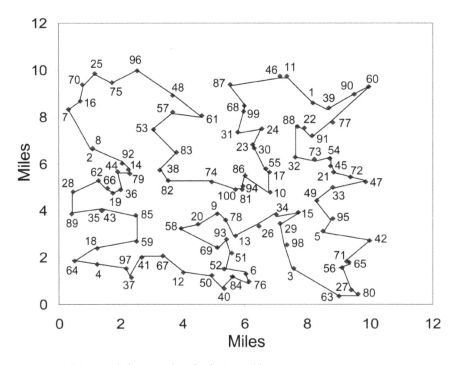

Figure 6. Solution path for a one hundred city problem.

6. Evaluation of Rule Selection

As was stated previously, no significant effort was put into selecting the rule set for this problem for the rule based genetic algorithm. The performance of the algorithm could potentially be enhanced significantly by careful evaluation of which rules factored into the solution process and then modifying rules or selecting new rules based on this information. As the genetic algorithm is capable of maintaining a solution history, an evaluation of the implemented rules may be made following single or multiple problem solutions. The following **Figures 7-10** present the percentage of the time a successful new path was located with each of the rules, averaged over the ten problems in each set. A successful new path is simply a path which is better than the current best path in the population.

From **Figures 7-10**, several observations may be made. First of all, each of the rules was utilized in the solution process of the rule based genetic algorithm. Each of the five rules is fairly equally utilized for the ten and twenty city problem sets. As the problem size increases, it appears that rules 2, 3 and 4 begin to be-

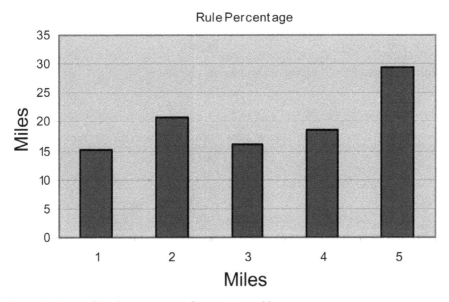

Figure 7. Successful rule percentages for ten city problem.

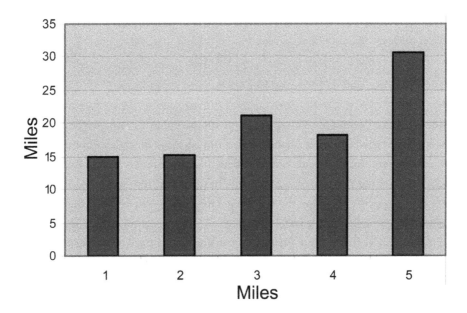

Figure 8. Successful rule percentages for twenty city problem.

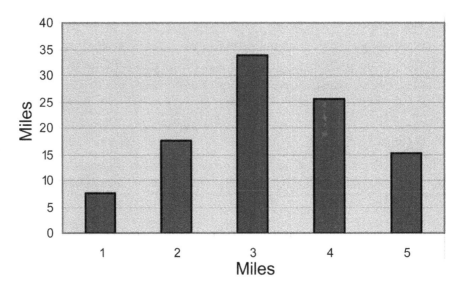

Figure 9. Successful rule percentages for fifty city problem.

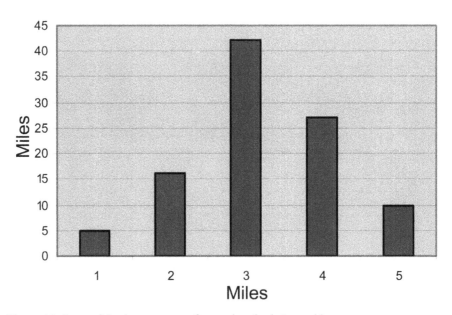

Figure 10. Successful rule percentages for one hundred city problem.

become more dominant. This points out the fact that as the problem size increases, the type of rules implemented may need some modification to maintain an efficient solution. The advantage is that this information is available and can help improve the performance of the rule based algorithm on a particular problem class. Specific rules for the traveling salesman problem are difficult as the minimum distance path leaves little room for interpretation. The rule set for a scheduling or delivery route planning problem would have obvious rules which could be productively implemented. For example, in a manufacturing scheduling problem with machine setups, one rule might be to try and group jobs which require little or no set-up time on a specific machine. Rules such as this will guide the solution through local minima, to a representative, global solution. It certainly makes sense to include as much problem specific information as possible for a particular problem class. On the other hand, one must guard against generating a greedy algorithm which quickly locates a local, rather than a global solution, unless a local solution is all that is desired. Local solutions can be avoided by maintaining some rules which can perform generic alteration in a design string which will help maintain the global character of the genetic solution process.

In order to demonstrate the robust nature of the rule based evolutionary approach, an additional 15 problems were solved. These problems were selected from the test problem set maintained by the University of Heidelberg and represent traveling salesman problems varying in the number of cities. The best known solution for each of the problems is also recorded. Fifteen problems ranging from fifty to 200 cities were selected and solutions were generated. The results generated by the rule based algorithm are documented in **Table 2**. From this table it can be seen that the rule based algorithm located the global solution in every case. This is further confirmation that the algorithm is robust and is able to locate a global optimum for most cases.

7. Summary and Conclusions

The framework for a general rule based, evolutionary environment is presented which can be utilized as an intelligent platform for the investigation of heuristic approaches for solving the traveling salesman and other related decision support problems. A set of five simple rules was embedded into the encoding of the ge-

Table 2. Results on TSPLIB problems.

Problem	Number of Cities	Best known Solution	Rule Based GA Result
Eil 51	51	426	426
Berlin 52	52	7542	7542
Eil 76	76	538	538
Rat 99	99	1211	1211
KroA 100	100	21282	21282
KroB 100	100	22141	22141
KroC 100	100	20749	20749
Eil 101	101	538	538
Pr 107	107	44303	44303
Bier 127	127	118282	118282
Ch 130	130	6110	6110
Ch 150	150	6528	6528
D198	198	15780	15780
Pr 226	226	80369	80369
A280	280	2579	2579

netic algorithm for the evaluation of the feasibility of the approach. The rule based algorithm was tested on sets of ten problems with randomly generated city locations for problem sizes including ten, twenty, fifty and one hundred cities. For comparison purposes, a traditional genetic algorithm and a simple simulated annealing algorithm were utilized to solve the same problem sets. The results demonstrate the potential of the rule based genetic approach. None of the tested algorithms were tuned or tailored for efficiency on the problem set. The rule based approach was able to consistently locate better quality solutions with less computational effort that the other two algorithms tested. Additionally, fifteen problems from a recognized test set of traveling salesman problems were solved and compared to the best known solutions. In every case the new algorithm located the global optimum.

The post evaluation of the results from the test problem sets point out which of the rules applied had the most positive impact on the search process. This analysis allows for the replacement of non-effective rules and for refinement of rules to increase their impact of the process. The effectiveness of individual rules was shown to be a function of problem size which is an indication that the rule set may have to be more sophisticated in order to solve problems involving one thousand cities or more. Additional tracking of rule combinations that proved to be effective could be easily accomplished. The concept is to provide an open computational platform which can be improved in performance over time to become increasingly effective in solving a particular problem class. A wide range of heuristic options may be provided initially and paired down over time.

The proposed algorithm executes a population of rules on a small population of potential city routes. This allows for large problems to be executed with a limited population size that need not grow significantly as the problem size increases. Currently, the initial city route population is generated randomly, but the possibility of utilizing a two phase approach is real option. This approach would cycle between a conventional genetic approach operating upon the specified city order encoding and the rule based approach improving the members of the phase one population. Additional rules such as the so called double bridge move proposed by Martin, Otto and Felton [20] may be easily incorporated. The existing framework, even with the simplistic rule set employed provides the basis for continued development and application to larger sets of problems.

References

[1]   Dantzig, G.B., Fulkerson, D.R. and Johnson, S.M. (1954) Solution of a Large-Scale Traveling Salesman Problem. *Operations Research*, **2**, 393. https://doi.org/10.1287/opre.2.4.393

[2]   Balas, E. and Toth, P. (1985) Branch and Bound Methods. In: Lawler, E.L., Lenstra, J.K., Rinnooy Kan, A.H.G. and Shmoys, D.B., Eds., *The Traveling Salesman Problem: A Guided Tour of Combinatorial Optimization*, John Wiley & Sons, New York, 80-147.

[3]   Lo, C.C. and Hus, C.C. (1998) Annealing Framework with Learning Memory. *IEEE*

Transactions on System, Man, Cybernetics, Part A: Systems and Humans, **28**, 1-13.

[4] Pepper, J.W., Golden, B.L. and Wasil, E.A. (2002) Solving the Traveling Salesman Problem with Annealing-Based Heuristics: A Computational Study. *IEEE Transactions on System, Man, Cybernetics, Part A: Systems and Humans*, **32**, 72-77. https://doi.org/10.1109/3468.995530

[5] Glover, F. Tabu Search—Parts I and II. *ORSA J. Computing*, Vol. 1, 190-206, 1989 and Vol. 2, 4-32, 1990.

[6] Tsai, C.F. and Tsai, C.W. (2002) A New Approach for Solving Large Traveling Salesman Problem Using Evolutionary Ant Rules. *Neural Networks*, 2002 *IJCNN'02 Proceedings of the* 2002 *International Joint Conference*, **2**, 1540-1545.

[7] Modares, A., Somhom, S. and Enkawa, T. (1999) A Self-organizing Approach for Multiple Traveling Salesman and Vehicle Routing Problems. *International Transactions in Operations Research*, **5**, 591-606. https://doi.org/10.1111/j.1475-3995.1999.tb00175.x

[8] Julstrom, B.A. (1995) Very Greedy Crossover in a Genetic Algorithm for the Traveling Salesman Problem. SAIC '95: Proceedings of the 1995 ACM Symposium on Applied Computing, Nashville, Tennessee, 26-28 February 1995, 324-328. https://doi.org/10.1145/315891.316009

[9] Wang, L.Y., Zhang, J. and Li, H. (2007) An Improved Genetic Algorithm for TSP. *Machine Learning and Cybernetics*, 2007 *International Conference*, 2, 925-928. https://doi.org/10.1109/icmlc.2007.4370274

[10] Kindervater, G.A.P. and Lenstra, J.K. (1985) Parallel Algorithms. In: O'hEigeartaigh, M., Lenstra, J.K. and Rinnooy, A.G., Eds., *Combinatorial Optimization: Annotated Bibliographies*, Wiley, Chichester, 106-128.

[11] Osman, I. and Kelly, J. (1996) Meta-Heuristics: An Overview. In: Osman, I. and Kelly, J., Eds., *Meta-Heuristics: Theory and Applications*, Kluwer, Boston, 1-21.

[12] Katayama, K., Hirabayashi, H. and Narihisa, H. (1998) Performance Analysis of a New Genetic Crossover for the Traveling Salesman Problem. *IEICE Transactions on Fundamentals of Electronics, Communications and Computer Sciences*, **E81-A**, 738-750.

[13] Applegate, D.L., Bixby, R.E., Chvatal, V. and Cook, W.J. (2007) The Traveling Salesman Problem: A Computational Study. Princeton University Press, Princeton.

[14] Agharghor, A., Riffi, M.E. and Chebihi, F. (2016) A Memetic Hunting Search Algorithm for the Traveling Salesman Problem. 2016 4*th IEEE International Colloquium on Information Science and Technology*, Tangier, 206-209. https://doi.org/10.1109/cist.2016.7805043

[15] Kaur, D. and Murugappan, M.M. (2008) A Genetic Algorithm Balancing Exploration and Exploitation for the Traveling Salesman Problem. *Annual Meeting of the North American Fuzzy Information Processing Society Fuzzy Information Processing Society*, Annual Meeting of the North American, 1-6 May 2008.

[16] Reinelt, G. TSBLIB 95, Universitat Heidelberg, Institut fur Angewandte Mathematik.

[17] Metropolis, N., Rosenbluth, A., Teller, M. and Teller, E.J. (1953) Equations of State Calculations by Fast Computing Machines. *The Journal of Chemical Physics*, **21**, 1087-1092. https://doi.org/10.1063/1.1699114

[18] Press, W.H., Flannery, B.P., Teukolsky, S.A. and Vetterling, W.T. (1986) Numerical Recipes. Cambridge University Press, New York.

[19] Lin, S. (1965) Computer Solution of the Traveling Salesman Problem. *The Bell System Technical Journal*, **44**, 2245-2269.
https://doi.org/10.1002/j.1538-7305.1965.tb04146.x

[20] Martin, O., Otto, S.W. and Felten, W. (1992) Large-Step Markov Chains for the TSP Incorporating Local Search Heuristics. *Operations Research Letters*, **11**, 219-224.

8

Brokers as Catalysts for the E-Health Market

Vivian Vimarlund[1,2], Craig Kuziemsky[3], Christian Nøhr[4], Pirkko Nykänen[5], Nicolas Nikula[6]

[1]International Business School, Jönköping University, Jönköping, Sweden
[2]Department of Computer and Information Science/Human-Centered Systems, Linköping University, Linköping, Sweden
[3]University of Ottawa, Ottawa, Canada
[4]Aalborg University, Aalborg, Denmark
[5]University of Tampere, Tampere, Finland
[6]Post-Nord, Stockholm, Sweden
Email: Vivian.Vimarlund@liu.se, Vivian.Vimarlund@ju.se

Abstract

In this study we use the experiences from the service industry and explore pre-requisites of the e-health market which will need to achieve to stimulate both sides of the market (vendors, healthcare organizations, government, institutions, corporations and services organizations) to interact with each other and develop demand driven services and social innovations. The results presented in this paper may be of interest for decision makers, industries (e.g. software or technology designers), small and medium enterprises (SME) and entrepreneurs with an interest in becoming a part of the e-health market, and for consumers (e.g. healthcare personnel and patients) that are willing to influence the market through their choices. The outcomes of the study shown that the role of virtual brokers is essential to the further development of a sustainable e-health market globally because its role as catalyst for interaction between the two-sides of the markets, its effects on the reduction of competitive constrains, its effects on the accessibility to broader network of actors and its effects on the support of public-private exchanges of knowledge and experience.

Keywords

Virtual Brokers, Two-Sided E-Health Market, Demand Driven Services, Social Innovations

1. Introduction

Over the last few years, the trend has been to innovate healthcare delivery through increasing patient involvement and engagement as part of developing a patient-centered e-health system [1] [2] [3] [4]. For this reason, much effort has been put to improve interactions between and within producers and consumers of healthcare services in order to co-create social innovations[1] [4] [5]. Strategies have been developed around the world to meet the challenges that the transition to a more patient-centered system demands [6] [7]. In parallel with this, the e-health industry[2] continues to expand as a push market[3]. Vendors develop products that are aimed to address the healthcare challenges of the millennium (e.g. *Improve productivity, personalized medicine, round the clock monitoring, and empowerment of patients*) and to find arenas for interaction between producers and consumers and private and public actors to identify and co-create demand driven services that match preferences and needs of consumers (e.g. healthcare organizations and patients) [8].

Demand driven innovations are essential for companies to remain competitive in an increasingly complex, uncertain and changing environment such as the e-health market. While the possibility exists to increase adaptability while providing several direct benefits to the producers and, consequently, to its customers, e.g. quicker and cheaper innovation cycles, reduction of transaction costs, access to embedded information, etc., the co-creation of social innovations presupposes the existence of catalysts that make the right connections and links between producers and seekers of services while also facilitating the interaction between the two sides of the market. In the past, the discussion about issues that can contribute to developing a sustainable market for e-health services has been limited to identifying issues related to defining, designing and implemented specific e-health services. The market for social e-health innovations, however, in addition to offer good comercializable ideas that spin out new business, or that improve existing business, has shown the need to more proactively use virtual platforms as tools for to facilitate matching between the two sides of the market [12] [13] [14] and as a mediator that bring benefits, tangible and intangible, to both sides [15].

In this study we use the experiences from the service industry to explore pre-requisites the e-health market needs to achieve to stimulate both sides of the market (vendors, healthcare organizations, government, institutions, corporations and services organizations) to interact with each other, and to develop demand driven services and social innovations. The results of this study may be of interest for decision makers, industries (e.g. software or technology designers), small and medium enterprises (SME) and entrepreneurs who are interested in

[1]Social innovations include several different actors that cross the boundaries of organizations to innovate and co-produce services. Social innovations in a healthcare context include actors from both public and private organizations [9].

[2]E-health refers to health services and information delivered or enhanced through the Internet and related technologies. In a broader sense, the term characterizes not only a technical development, but also a state-of-mind, a way of thinking, an attitude, and a commitment for networked, global thinking, to improve health care locally, regionally, and worldwide by using information and communication technology [10].

[3]The e-health market was estimated to have a market size of approximate USD 85.44 billion in 2014 and is expected to reach USD 308.0 billion by 2022 [11].

becoming a part of the e-health market in the future, and for consumers (e.g. healthcare personnel and patients) who are willing to influence the market through their choices.

2. Method

The present study is based on previous research that was performed by the authors and reported in a book entitled "E-health two sided markets: Implementation and business models, 2016". We use also experiences from one service industry that uses virtual platforms as brokers which enable parties to benefit from trade or from interactions with partnerships. These benefits arise because the parties enjoy a reduction of transactions costs by minimizing costs for duplication, advertising and media support. We also use information that was obtained from a series of interviews and from a literature review that was performed in two previous studies [16] [17]. The first of these studies identified the challenges that customers and providers consider of importance to develop a sustainable market for social innovations. The second study sampled knowledge about challenges and opportunities associated with the development of a market for social innovations. We use the knowledge gained in those studies to illustrate the demands and expectations consumers and entrepreneurs have to join the e-health market and to compare expectations from the two sides of the e-health market with the goals the service market has when using brokers.

The paper has the following structure. First we discuss virtual brokers and the service industry and identify a list of outcomes that enable the development of social innovations. We then discuss the e-health market and describe how the aforementioned outcomes could enable the development and co-creation of social innovations for e-health. We then suggest specific requisites that the e-health market should guarantee to attract the two sides of the market.

2.1. Virtual Brokers and the Service Industry

The number of stakeholders in the service industry have greatly increased and their interactions between these stakeholders has become more complex [18] [19]. This increase in complexity has made cooperation for innovation less straightforward. Virtual brokers[4] are thus required to established links and to support the flow of information among the actors, but also to incentive them to enhance cooperation.

For many years the service industry has moved from push market to pull market that begins with the demand rather than the supply. In such a market, virtual platforms, are used as brokers that remove barriers for communication, build arenas for interaction between the two sides of the market, consumers and producers, and also offer the necessary marketing infrastructure that allows to

---

[4]The term "broker" has given rise to the connotation of virtual platforms that brings people together and that offers the possibility to strategically interact and match actors that pursue similar objectives. Brokers are facilitators of interaction and cooperation in innovation systems, and their activities extend throughout the two-sides of the market.

diminishing commercialization efforts, the develop of innovative business models, the use of distribution channels that made the services universally accessible and that at the same time offer demand driver services [19]. The use of brokers has facilitate the development of a space where interactions can take place between stakeholders that are different enough to have new knowledge but related enough to understand each other. This leads to the creation of innovations in a many to many relationship as demanded by the service industry [20] where brokers are expected to have the role of "systemic intermediaries".

Brokers in the service industry, are however, not only platforms that facilitate interaction between different stakeholders, they also offer software applications, innovative supply chain models [12], and mechanism or strategies that allow the follow up and re-use of services for further innovate. The use of virtual brokers has resulted in that firms of different sizes can enter to the market and benefit from using common virtual platforms (the broker). Some of the benefits include the reduction of competitive constrains, access to broader network of actors who exchange ideas and values, and the support of public-private exchanges of knowledge and experience [17].

The use of brokers in the service industry has made it possible to:

- Provide a platform that enables producers and consumers interact with each other as they identify demand driven services.
- Provide access to an infrastructure that the consumers cannot access in single markets (one producer, one consumer).
- Signal relevant market activity that make the both sides valuable to join up the platform.
- Apply principles, policies, and use networks that encourage consumers to use and trust the broker.
- Use innovative business and payment models.
- Offer multi-homing alternatives through the presence of several providers and suppliers (multi-homing) that offer comparable services and that have similar degrees of acceptance among the consumers.

Virtual brokers further allow the service industry the possibility to change the structure of the industry. This has been realized in terms of vertical integration (for tighter control and higher profit extraction power) and in terms of vertical disintegration (by using licenses that help to expand the market) [19].

One of the most important characteristic that virtual brokers possessed is the fact that they are entrepreneur-focused (as opposed to simple business focused). They help innovators and entrepreneurs realize their initial ideas all the way through to products that directly benefit from such collaboration and networking. Consequently, the sustainability of the brokers , much depends on factors such as: the existence of corporate social responsibility, the existence of policies and guidelines to guarantee quality, security and safety issues of relevance for the two sided of the market, the existence of networks that guarantee transparency and prevent market inefficiencies (e.g. monopolies, cartel, and negative external effects) [21], and the capacity to guarantee the development of long-term strategic planning and a dynamic evolution of the market [22].

2.2. Virtual Brokers and Social Innovations: Is the E-Health Market Ready to Use Virtual Brokers to Stimulate the Co-Creation of Social Innovations?

Technological developments, innovations, and the use of electronic devices across the world provide numerous opportunities for prominent players in to the e-health market to achieve the goals of the e-Health Acton Plan, namely to innovate healthcare for the 21 century [6]. The increasing use of tablets, smart phones, as a quick and easy mode of communication is likely to supplement the growth of the market. However, concerns related to the lack of reimbursement policies and the absences of brokers who can facilitate interaction of the two sides of the market currently hamper growth in the e-health market place. Note that in this market innovations are created by using embedded knowledge from actors outside the boundaries of the organization [23] [24] [25] [26].

To meet the demands of this marketplace, a series of portals and virtual platforms, normally owned by healthcare authorities, county councils, insurance companies etc, has been globally and national developed. These portals and platforms usually allow free access for patients to, for instance, health record systems and advice from healthcare personnel. They are, however, not specifically built arenas or forum where interoperability or an interchange of knowledge between the two sides of the market can take place. Outputs from interviews with representatives from the two sides of the markets (customers and suppliers) and from the literature review performed in previous studies, as mentioned in the method chapter, shown that there are a number of challenges that are of key relevance for to achieve and develop a sustainable e-health market that can stimulate co-creation and at the same time produce and deliver social innovations.

In general it seems that the lack of arenas in which consumer and producers can communicate and interact [26] to reduce costs related to interoperability to develop demand driven social innovations, are the major issues that constrain the development of the e-health market today. Further, there seems to be a need for to clarify rules and for to develop structures and arena that can be used to support interoperability and interaction between consumers and providers to be able to access and use the embedded knowledge they have in order to develop demand driven services and social innovations [13] [24] [26]-[31]. The development of innovative and alternative business models that sustain alternative payment and reimbursement alternatives also seems to be important [32] for the two sides of the market. Not with standing this, the absence of information of specific laws and regulations for different contexts and organizations, as well as obstacles to communication due to a changing environmental and changes in the actors also poses problems for those who has the ambition to join the e-health two-sided market of today [27] [28].

Comparing the outputs identified by providers and consumers in the studies focused in the e-health market, with the outcomes the use of virtual brokers have made possible for the service industry, it seems that there are no major differences between them (See the **Table 1**). An important question is how virtual brokers in e-health can meet demands of transparency in ownership, security and safety, and trust in communication [33]. Whilst simultaneously being subject to an open market that follows rules for the supply of services and regulates the entrance into the market.

Table 1. List of issues that are considered of key relevance by both sides of the e-health market and its correspondence with the main outcomes identified in the service industry as a consequence of the use of virtual brokers.

Lists of issues considered of key relevance by both sides of the e-health market to produce and deliver social innovations	Main outcomes to use brokers in the service industry
• A new view of doing business	• Provide a platform that enables producers and consumers interact with each other as they identify demand driven services
• Accessibility to equivalent services • Information about the type of services offered (complementary, substitutes, equivalent, belonging a base basket or considered as "luxury services" not necessary but useful to sample and register individual based information)	• Offer multi-homing alternatives through the presence of several providers and suppliers (multi-homing) that offer comparable services and that have similar degrees of acceptance among the consumers.
• An open market that allows actors to compete and collaborate with each other • Rules for the supply of services and entry to market	• Signal relevant market activity that made the both sides valuable to join up the platform
• Interoperable structures that reduce transaction costs • Structures that allow to use consumers' embedded knowledge	• Provide access to an infrastructure that the consumers cannot access in single markets (one producer, one consumer)
• Alternative innovative business, payment and reimbursement models • Knowledge to create new services that bring added value • Knowledge about the needs and the kind of services that match inter- and intra organizational demands • Shared accesses to individual data for personalization of services • Organizational demands and eventual legal differences between different kinds of organizations	• Use innovative business and payment models • Apply principles, policies, and use networks that encourage consumers to use and trust the broker

From the above, it seems rational to argue that brokers in the e-health market, in addition to facilitate an arena for interaction and co-creation of social innovations, need to guarantee the match between specific request that the e-health market presupposes and the demand of attracting firms and organization to produce and co-produce demand driven services. We suggest therefore, that e-health brokers who want to develop a sustainable arena of interaction and co-creation where both sides of the market are present consider to:

• Develop guidelines and policies regarding ownership of services and pre-requisites for access to the market and clear stipulate whether.
o The services should be owned 1) by an intermediary (for example a county council, a healthcare unit, an insurance company, a pharmaceutical company); 2) by agents (for example a patient organization, or by the company that produce the service), or 3) whether an alternative ownership model should exist.

o Contractual arrangements and property rights should be 1) generic or 2) specific depending the type of the services.

o Access to any virtual broker should be restricted to a limited number stakeholders of whether the broker will use an open source principle.

o Property rights are to be regulated by contracts or whether the services be open source.

- Offer Multi-home alternatives. In a market in which consumers' preferences are sufficiently homogenous (due the nature of the services offered) and given that they will guarantee quality, safely and privacy, the existence of several providers can contribute to an increase in social welfare. This is especially the case; if there are several providers of the same type of services that can guarantee the access to alterative that are equal equivalent to each other ("*multi-homing*") Multi-homing alternatives should further increase the degree of competition while contributing to diffuse innovations to a higher number of customers.

- Develop networks that diminish risks. The main challenge is the development of a coherent, sustainable and trusting arena were all relevant information can be transferred from all producers to all consumers in a structured, well defined, complete, and undistorted manner. To offer an arena for interaction that will attract risk-adverse actors, brokers will further need to guarantee the existence of several types of networks such as:

o *Knowledge networks* to develop new ways of thinking, where security and safety issues that can be helpful in solving transnational problems can be discussed. Knowledge networks should further support knowledge creation around products, services, goods and disseminate ideas for social innovation and order to align developers and customers" needs in a realistic manner.

o *Policy networks* to create policies even though they are not necessarily networks for government policy makers. Networks activities should cover the full range of steps in policy process (beyond to policy proposals) including agenda setting, policy formulation, rulemaking, coordination, implementation, and evaluation and developing of security policies and principles.

o Advocacy *networks* to change the agenda or policies of governments, corporations or other institutions. An advocacy network challenges business leaders to rethink not only their business strategy, but also their larger purpose and role in the global marketplace. Such a network should contributes to the visualization of important issues for the e-health area as well as the pre-requisites different health-care systems demand.

o *Watchdog networks* to ensure business of transparency, where institutions are scrutinized so as to ensure that they behave appropriately. Topics range from corruption and the environment to financial services. Customers and producers can evaluate the value of services at levels not possible before. The area for interaction the brokers offer should characterized as transparent, prepared for developing a brand or reputation that is sustainable over time, facilitates management systems, early warning systems and the visualization of open source support systems.

3. Discussion

While the e-health market is rapidly becoming fundamental to the provision of health and social care, efforts to establishing a market in which consumers and providers can interact with each other, benefit from each other and co-produce social innovations has increase. In view of the challenges the e-health market is confronted with as it strives to achieve sustainability, virtual brokers can have an strategic role to both accelerating the diffusion of services, and in facilitating interaction and in sustaining collaboration between the two sides of the market [34]. We thus consider the e-health market as a "pull market" in which consumers and producers interact with each other as they develop demand-driven services.

A mayor difficulty for the e-health market today, is the fact that many innovations are often incremental and form part of a continuous process of numerous small-scale advances. Outlooks of the-e-health market often discuss the need to covers several perspectives including political, technological, economic perspectives, and issues related to international cooperation, In addition, the needs to develop trust, security and cost-effectiveness of the services are also of importance. Furthermore, the e-health market needs to consider socio-technical and economic issues as it supports a sustainable relationship among the various industry participants, providers of e-health services and customers.

This is done so that the is able to solve externalities that affect the market, including laws, regulations, policies, market restrictions (for example, the price the consumers pay for the services, as in the case of the Scandinavian countries where the prices are regulated by policies and demand solutions such as subventions, roof prices , existence of public owned monopolies, etc.). The market must also improve operability so as to better maximize benefits for both sides of the market, namely the market and the individuals (consumers and patients) who use the e-health system.

From the interviews and the literature review that was previously performed, we learn that a general constrain for further development of the market is the absence of "connected services". The lack of information on whether some services will be complex, single, for example is also an issue because the level of responsibility providers can have. In today's market it is not clear who will be offering the services, how they will be accessible and how consumers' knowledge will be used to improve services. Entrepreneurs do not seems to be willing to both distribute and finance the services.

A central task for the future of the e-health market is, therefore, to actively investigate what services or social innovations consumers actually want. It is not longer an innovation to merely offer delivery of drugs or delivery of medical devices, or to offer "bank services" (*i.e.* online payment, etc.) and so on. The lack of capacity to capture embedded knowledge, individual preferences and attitudes [34], or knowledge about the inter-temporal use of e-health services, are major hurdles to enter the market. Consequently, considerable effort needs to be made in the future, if we are to better understand and integrate customer orientation into the design and deployment of e-health services and intermediary platforms.

Innovation researchers emphasize the importance of brokers in networks. Brokers connect stakeholders who are not familiar to each other but also allow them to improve upon the new combinations that are essential to the demand of innovation [34]. Virtual e-health brokers may bundle features that provide value to both sides of the market and maximize social welfare. Finally, because sustainable development of the e-health market depends a great deal upon the market structures that will be developed, the intermediaries will take the role as brokers and the development of infrastructures that allow information to flow within and between the two sided of the market. Learning from the service industry and extrapolating good experiences from this industry will allow us to avoid continuing to work with explorative approaches. Instead, concrete market innovations should be made. Much of the desired improved collaboration between the two sides of the e-health market requires a long-term perspective, and a willingness in investors that is based on the expectation that the collaboration will continue for a long time. It is rarely possible to specify in advance exactly how this might take place. If the service industry succeeds 1) in developing virtual brokers that work and 2) in developing co-owned joint ventures with guarantees of continued cooperation between their business partners, then the e-health market should definitely benefit from their experiences. The current imperfect interaction between the two sides of the e-health market is often not a result of unwillingness of the concerned parties to interact with each other, but of a lack of capacity, structures, and incentives to interact effectively. Enterprises or organizations that will play a role as virtual brokers in the future can close the gap. This will especially be the case if brokers can be shown to have a good reputation and a degree of independence from the major stakeholders in the process and the overall innovation system. This does not mean that brokers necessarily need to belong to specialized organizations, as is the case for the majority of the portals that have been developed in the area today. It can also be possible that organizations with legitimacy in the service area act at watchdog networks and guarantee the legitimacy of the brokers. In this context, they have an important potential role in contributing to the development of policies and guidelines and to the discussion of these policies and guidelines with industries and stakeholders who are interested in becoming brokers, locally and even globally.

4. Conclusion

The role of virtual brokers is essential for the evolution of the service market. They have contributed to the promotion of services; they match the demand with the best available services (based on customer needs and wants) and they provide the infrastructure that is needed to allow different parties to come into contact with each other, thereby reducing transaction costs and duplication costs. Virtual brokers also offer alternative business models. Virtual brokers have taken on the role of being "watchdogs", ensuring that the ecosystem that the broker offers are used to provide "good things", for example, by preventing market inefficiencies (e.g., monopolies, cartels, and negative external effects). Virtual brokers help in the continuous scaling of new collaborative ideas, encourage interoperability and cooperation among individuals, organizations and companies as they share information, build alliances, and develop complementary products and services. In further research it will be of interest to investigate if and how the two sides of the market are willing to use the brokers developed in the service industry to interact with each other and develop social innovations. It is also of importance to validate the theoretical assumptions that are presented in this paper with the industries, organizations, and customers, and to enquire of them which additional pre-requisites, if any, are necessary to consider as the e-health market continues to expand. Finally, it is also of relevance to sample knowledge about preferences regarding the type of brokers that will be chosen, whether they are private or public, or belong to companies that have not traditionally been active in the e-health market, but have experience in creating a space where providers and customers can meaningfully interact with each other.

References

[1]   Koch, S. (2012) Improving Quality of Life through E-Health—The Patient Perspective. *The 24th Medical Informatics in Europe Conference*, Pisa, 2012, 25-29.

[2]   Barry, M.J. and Edgman-Levitan, S. (2012) Shared Decision Making, the Pinnacle of Patient-Centered Care. *New England Journal of Medicine*, **366**, 780-781. https://doi.org/10.1056/NEJMp1109283

[3]   Berwick, D.M., Nolan, T.W. and Whittington, J. (2008) The Triple Aim: Care, Health, and Cost. *Health Affairs*, **27**, 759-769. https://doi.org/10.1377/hlthaff.27.3.759

[4]   Dwamena, F., Holmes-Rovner, M., Gaulden, C.M., Jorgenson, S., Sadigh, G., Sikorskii, A., Lewin, S., Smith, R.C., Coffey, J., Olomu, A. and Beasley, M. (2012) Interventions for Providers to Promote a Patient-Centred Approach in Clinical Consultations. Cochrane Database of Systematic Reviews, Cochrane.

[5]   Tang, C., Lorenzi, N., Harle, C.A., Zhou, X. and Chen, Y. (2016) Interactive Systems for Patient-Centered Care to Enhance Patient Engagement. *Journal of the American Medical Informatics Association*, **23**, 2-4. https://doi.org/10.1093/jamia/ocv198

[6]   Health IT (2016) Meaningful Use Regulations. https://www.healthit.gov/policy-researchers-implementers/meaningful-use-regulations

[7]   European Commission (2012) E-Health Action Plan 2012-2020—Innovative Healthcare for the 21st Century. Brussels, 1-14.

[8]   Acheampong, F. and Vimarlund, V. (2014) Business Models for Telemedicine Services: A Literature Review. *Health Systems*, **4**, 189-203.

https://doi.org/10.1057/hs.2014.20

[9] Chesbrough, H.W. (2003) Open Innovation: The New Imperative for Creating and Profiting from Technology. Harvard Business School Press, Boston.

[10] Eysenbach, G. (2001) What Is E-Health? *Journal of Medical Internet Research*, **2001**, 3. https://doi.org/10.2196/jmir.3.2.e20

[11] Grand View Research Inc (2016) Healthcare Mobility Solutions Market Size & Forecast By Product & Services (Mobile Devices, Mobile Applications, Enterprise Mobility Platforms) by Application (Enterprise Solutions, mHealth) by End Use, and Trend Analysis from 2014-2025.
http://www.grandviewresearch.com/industry-analysis/healthcare-mobility-solutions-market

[12] Bullinger, A.C., Rass, M., Adamczyk, S., *et al.* (2012) Open Innovation in Health Care: Analysis of an Open Health Platform. *Health Policy*, **105**, 165-175.
https://doi.org/10.1016/j.healthpol.2012.02.009

[13] Bullinger, A.C., Rass, M. and Moeslein, K. (2012) Towards Open Innovation in Health Care. *The European Conference on Information Systems*, Barcelona, 2012, 5-15.

[14] Kuenne, C.W., Moeslein, K. and Bessant, J. (2013) Towards Patients as Innovators: Open Innovation in Health Care. In: Mukhopadhyay, C., Akhilesh, K.B., Srinivasan, R., *et al.*, Eds., *Driving the Economy through Innovation and Entrepreneurship*, Springer, New York, 315-327. https://doi.org/10.1007/978-81-322-0746-7_26

[15] Leonard, D. (1995) Wellsprings of Knowledge: Building and Sustaining the Sources of Innovation. Harvard Business School Press, Boston.

[16] Was. S and Vimarlund, V. (2016) Healthcare in the Age of Open Innovation. A Literature Review. *Health Information Management Journal*, 1-13.

[17] Was. S and Vimarlund, V. (2015) Challenges of Stimulating a Market for Social Innovation-Provision of a National Health Account. *Proceedings of European Federation for Marical Informatics*, Amsterdam, Madrid, 546-549.

[18] World Bank (2006) World Development Report.
http://documents.worldbank.org/curated/en/435331468127174418/pdf/322040World0Development0Report02006.pdf

[19] Nord, P. (2016) Consumer-Driven Logistics: Driving Forces and Challenges. White Paper.
http://www.postnord.com/globalassets/global/english/document/publications/2016/whitepaper-about-consumer-driven-logistics-october-2016.pdf

[20] Granovetter, M. (1985) Economic Action and Social Structure: The Problem of Embeddedness. *American Journal of Sociology*, **91**, 481-510.
https://doi.org/10.1086/228311

[21] Shapiro, C. and Variant, H.R. (1991) Information Rules. Harvard Business School Press, Boston.

[22] Evans, D.S. (2007) Some Empirical Aspects of Multi-Sided Platform Industries. *Review of Network Economics*, **2**, 191-209.

[23] Gassmann, O. and Enkel, E. (2004) Towards a Theory of Open Innovation: Three Core Process Archetypes. *The R&D Management Conference*, Lisbon, 7-9 July 2004.

[24] Rubinelli, S., Collm, A., Glassel, A., *et al.* (2013) Designing Interactivity on Consumer Health Websites: Paraforum for Spinal Cord Injury. *Patient Education and*

Counseling, **93**, 459-463. https://doi.org/10.1016/j.pec.2013.09.015

[25] Salge, T.O., Farchi, T., Barrett, M.I., *et al.* (2013) When Does Search Openness Really Matter? A Contingency Study of Health-Care Innovation Projects. *Journal of Product Innovation Management*, **30**, 659-676. https://doi.org/10.1111/jpim.12015

[26] Zachariadis, M., Oborn, E., Barrett, M., *et al.* (2013) Leadership of Healthcare Commissioning Networks in England: A Mixed Methods Study on Clinical Commissioning Groups. *BMJ Open*, **3**, e002112.
https://doi.org/10.1136/bmjopen-2012-002112

[27] Davey, S., Brennan, M., Meenan, B.J., *et al.* (2001) Innovation in the Medical Device Sector: An Open Business Model Approach for High-Tech Small Firms. *Technology Analysis and Strategic Management*, **23**, 807-824.

[28] Dias, C. and Escoval, A. (2012) The Open Nature of Innovation in the Hospital Sector: The Role of External Collaboration Networks. *Health Policy and Technology*, **1**, 181-186. https://doi.org/10.1016/j.hlpt.2012.10.002

[29] Dandonoli, P. (2013) Open Innovation as a New Paradigm for Global Collaborations in Health. *Globalization and Health*, **9**, 1-5.
https://doi.org/10.1186/1744-8603-9-41

[30] Kuenne, C.W., Moeslein, K. and Bessant, J. (2013) Towards Patients as Innovators: Open Innovation in Health Care. In: Mukhopadhyay, C., Akhilesh, K.B., Srinivasan, R., *et al.*, Eds., *Driving the Economy through Innovation and Entrepreneurship*, Springer, New York, 315-327. https://doi.org/10.1007/978-81-322-0746-7_26

[31] Meersman, D. and Leenheer, P. (2012) Open Innovation in Health Service Value Networks: A Methodology for the Innovation of Ambient Assisted Living Platforms and Services, Abramowicz Health Information. Business Information Systems Workshops, Springer, Berlin, 25-36.

[32] Zott, C., Amit, R. and Massa, L. (2011) The Business Model: Recent Developments and Future Research. *Journal of Management*, **37**, 1019-1042.
https://doi.org/10.1177/0149206311406265

[33] Anandajayasekeram, P. (2011) Agricultural Services and Technology Innovations.
https://innovationpolicyplatform.org/sites/default/files/rdf_imported_documents/Agricultural_Innovation_Brokers.pdf

[34] Vimarlund, *et al.* (2016) E-Health Two-Sided Markets-Implementation and Business Models. Elsevier, Amsterdam.

9

Application of the SECI Model using Web Tools to Support Diabetes Self-Management and Education in the Kingdom of Saudi Arabia

Saleh Almuayqil[1,2], Anthony S. Atkins[2], Bernadette Sharp[2]

[1]College of Computer Sciences and Information, Aljouf University, Sakaka, KSA
[2]School of Computing and Digital Technologies, Staffordshire University, Stoke-on-Trent, UK
Email: saleh.naif@ju.edu.sa

Abstract

The area of knowledge management, the SECI mode in particular, has great value in terms of enriching patients' knowledge about their diseases and its complications. Despite its effectiveness, the application of knowledge management in the healthcare sector in the Kingdom of Saudi Arabia seems deficient, leading to insufficient practice of self-management and education of different prevalent diseases in the Kingdom. Moreover, the SECI model seems to be only focusing in the conversion of human knowledge and ignore knowledge stored in databases and other technological means. In this paper, we propose a framework to support diabetic patients and healthcare professionals in the Kingdom of Saudi Arabia to self-manage their disease. Data mining and the SECI model can provide effective mechanisms to support people with diabetes mellitus. The area of data mining has long been utilised to discover useful knowledge whereas the SECI model facilitates knowledge conversion between tacit and explicit knowledge among different individuals. The paper also investigates the possibilities of applying the model in the web environment and reviews the tools available in the internet that can apply the four modes of the SECI model. This review helps in providing a new median for knowledge management by addressing several cultural obstacles in the Kingdom.

Keywords

SECI Model, Framework, Saudi Arabia, Diabetes Mellitus

1. Introduction

The Kingdom of Saudi Arabia (KSA) has been associated for increased prevalence of number of diseases including diabetes mellitus. The prevalence of these diseases in KSA requires daily monitoring and continuous care to prevent its complications. An effective way to manage these diseases is the application of self-management and education strategies. The term self-management in the medical domain is used to emphasize the patients' role to control their diseases. The term has been used to enable individuals to deal with their chronic illnesses, and its resulted complications, by increasing their knowledge, skills and confidence [1]. Self-management also empowers people with different diseases to manage their negative emotions and maintain life roles. It has been applied globally and has proved its usefulness to a number of diseases including different chronic conditions. However, its application in KSA is deficient and doesn't meet the required effort to control these diseases.

The application of self-manage and education in healthcare can be supported by Knowledge Management (KM). KM is a dynamic process of capturing, storing, sharing and creating knowledge [2]. KM facilitates sharing of knowledge among different organizations and individuals through communications and offers useful means for creating and disseminating knowledge [3]. Despite its advantages, KM in KSA face several factors related to national and organisational aspects that hinder its implementation and limit its practices in different domains including healthcare. Lack of KM practice in KSA limits application of several activities associated with the idea of self-management and education to support patients of different diseases in the Kingdom.

Nonaka and Takeuchi [4] proposed the knowledge creation model that facilitates interaction of tacit and explicit knowledge by applying the four conversion modes Socialization, Externalisation, Combination and Internalisation (SECI). The SECI model is well-known theory in the area of KM and has been successfully applied to manage knowledge in a variety of domains including healthcare. The SECI model can be utilised to integrate KM and Knowledge Discovery (KD) to support patients and healthcare professionals in KSA in managing several chronic diseases such as diabetes mellitus. Such integration applies KD to elicit tacit complications encountered by diabetic individuals whereas KM helps overcome these complications through the transfer of useful guidelines and best practices among patients with diabetes and healthcare professionals.

DM implementation in healthcare is well documented in the literature [5] [6]. However, the utilisation of the SECI model in the healthcare domain is still deficient. The SECI model explores the interrelationship between the two different types of knowledge, tacit and explicit, and facilitates the conversion between them. Such a process is necessary to benefit from knowledge availability in the healthcare domain [7]. The SECI model has been utilised in different domains for the purpose of knowledge creation and dissemination. Several studies have shown successful applications of the knowledge creation model successfully. For example, the SECI model was proposed to be applied in a library to build a system for knowledge sharing [8]. In another study, the SECI model was utilised in the field of software development in order to assist stakeholders in the process of elicitation, specification and validation of software requirements [9]. Additionally, another study examined the SECI model utilisation in the manufacturing sector and proved its successful utilisation [10]. Nevertheless, the successful implementation in different domains requires similar application within the healthcare sector in KSA, which is seen to have slower KM practice than other healthcare sectors in developed countries [11] [12] [13].

Although the SECI model is recognized as valuable approach for knowledge creation, the concentration of the model tends to primary focus on social interactions to share human knowledge; yet there is a rich knowledge embedded in databases and documents to be mined and shared using this model, making use of many available software tools. In this paper, the focus is how the SECI model can disseminate such knowledge using a set of web tools. Internet technologies are widely utilised in order to self-manage illnesses and learn from other patients' experiences [14]. Therefore, the application of the SECI to support effective interaction between patients and healthcare professionals can be achieved through the utilisation of many related web tools. Such an approach can assist promote the sharing of guidelines and best practices among patients and healthcare professionals to manage diseases and improve their wellbeing.

This paper presents an integrated framework of KM and KD to support he community of diabetes mellitus in KSA. The framework utilises the SECI model to fulfil two main issues in the context of KSA. Firstly, the lack of KM practices in healthcare. Secondly, the lack of diabetes self-management and education initiatives. The paper is organised as follows: Section 2 highlights diabetes mellitus in KSA. Section 3 discusses the application of KM in the healthcare domain in KSA. Section 4 defines the SECI model. Section 5 introduces our integrated framework. Section 6 provides a literature review of the web tools that can be applied to the SECI model. Section 7 draws the conclusion of this paper and highlights areas of future work.

2. Diabetes Mellitus in the Kingdom of Saudi Arabia

Diabetes mellitus is a group of metabolic disorders known by hyperglycaemia which is caused by deficient insulin secretion and/or insulin actions [15]. People in different ageing, gender and in developing and even developed countries are being diagnosed with diabetes and the prevalence of diabetes mellitus is expected to increase internationally to 592 million in 2035 [16].

KSA, like other developing countries, has a considerable number of patients who are suffering from different kind of chronic diseases. One of those diseases is diabetes mellitus, which has high percentage of appearance among citizens in almost every part of the Kingdom. According to [17], KSA is in the third place among the top 10 countries for diabetes prevalence. In 2010, the prevalence percentage for diabetes mellitus in KSA was 16.8% among adults in the ages of 20 - 79 years old. This percentage is expected to rise in 2030 to reach 18.9% [18]. The number of outpatient visits made by diabetic individuals to Primary Healthcare Centres (PHCs) is 1.8 million out of 29.3 million overall outpatient visits to PHCs in KSA. This number of diabetic people's visits represents 6.44% of the overall number of visits to all PHCs in KSA and put diabetic people in third place in the scale of all outpatient visits in the Kingdom [19].

Official reports from the MOH in KSA show increasing numbers of visits to public hospitals over the years. The number of visits to MOH hospitals due to diabetes mellitus was over 434 thousands in 2011 [19]. The number has increased through 4 years to exceed 477 thousand visits to MOH hospitals in 2014 [20].

In a recent statistical study, the International Diabetes Federation revealed that KSA has more than 3.8 million cases of diabetes mellitus in 2014 and the prevalence of this disease among individuals represents 20.5% [21]. Those diabetic people are not limited to a particular age. In 2015, KSA is in the list of top countries in terms of the prevalence of type 1 diabetes among children under 14 years old with 16,100 cases [22]. In the same year, the prevalence of diabetes mellitus among people from 20 to 79 years old is 20%. Diabetic people in KSA suffer from various complications of diabetes. However, the most serious complication encountered by diabetics in KSA is mortality. According to the Centers for Disease Control and Prevention, diabetes mellitus is considered the first cause of death in KSA among all other diseases in 2013 [23].

Beside many complications which could result from this disease, diabetic individuals also face other difficulties and issues related to controlling the disease and its consequences through different lifestyle activities. These issues are known by the non-health related complications of diabetes mellitus. Péres *et al.* [24] reported some of those challenges people with diabetes mellitus can have in their daily life including difficulties controlling impulses related to eating habits, doubts in the correct way of using medications, refusal to take insulin because of concerns regarding dose preciseness and doubts regarding time schedules for antidiabetics. Blonde [25], in addition, indicated patient deficiency in adherence to lifestyle measures and pharmacologic therapies as one of the most common reasons cited for failure to achieve glycaemic goals. Patients of diabetes face problems in identifying medications and understanding prescriptions especially when patients asked to change medication. Most patients could not remember their blood glucose and blood pressure target. According to Onwudiwe *et al.* [26], the lack of knowledge of desired blood glucose level is the major barrier of diabetes self-management. Another study suggested that appropriate knowledge about diabetes mellitus is essential to ensure patients' adherence to medication [27]. The study found that diabetic individuals expressed their concerns regarding the adverse effects of multiple anti-diabetes medications. In addition, participants in the study believe that diabetes medications can be harmful, which suggests assessment of patients' knowledge and education about diabetes mellitus prior to medication intake to ensure adherence of patients to medications.

In addition to the above complications, diabetic patients in Muslim countries face difficulties related to controlling diabetes during the Holy month of Ramadan. Since people in Muslim countries fast every day of the month of Ramadan from sunrise until sunset, Muslims who have diabetes mellitus might be at risk of considerable fluctuations in the blood glucose level [28]. Muslims in Ramadan change their eating routines, which includes changing the types and timing of almost all meals during this month. This can affect fasting people with diabetes mellitus in terms of identifying the appropriate diet, medication time and amount [29].

Diabetes mellitus has wider attention in the area of self-management and education from variety of studies which have demonstrated such programs in different countries [25] [30] [31]. However, the implementation of diabetes self-management and education in KSA is still deficient especially when considering the vast prevalence of the disease in the Kingdom.

3. Knowledge Management in Healthcare in the Kingdom of Saudi Arabia

The healthcare domain utilises tacit and explicit knowledge in different ways. Explicit knowledge is communicable in systematic language whereas tacit knowledge is obtained through experience and cannot be easily articulated [4]. Researchers have demonstrated the importance of the two types of knowledge in different studies. Tacit knowledge is valuable for many healthcare practitioners in addressing a medical problem [32]. Tacit knowledge is also beneficial in clinical care as it is the basis for decision-making even though these decisions guidelines are made available in an explicit form [33]. The value of tacit knowledge in this context resides in capturing such a form of knowledge which can contribute to the performance and training of practice, typically based on experience [34]. More precisely, utilisation of tacit knowledge in healthcare has more connotations to healthcare delivery by promoting or rejecting of explicit medical expertise [35]. Moreover, the capture of tacit knowledge, and its transformation into explicit, seems to benefit the performance not only for clinicians, but also for hospital leadership and other individuals in different departments in the hospital [36].

Explicit knowledge is also useful to capture critical issues in the healthcare sector. Knowledge is the driving force for enhancing practice management [37]. Therefore, making this knowledge explicit can make healthcare organisations better equipped to deal with constraints such as increased cost and the pressure for delivering high quality and effective care. In addition, explicit knowledge is valuable for the practice of evidence based medicine, which is based on research evidence, clinical expertise and patients' preferences and values for the purpose to achieve best medical decision-making [37].

The advantages of tacit and explicit knowledge as well as the case of evidence based medicine raise the importance of utilising a conversion mechanism for the two types of knowledge in healthcare. Evidence based medicine is primarily based on the explicit evidence from research. However, it is important to consider the tacit knowledge which represents both the clinical expertise of medical staffs and the patients' preferences. According to Wickramasinghe and Davison [37], the tacit knowledge of medical expertise and patients' preferences are not utilised sufficiently. More importantly, it is almost impossible for healthcare professionals to rely on solely tacit knowledge in supporting their medical decisions and practices. Wickramasinghe and Davison also stated that ignoring the tacit knowledge of healthcare professionals, which is gained from daily practices, might not be the solution as that tacit knowledge can provide great significance to the healthcare system. Therefore, the best solution to tackle this problem is to adopt a knowledge conversion theory that can convert tacit and explicit knowledge to support relevant activities in the healthcare domain.

Conversion between tacit and explicit knowledge not only benefits healthcare professionals and medical staff in healthcare, it can also benefit patients by facilitating sharing and converting tacit and explicit knowledge about their diseases, and its associated aspects such as diagnosis and medication. The knowledge which patients have about their diseases is the first step in their treatment journey; it can affect their lives as it can determine their activities and lifestyle [11]. This can contribute to their control and management of their diseases. Application of KM in the healthcare sector can be effective in sharing knowledge to educate patients about their diseases and how to manage them efficiently.

The education influence, offered to patients and other stakeholders, is well documented in developed countries; which plays significant role in empowering patients and enriching their knowledge about their diseases. However, such an influence is still deficient in Saudi Arabian healthcare sector [11]. More precisely, small number of large healthcare organisations in the Kingdom has documented education efforts to support their patients about their diseases and medication. For example, Al-Ghamdi *et al.* [38] assessed a medication counselling program provided for discharged patents from a hospital in Saudi Arabia to avoid adverse drug events. The study showed that the knowledge and education effort provided for patients prevented them from adverse drug events. In another study conducted in another major hospital in the Kingdom, the education and counselling program increased the medical knowledge of patients in relation to their recognition of medication and its side effects [39].

Nevertheless, the majority of healthcare organisations in KSA lack an effort in relations to educate their patients about the different diseases they suffer from. The reason beyond this deficiency can be linked to poor KM practice due to a number of factors. The literature indicates these factors are uniquely derived from the national and organisational cultures in most organisations in the Arabic, Middle Eastern and Saudi Arabian Context. These factors are highlighted as follows:

• Trust is a strong factor that influences the sharing of knowledge among members in an organisation [40] [41]. Trust creates the atmosphere necessary for engaging with others especially when the regulations and rules insufficiently ensure their perceived behaviour [40]. The presence of trust among members is the core factor towards successful knowledge sharing among them [42]. In addition, trust will enable the availability of knowledge to partners and colleagues even though the individuals who own that knowledge prefer to keep it for themselves [43].

- Openness to change is important for promoting, managing and sharing knowledge [28] [29] [44] [45]. Openness is defined by Bradley [46] as improving performance or obtaining high absorptive capacity through recognising and responding to the needs for change.

- Team-work is having the members of any organisation to work as a team. Team-working facilitates the success of knowledge sharing process by fostering members to contact and eventually learn from each other's [47]. Previous studies have shown the positive effect of working as a team and emphasised that it improve and enable knowledge sharing and management among members [48] [49]. However, organisations in Saudi Arabia provide limited opportunities to engage members from different departments to engage in teamwork practices [50].

- Communication and interaction between members inside and outside the organisation is essential for sharing knowledge [41]. One of the barriers of KM practices in Saudi Arabian context is the lack of effective organisational communication [51]. Glisby and Holden [52] suggested that cooperative work environment is necessary for Knowledge Sharing (KS). Individuals who experience competition in organisation feel the stress leading to discouraging KS in their organisation [53].

- The structure of an organisation is another factor in the organisational culture that influences KM practices in different organisations [54]. Middle Eastern cultures are considered to have high level of bureaucracy which can hinder KS activities within any organisation [55].

- Some organisations have insufficient KS practice due to the high power distance barrier, which is an attribute driven by the tradition [56] [57]. In high power distance cultures, managers normally control their employees, and workers in the workplace are reluctant to speak with their managers openly. Employees in those cultures fear the communication with their managers because of the high level of inequality in power distribution among individuals. Consequently, sharing of knowledge is negatively influenced. Countries in the Arab world are regarded as high power distance cultures and this will affect externalisation and internalisation of knowledge [53].

4. About the SECI Model

As Nonaka and Takeuchi explain in their paper that though organisations actually create and manage knowledge dynamically, there is little understanding of how to capture it and share it. They propose a model of knowledge creation consisting of three elements: the SECI (Socialisation, Externalisation, Combination, and Internalisation) process, knowledge creation through the conversion of tacit and explicit knowledge, the shared context for knowledge creation, and knowledge assets [58]. The knowledge creation process is a spiral which grows out of these three elements and can lead to dialectical thinking. Using existing knowledge assets, organisations create new knowledge through the SECI process that takes place in the share context; new created knowledge becomes in turn the basis for a new spiral of knowledge creation. They identify two types of knowledge, explicit and tacit, which are important to share and convert them in order to create knowledge. The four SECI conversion modes are explained below and illustrated in **Figure 1**.

Socialisation. Socialisation is the first mode in the SECI model and involves social interaction to enable the conversion of tacit knowledge from one to another without use of language [59]. Observation, imitation and brainstorming are useful tools to perform such a conversion.

Externalisation. The second mode of the SECI model is externalisation which enables the conversion from tacit to explicit knowledge [59]. It translates tacit knowledge to forms to be understandable and interpretable by other users via interaction, namely dialogues and informal meetings. The new produced explicit knowledge can then can be codified and recorded through different means such documentation and recording.

Combination. The conversion of explicit knowledge to another explicit knowledge is the third mode of the SECI model [59]. This process can be performed through combining different explicit knowledge and reconfiguring a new form of explicit knowledge. Formal meetings in organisations are considered as a very assistive combination tool [4].

Internalisation. Internalisation is the mode where explicit knowledge is converted to tacit knowledge and become part of an individual's brain [4]. The im-

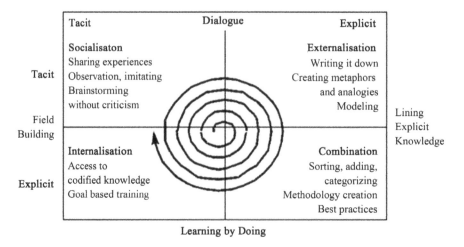

Figure 1. The SECI model [1].

plementation of internalisation involves "learning by doing" and individuals who successfully internalise tacit knowledge will eventually acquire "know how" skills.

An important factor that must be considered when discussing the SECI model is the concept of "Ba". Ba is a platform where each conversion mode of the SECI model takes place. There are four types of Ba defined by [60]. Ba is the space where individuals share their experiences, feelings and emotions. This type of Ba offers the space where socialisation can be accomplished through physical and face-to-face interactions. Interacting Ba is the space where mental skills are transformed into explicit form through dialogues. Communication skills and metaphor are essential in this stage of knowledge conversion for successful dissemination of knowledge with respect to its sensitive meanings. Cyber Ba is the third space where combination mode is accomplished through interaction in a virtual world instead of real place and time. The combination mode is performed more efficiently through the utilisation of technology. The fourth type of Ba is the exercising Ba which is the space that facilitates internalisation through training and practical learning.

Although the application of KM seen to be hindered due to several factors in KSA, the SECI model offer a solid basis to encourage KM to empower patients' of diabetes mellitus in the Kingdom in terms of self-management and education; the SECI model can be tailored and adapted to meet the cultural constraints associated with the Saudi societies to ensure healthcare organisations. Individuals can survive in the knowledge economy environment and that knowledge can be effectively managed and shared among the diabetic individuals. Solutions have been suggested to support KM practices through the adoption of the SECI model [61]. These solutions provide useful tools that can emphasize human interactions, an essential component of KM in healthcare organisations and other sectors in KSA. Therefore, the current research has applied the SECI model to increase the knowledge of citizens who struggle from diabetes mellitus in KSA to fulfil the gap of deficient KM utilisation in the Saudi Arabian healthcare sector.

5. The Framework

The framework is designed in three layers (see **Figure 2**). The first layer focuses on the barriers related to e-health in KSA and the complications that can be related to different diseases. The framework is applied to the domain of diabetes mellitus in KSA. Therefore, the framework aims to overcome several non-health related complications related to diabetes mellitus. The second layer is related to KD and DM in particular, where the diabetes mellitus non-health related complications obtained from the first layer are data mined. The third layer is the KM layer where the SECI model is applied to capture these complications and disseminate useful diabetes self-management and provide education guidelines and best practices to diabetic citizens in KSA.

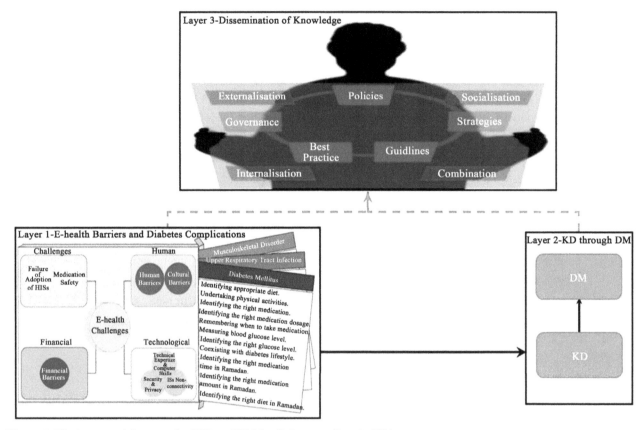

Figure 2. The integrated framework of KD and KM for diabetes mellitus in KSA.

5.1. The First Layer: Issues and Complications

In this layer, there are two categories of issues, firstly the e-health barriers and secondly the complications related to a particular disease in KSA. The e-health issues are discussed in details in [62], eliciting several e-health issues to the majority of Information and Communication Technologies (ICTs) being adopted in healthcare in KSA. In this paper, the second issue is discussed. The framework is applied to overcome the non-health related complications encountered by diabetic patients in KSA. Diabetes non-health related complications relate to difficulties encountered by diabetes mellitus sufferers in KSA in their daily life. A survey was undertaken to investigate these complications related to lifestyle issues and the medication aspects and profile attributes of diabetic citizens (e.g. age, gender, educational level, etc.). In this survey, we focused on 11 complications, namely diet, physical activities, medication (*i.e.* dosage intake), blood glucose level, identifying the right glucose level, lifestyle, identifying the right medication time, amount and the appropriate diet in Ramadan (see **Figure 3**).

5.2. The Second Layer: Knowledge Discovery and Data Mining

The aim of this layer is to mine the data acquired from the survey and elicit new knowledge that can link the non-health related complications encountered by diabetic citizens in KSA with the their profile characteristics. Consequently, the

Diabetes Mellitus
• Identifying appropriate diet.
• Undertaking physical activities.
• Identifying the right medication.
• Identifying the right medication dosage.
• Remembering when to take medication.
• Measuring blood glucose level.
• Identifying the right glucose level.
• Coexisting with diabetes lifestyle.
• Identifying the right medication time in Ramadan.
• Identifying the right medication amount in Ramadan.
• Identifying the right diet in Ramadan.

Figure 3. Diabetes non-health related complications.

DM method employed is association rule mining, which is appropriate to the structure of our survey which contains nominal attributes and instances.

The findings from the DM study can include different associations among diabetes non-health related complications and the profile information of patients who encounter these complications. For example, the DM study in this layer can link the difficulty of identifying the appropriate diet with diabetic patients who are male, married and have type 1 diabetes.

5.3. The Third Layer: Knowledge Management

The third layer in the framework is designed to enable effective provision of useful strategies, guidelines and best practices to citizens relevant to these complications related to different illness. In addition, this layer facilitates the exchange and conversion of tacit and explicit knowledge between patients and healthcare professionals in order to provide useful recommendations that can empower patients to control their diseases. The SECI model is applied in this layer to provide an effective self-management and education tips of diabetes mellitus (see **Figure 4**).

Policies, strategies, guidelines, best practice and governance are useful recommendations to be shared between stakeholders: patients and healthcare professionals. These aspects provide promising solutions to overcome every non-health related complication of diabetes mellitus. Some of these solutions, such as medication intake guidelines, might be in explicit form of knowledge whilst others, such as physical activities best practices, can be tacit. The SECI model enables knowledge creation as the solution presented in one form of knowledge (tacit or explicit) can be transformed to another in order to facilitate effective diabetes self-management for every diabetic citizen in KSA and successful e-health utilisation in the healthcare sector in the Kingdom.

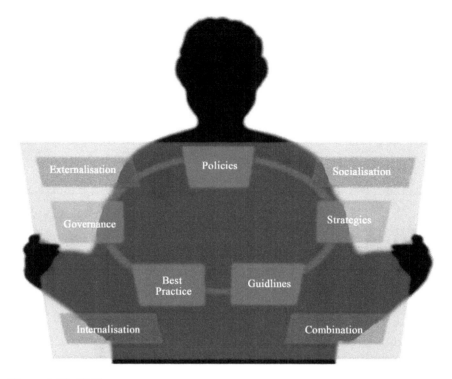

Figure 4. The KM layer.

The first mode in the SECI model, socialization, can overcome the complication of undertaking physical activity as diabetic citizens can socialise with other diabetics who match their diabetes type and profile information such as age, gender and education level. The externalisation mode can be applied to overcome the complication of identifying the right medication dosage through sharing medication guidelines from healthcare professionals to diabetic citizens of a particular diabetes type. The combination mode can overcome the complication of identifying the appropriate medication time in Ramadan through dissemination of different explicit strategies in relation to how to deal with diabetes in the holy month of Ramadan. The internalisation mode can help overcome the complication of identifying the diet appropriate to the health condition through the provision of best practices related to diet by individuals of the same profile information and diabetes type.

6. Web Tools for the SECI Model

The above KM layer is supported by a web portal which includes a number of tools to capture the four modes of the SECI model. This portal captures valuable guidelines, strategies and best practices that can help diabetic citizens to control their disease. The portal is named Diabetes Self-Management in the Kingdom of Saudi Arabia (DSMKSA) and is designed with respect to barriers affecting e-health initiatives in KSA as discussed in [62] (see **Figure 5**).

Researchers have demonstrated that socialisation, externalisation, combination and internalisation are performed through the internet by various tools

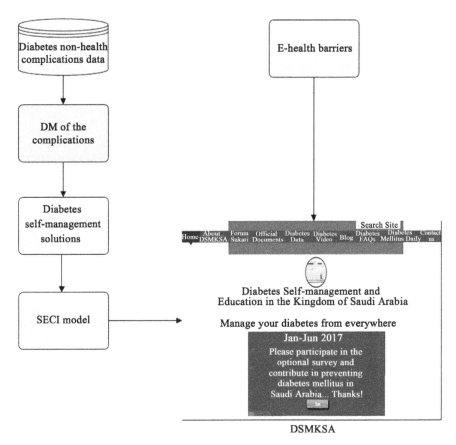

Figure 5. Embodiment of the KM layer of our framework in a web portal.

provided by the web 2.0 technologies [63] [64]. Web 2.0 is an open source and interactive applications, generated and controlled by the users, which in turn expand their knowledge skills as participants in business and social processes [65]. Web 2.0 enhances the flow of knowledge as it enables the creation of informal networks of users which facilitates the generation, dissemination and editing of knowledge and informational contents. There are a number of web tools, such as blogs, wikis, forums, etc. that can support the four modes of the SECI model. These tools apply the four modes on Nonaka and Takeuchi and address several cultural factors that hinder KM in KSA as outlined below (see **Figure 6**):

Socialisation:

1) Forums are a very useful tool to enable socialisation among individuals. Reward incentives can be used for the posts which are highly rated, and will encourage participation [53]. Forums can allow anonymous participation which enables individuals who fear judgments and the loss of face to engage in discussions. This encourages participants' willingness to share their concerns about diet or medication side effects [4].

2) Community of Practice (CoP) and wikis are useful tools to perform socialisation. According to Ray [53] and Hoadley [66], CoP provided via wikis enables individuals to provide valuable knowledge related to their areas of expertise. Similar to web forums, wikis can enable anonymous participations. This can-

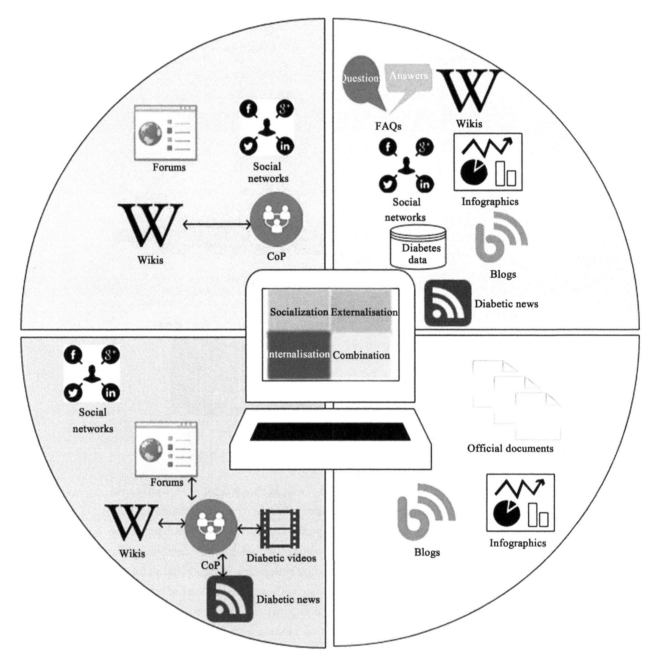

Figure 6. Web tools to apply the SECI model in the internet.

enable KM practices in cultures who are seen as high power distance cultures such as KSA.

3) Social media is another web tool that can enhance socialisation in the internet platform. Social media provides feasible way of sharing tacit knowledge such as expertise, understanding, experience and skills without the utilisation of language. For example, it can disseminate best practices of appropriate exercises. In addition, different social media enable observations, imitation and practice by providing opportunities to individuals to participate in formal and informal communities, which are the space required for socialisation [63].

Externalisation:

1) According to Chatti *et al.* [63], blogs support externalisation by offering a space for everyone to capture knowledge. They also enable immediate documentation of thoughts through discussions in different blogs. They are powerful for knowledge sharing in individualistic cultures. They can be suitable for sharing best practices and offers indirect communication, which can overcome the fear of assessment and criticisms. Moreover, blogs allow anonymous participation to overcome the barrier of structure in organisations. Blogs utilisation in organisations can result in long term orientation organisations, which focus on long term goals [53]. Blogs can be utilised to support diabetic citizens by sharing guidelines related to medication intake from healthcare professionals.

2) Wikis are also seen to be useful web tool for externalisation [63]. They facilitate the capturing of collective knowledge where every user can share her/his experience. This increases social interaction and empower collaborative knowledge capturing as knowledge in wikis can be created and modified by different individuals. Therefore, wikis are seen as helpful tool to overcome individualism, which is the national attribute that hinders externalisation. This knowledge can be in various forms such as spoken or written words, different formats of images, sound tracks such as music and lectures. Furthermore, contributions in wikis, which also can be anonymous, can be supported by top management in organisations [53]. This can overcome the of high power distance which occurs in cultures such as KSA. Wikis can be great mean to share appropriate exercises and medications best practices in written forms.

3) Besides its support to socialisation, social media can also support externalisation. Social media enable users to share and capture different knowledge about diabetes and scientific findings that may be presented in different formats such as text, images, videos or audios. For example, it can convert tips of diabetes medication dosage and tips into codified guidelines. Moreover, it can be facilitated through newly developed devices and software for knowledge sharing and capturing [63].

4) Question and answers page is another web tool that can support externalisation. It facilitates externalisation as it allows articulation and codifying of tacit knowledge. This process enables the conversion of knowledge from tacit form to explicit [64]. Questions and answers are useful way to externalise medical knowledge in forms of patient's questions and answers provided by healthcare professional. For example, best practice of how to measure blood glucose level.

Combination:

1) One of the effective web technologies for combination is document system. According to Natek [64], a document system allows participants to upload and download important documents of interests. It facilitates access to information. Nonaka and Takeuchi [4] indicated that open source to information is an important tool for combination. Moreover, uploading and downloading documents of interest ensures the practice of combination in Arabic culture, which per-

forms combination only when the knowledge is considered to be valuable [43]. Document system can disseminate strategies of coexisting with diabetes mellitus and policies related to diabetes prevention and treatments.

2) Wikis are also seen to be effective tool for combination in the online community. Wikis build searchable and up to date learning content that can be distributed among different organisational boundaries [63]. In addition, wikis enable collaborative decision-making and decrease bureaucracy. This is prerequisite for combination as a consultative decision making is effective practice for this mode [4].

3) Blogs can support combination in a similar way to wikis. Blogs can provide valuable learning assists that are searchable and up to date and can be transferrable into social context [63]. Furthermore, they allow collaborative decision making and decrease bureaucracy. Blogs can share different strategies related to appropriate diet plan.

Internalisation:

1) CoP is one of the effective web tools for internalisation [64]. CoP can be provided for participants through social media where work-groups transfer knowledge among staffs who share the same interests or who are looking for a particular knowledge. To overcome cultural boundaries such as low uncertainty avoidance, rewarding valuable contributions will lead the organisation's community to value KS and increase it. Another way to reward contributions is by linking posts to the organisations network to value knowledge and give those contributors reputations as experts, which also overcomes individualism and then increase KS. CoP can be integrated with web forums by allowing participants of common interests, *i.e.* diabetic individuals, to share their experiences and their best practices [53]. Anonymous participation can be valuable in this type of web technology especially in high power distance cultures such as KSA. Another way to apply CoP is to provide a shared repository for information resources, which can be used to support diabetics in a more tailored way, according to gender, age or lifestyle [66]. Therefore, instructional videos can be valuable repository for knowledge that can implement internalisation through a CoP. Such and implementation can include sharing of guidelines related diet and exercise, which can be mastered by diabetics through the practice of "learning by doing".

2) Wikis are also an effective web tool for internalisation. Wikis enable individuals to contribute by sharing their experience in their speciality [53]. Wikis can be implemented as a CoP. They help individuals to capture knowledge of others and enable users to easily edit webpage contents [67]. Wikis can be adopted by top management in organisations to facilitate KS. Also anonymous participation is effective to encourage KM practice in high power distance cultures, such as KSA.

In summary, the application of the SECI model via web tools can facilitate knowledge dissemination practice effectively through overcoming a number of national and organisational hinderers of KM. This will play significant role in the control of diabetes non-health related complications in highly prevalent country of diabetes mellitus such as KSA. The socialisation mode can play significant role in overcoming these complications by enabling diabetic individuals to socialise with each other via the portal. The outcomes from such an action result in engaging diabetic individuals in group discussion about their complications and best practices. Diabetic citizens can also socialise and interact with healthcare professionals. In terms of externalisation, healthcare professionals can help patients overcome their complications can be overcome through converting useful guidelines, best practices and recommendations to comprehensible and appropriate media. The externalised recommendations can empower diabetic individuals to deal with different types of non-health related complications of diabetes mellitus such as identifying appropriate time and/or dosage of medication. Moreover, the externalisation mode can disseminate our tacit DM findings and make them explicit. This can benefit the community of diabetes mellitus by providing data in explicit form and make them available for further research and studies related to diabetes mellitus. The combination mode provides flexible way to integrate different aspects of guidelines and strategies for appropriate diabetic citizens taken into consideration their specific lifestyle, diet, medication issues and Ramadan requirements. In the internalisation mode, CoPs can be created where diabetic citizens are learning by doing and following different guidelines related to dealing with several barriers such as identifying the right physical activity and coexistence with the life style of diabetes mellitus.

7. Conclusions

The prevalence of diabetes mellitus in KSA requires serious attention to raise the awareness of diabetes self-management and education. The current paper shows that current practices are limited in KM with respect to the healthcare domain in the Kingdom. The integrated framework of KM and KD, presented in this paper is an effective approach to support patients and healthcare professionals of diabetes mellitus in KSA. The SECI model is a valuable knowledge creation theory, which can address the factors hindering the practice KM and encourage diabetes self-management and education in the Kingdom through various technological means. The application of the SECI model can be supported by a number of web tools. These tools not only apply the four modes of the SECI model successfully, but they also have the ability to overcome a number of national and organizational factors that hinder knowledge dissemination in KSA. This will encourage KM practice in KSA in the domain of healthcare.

The current paper has two future research directions. The first future research direction is a DM study, which can reveal a number of non-health related complications of diabetes mellitus from a dataset of diabetic patients in KSA. The second future work opportunity includes development of a KM web portal to support diabetic patients to overcome the barriers extracted from the DM study.

The portal can utilise different web tools to apply the four modes of the SECI model in order to share useful guidelines and best practices related to diabetes self-management and education effectively.

References

[1]   Lorig, K.R., Sobel, D.S., Ritter, P.L., Laurent, D. and Hobbs, M. (2000) Effect of a Self-Management Program on Patients with Chronic Disease. *Effective Clinical Practice*, 4, 256-262.

[2]   Ni, G., Wang, W., Wang, J., Zong, Z. and Xie, M. (2010) Research on the Knowledge Management System of the Vicarious Management Corporation. *Information Science and Management Engineering*, Xi'an, 7-8 August 2010, 62-67.

[3]   McInerney, C.R. and Koenig, M.E.D. (2011) Knowledge Management (KM) Processes in Organizations: Theoretical Foundations and Practice. *Synthesis Lectures on Information Concepts, Retrieval, and Services*, 3, 1-96.

[4]   Nonaka, I. and Takeuchi, H. (1995) The Knowledge-Creating Company: How Japanese Companies Create the Dynamics of Innovation. Oxford University Press.

[5]   Aljumah, A.A., Ahamad, M.G. and Siddiqui, M.K. (2013) Application of Data Mining: Diabetes Health Care in Young and Old Patients. *The Journal of King Saud University Computer and Information Sciences*, 25, 127-136.

[6]   Esfandiari, N., Babavalian, M.R., Moghadam, A.M.E. and Tabar, V.K. (2014) Knowledge Discovery in Medicine: Current Issue and Future Trend. *Expert Systems with Applications*, 41, 4434-4463.

[7]   Dalkir, K. and Liebowitz, J. (2011) Knowledge Management in Theory and Practice. MIT Press.

[8]   Cao, J., Yao, Z., Li, Y., Zhai, C. and Xu, B. (2010) Utilizing SECI Model for Knowledge Management in Library. *International Conference on Educational and Information Technology*, Vol. 3, 62-64.

[9]   Chikh, A. (2011) A Knowledge Management Framework in Software Requirements Engineering Based on the SECI Model. *Journal of Software Engineering and Applications*, 4, 718-728. https://doi.org/10.4236/jsea.2011.412084

[10] Li, Y.-H., Huang, J.-W. and Tsai, M.-T. (2009) Entrepreneurial Orientation and Firm Performance: The Role of Knowledge Creation Process. *Industrial Marketing Management*, 38, 440-449.

[11] Alshammari, T.M. (2016) Patient's Medicinal Knowledge in Saudi Arabia: Are We Doing Well? *Saudi Pharmaceutical Journal*, 24, 560-562.

[12] Szulanski, G. (2001) Knowledge Creation: A Source of Value. *Academy of Management Review*, 26, 318-320. https://doi.org/10.2307/259128

[13] Scott, J.E. (1998) Organizational Knowledge and the Intranet. *Decision Support Systems*, 23, 3-17.

[14] Ziebland, S., Lavie-Ajayi, M. and Lucius-Hoene, G. (2014) The Role of the Internet for People with Chronic Pain: Examples from the DIPEx International Project. *British Journal of Pain*, 9, 62-64. https://doi.org/10.1177/2049463714555438

[15] American Diabetes Association (2013) Diagnosis and Classification of Diabetes Mellitus. *Diabetes Care*, 36, 67-74.

[16] Ministry of Health (2016) Health Days 2016—World Diabetes Day. http://www.moh.gov.sa/en/HealthAwareness/healthDay/2016/Pages/HealthDay-201

6-11-14.aspx

[17] Zhang, P., Zhang, X., Brown, J., Vistisen, D., Sicree, R., Shaw, J. and Nichols, G. (2010) Global Healthcare Expenditure on Diabetes for 2010 and 2030. *Diabetes Research and Clinical Practice*, **87**, 293-301.

[18] Shaw, J.E., Sicree, R.A. and Zimmet, P.Z. (2010) Global Estimates of the Prevalence of Diabetes for 2010 and 2030. *Diabetes Research and Clinical Practice*, **87**, 4-14.

[19] Ministry of Health (2011) Health Statistical Year Book 1432H. http://www.cdsi.gov.sa/english/

[20] Ministry of Health (2014) Statistical Year Book 1435H. http://www.moh.gov.sa/en/Ministry/Statistics/Book/Pages/default.aspx

[21] International Diabetes Federation (2014) Saudi Arabia International Diabetes Federation. http://www.idf.org/membership/mena/saudi-arabia

[22] International Diabetes Federation (2015) IDF Diabetes Atlas.

[23] Centers for Disease Control and Prevention (2016) Global Health—Saudi Arabia. https://www.cdc.gov/globalhealth/countries/saudi_arabia/

[24] Péres, D.S., dos Santos, M.A., Zanetti, M.L. and Ferronato, A.A. (2007) Difficulties of Diabetic Patients in the Illness Control: Feelings and Behaviors. *Revista Latino-Americana de Enfermagem*, **15**, 1105-1112. https://doi.org/10.1590/S0104-11692007000600008

[25] Blonde, L. (2005) Current Challenges in Diabetes Management. *Clinical Cornerstone*, **7**.

[26] Onwudiwe, N.C., Mullins, C.D., Winston, R.A., Shaya, F.T., Pradel, F.G., Laird, A. and Saunders, E. (2014) Barriers to Self-Management of Diabetes: A Qualitative Study among Low-Income Minority Diabetics. *South African Journal of Diabetes and Vascular Disease*, **11**, 61-65.

[27] Sweileh, W.M., Zyoud, S.H., Abu Naba, R.J., Deleq, M.I., Enaia, M.I., Nassar, S.M. and Al-Jabi, S.W. (2014) Influence of Patients? Disease Knowledge and Beliefs about Medicines on Medication Adherence: Findings from a Cross-Sectional Survey among Patients with Type 2 Diabetes Mellitus in Palestine. *BMC Public Health*, **14**, 94. https://doi.org/10.1186/1471-2458-14-94

[28] Zargar, A. (2017) Diabetes Control during Ramadan Fasting. *Cleveland Clinic Journal of Medicine*, **84**, 352-356. https://doi.org/10.3949/ccjm.84a.16073

[29] Hassanein, M., Al-Arouj, M., Hamdy, O., Bebakar, W.M.W., Jabbar, A., Al-Madani, A., Hanif, W., Lessan, N., Basit, A., Tayeb, K., Omar, M., Abdallah, K., Al Twaim, A., Buyukbese, M.A., El-Sayed, A.A. and Ben-Nakhi, A. (2017) Diabetes and Ramadan: Practical Guidelines. *Diabetes Research and Clinical Practice*, **126**, 303-316.

[30] Powers, M.A., Bardsley, J., Cypress, M., Duker, P., Funnell, M.M., Fischl, A.H., Maryniuk, M.D., Siminerio, L. and Vivian, E. (2017) Diabetes Self-Management Education and Support in Type 2 Diabetes. *The Diabetes Educator*, **43**, 40-53. https://doi.org/10.1177/0145721716689694

[31] Deakin, T., McShane, C.E., Cade, J.E. and Williams, R.D.R.R. (2005) Group Based Training for Self-Management Strategies in People with Type 2 Diabetes Mellitus. *The Cochrane Database of Systematic Reviews*, **2**, CD003417. https://doi.org/10.1002/14651858.CD003417.pub2

[32] Herbig, B., Bussing, A. and Ewert, T. (2001) The Role of Tacit Knowledge in the Work Context of Nursing. *Journal of Advanced Nursing*, **34**, 687-695. https://doi.org/10.1046/j.1365-2648.2001.01798.x

[33] Thornton, T. (2006) Tacit Knowledge as the Unifying Factor in Evidence Based Medicine and Clinical Judgement. *Philosophy, Ethics, and Humanities in Medicine*, 1, 2. https://doi.org/10.1186/1747-5341-1-2

[34] Kothari, A., Rudman, D., Dobbins, M., Rouse, M., Sibbald, S. and Edwards, N. (2012) The Use of Tacit and Explicit Knowledge in Public Health: A Qualitative Study. *Implementation Science*, 7, 20. https://doi.org/10.1186/1748-5908-7-20

[35] Boateng, W. (2008) Knowledge Management in Evidence-Based Medical Practice: Does the Patient Matter? *Electronic Journal of Knowledge Management*, 8, 281-292.

[36] Hovlid, E., Bukve, O., Haug, K., Aslaksen, A.B. and von Plessen, C. (2012) Sustainability of Healthcare Improvement: What Can We Learn from Learning Theory? *BMC Health Services Research*, 12, 235. https://doi.org/10.1186/1472-6963-12-235

[37] Wickramasinghe, N. and Davison, G. (2004) Making Explicit the Implicit Knowledge Assets in Healthcare: The Case of Multidisciplinary Teams in Care and Cure Environments. *Health Care Management Science*, 7, 185-195. https://doi.org/10.1023/B:HCMS.0000039381.02400.49

[38] Al-Ghamdi, S.A., Mahmoud, M.A., Alammari, M.A., Al Bekairy, A.M., Alwhaibi, M., Mayet, A.Y. and Aljadhey, H.S. (2012) The Outcome of Pharmacist Counseling at the Time of Hospital Discharge: An Observational Nonrandomized Study. *Annals of Saudi Medicine*, 32, 492-497. https://doi.org/10.5144/0256-4947.2012.492

[39] Alkatheri, A. and Albekairy, A. (2013) Does the Patients' Educational Level and Previous Counseling Affect Their Medication Knowledge? *Annals of Thoracic Medicine*, 8, 105. https://doi.org/10.4103/1817-1737.109823

[40] Ridings, C., Gefen, D. and Arinze, B. (2002) Some Antecedents and Effects of Trust in Virtual Communities. *The Journal of Strategic Information Systems*, 11, 271-295.

[41] Al-Alawi, A.I., Al-Marzooqi, N.Y. and Mohammed, Y.F. (2007) Organizational Culture and Knowledge Sharing: Critical Success Factors. *Journal of Knowledge Management*, 11, 22-42. https://doi.org/10.1108/13673270710738898

[42] Hutchings, K. and Michailova, S. (2003) Facilitating Knowledge Sharing in Russian and Chinese Subsidiaries: The Importance of Groups and Personal Networks.

[43] Weir, D. and Hutchings, K. (2005) Cultural Embeddedness and Contextual Constraints: Knowledge Sharing in Chinese and Arab Cultures. *Knowledge and Process Management*, 12, 89-98. https://doi.org/10.1002/kpm.222

[44] Gold, A.H., Malhotra, A. and Segars, A.H. (2001) Knowledge Management: An Organizational Capabilities Perspective. *Journal of Management Information Systems*, 18, 185-214. https://doi.org/10.1080/07421222.2001.11045669

[45] Alavi, M., Kayworth, T.R. and Leidner, D.E. (2015) An Empirical Examination of the of Organizational Influence Culture on Knowledge Practices Management. *Journal of Management Information Systems*, 22, 191-224.

[46] Bradley, M. (2000) Working Knowledge: How Organizations Manage What They Know. New Library World, Emerald Group Publishing Limited, 282-287.

[47] Schein, E.H. (2004) Organizational Culture and Leadership. 3rd Edition.

[48] Park, H., Ribière, V. and Schulte, W.D. (2004) Critical Attributes of Organizational Culture That Promote Knowledge Management Technology Implementation Success. *Journal of Knowledge Management*, 8, 106-117. https://doi.org/10.1108/13673270410541079

[49] Mowery, B. (2015) Report Information from ProQuest.

[50] Albrithen, A. and Yalli, N. (2015) Medical Social Workers' Perceptions Related to

Interprofessional Teamwork at Hospitals. *Journal of Social Service Research*, **41**, 722-731. https://doi.org/10.1080/01488376.2015.1068723

[51] ALHussain, A.Z. (2011) Barriers to Knowledge Management in Saudi Arabia.

[52] Glisby, M. and Holden, N. (2003) Contextual Constraints in Knowledge Management Theory: The Cultural Embeddedness of Nonaka's Knowledge-Creating Company. *Knowledge and Process Management*, **10**, 29-36. https://doi.org/10.1002/kpm.158

[53] Ray, D. (2014) Overcoming Cross-Cultural Barriers to Knowledge Management Using Social Media. *Journal of Enterprise Information Management*, **27**, 45-55. https://doi.org/10.1108/JEIM-09-2012-0053

[54] Sabri, H. (2005) Knowledge Management in Its Context: Adapting Structure to a Knowledge Creating Culture. *International Journal of Commerce and Management*, **15**, 113-128.

[55] Nazari, J.A., Herremans, I.M., Isaac, R.G., Manassian, A. and Kline, T.J. (2009) Organizational Characteristics Fostering Intellectual Capital in Canada and the Middle East. *Journal of Intellectual Capital*, **10**, 135-148. https://doi.org/10.1108/14691930910922950

[56] Hofstede, G. (2003) Culture's Consequences: Comparing Values, Behaviors, Institutions, and Organizations across Nations. *Behaviour Research and Therapy*, **41**, 861-862.

[57] Hofstede, G. (2001) Culture's Consequences: Comparing Values, Behaviors, Institutions and Organizations across Nations. SAGE, Thousand Oaks, London, New Delhi.

[58] Nonaka, I., Toyama, R. and Konno, N. (2000) SECI, Ba and Leadership: A Unified Model of Dynamic Knowledge Creation. *Long Range Planning*, **33**, 5-34.

[59] Nonaka, I. (1994) A Dynamic Theory of Organizational Knowledge Creation. *Organization Science*, **5**, 14-37. https://doi.org/10.1287/orsc.5.1.14

[60] Nonaka, I. and Konno, N. (1998) The Concept of Ba: Building a Foundation for Knowledge Creation. *California Management Review*, **40**, 40-54. https://doi.org/10.2307/41165942

[61] Almuayqil, S., Atkins, A.S. and Sharp, B. (2015) Integrated Framework of Knowledge Management and Knowledge Discovery to Support E-Health for Saudi Diabetic Patients. *International Journal of Advanced Life Sciences*, **7**, 111-121.

[62] Almuayqil, S., Atkins, A.S. and Sharp, B. (2016) Ranking of E-Health Barriers Faced by Saudi Arabian Citizens, Healthcare Professionals and IT Specialists in Saudi Arabia. *Health*, 1004-1013. https://doi.org/10.4236/health.2016.810104

[63] Chatti, M.A., Klamma, R., Jarke, M. and Naeve, A. (2007) The Web 2.0 Driven SECI Model Based Learning Process. *Advanced Learning Technologies*, Niigata, 18-20 July 2007, Vol. 5, 780-782. https://doi.org/10.1109/ICALT.2007.256

[64] Natek, S. (2016) Knowledge Management Systems Support Seci Model of Knowledge-Creating Process Abstract.

[65] Constantinides, E. and Fountain, S.J. (2008) Special Issue Papers Web 2.0: Conceptual Foundations and Marketing Issues. *Journal of Direct*, **9**, 231-244.

[66] Hoadley, C. (2012) What Is a Community of Practice and How Can We Support It? In: *Theoretical Foundations of Learning Environments*, 286.

[67] Dickson, D. (2009) Using Wiki Technology to Create Communities of Practice. Rochester Institute of Technology, Rochester.

10

Exploring the Benefits of an Agile Information System

Pankaj Chaudhary, Micki Hyde, James A. Rodger

Information Systems and Decisions Sciences Department, Eberly College of Business & IT, Indiana University of Pennsylvania, Indiana, USA
Email: pankaj@iup.edu

Abstract

Information Systems (IS) agility is a current topic of interest in the IS industry. The study follows up on work on the definition of the construct of IS agility and attributes for sensing, diagnosis, and selection and execution in an agile IS. IS agility is defined as the ability of an IS to sense a change in real time; diagnose it in real time; and select and execute a response in real time. Architecting an agile IS is a complex and resource-intensive task, and hence examination of its benefits is highly desired and appropriate. This paper examines the benefits of an Agile Information System. Benefits of an agile IS were derived from related academic literature and then refined using practitioner literature and qualitative data. The benefits considered were the first order or direct benefits. These benefits were then empirically validated through a survey of IT practitioners. The results of the survey were analyzed and a rank order of the benefits was arrived at. An exploratory factor analysis was also done to find the common dimensions underlying the benefits. It is suggested that organizations can use the empirically validated benefits from this study to justify and jump-start their capital and labor expenditure to build agility into their Information System.

Keywords

Information Systems Agility Benefits, Agile Information Systems Benefits, Agility

1. Introduction

Change is the rule of the game in the current business environment. Not only are the changes occurring at an increasing rate, they are becoming increasingly unpredictable. This unpredictability can involve when a known change will occur, what an unknown change will look like, or the combination of these. The rapid rate of change implies that an organization needs to become an expert at changing and morphing itself rapidly in response to a change. As per the ORACLE cloud agility survey [1] the ability of the competitor to launch innovative services more rapidly was identified as a top threat by 27% of the respondents. Also, as per the survey, a majority of businesses believe they are agile but cannot flexibly manage workloads or rapidly develop, test, and launch new applications, leaving them poorly prepared to deal with competitive threats. Retention of leadership and/or competitive position requires that an organization should be able to change at will in any direction, without significant cost and time, to counter a threat or capitalize on an opportunity. Such an organization may be characterized as an agile organization. For most of organizations the survival and/or retention of market share demands that the organization should be able to change faster than, or as fast as, new entrants and rivals. The ORACLE survey found that the impact of agility on competitiveness is critically important to businesses.

Information Systems (IS) pervade all aspects of modern organizational functioning and play an integral role in information processing activities of an organization. Information Systems are needed for organizational agility on account of their ability to provide shared, distributed and integrated, current, and fast-flowing information [2]-[8].

Modern business processes in organizations use IS as a core resource or component. In many and most of cases, IS may completely or significantly embed a business process (e.g., Internet banking). The pivotal role of IS in modern organizational business processes means that an organization (agile or striving to be) cannot change its business processes unless the IS changes as well. Thus an agile organization would need an agile IS. As per the ORACLE cloud agility survey, 81% of the respondents stated that the ability to rapidly develop, test, and launch new business applications is critically important or important to the success of the business. In particular 29% of the respondents believed that effective mobilization of applications and services is the most important factor in business success today [1]. What Brandt and Boynton [9] indicated in 1993 still holds true—current IS are not easy to change though several are getting better at it in some aspects.

So what is an agile IS? We arrive at the definition or construct of an agile IS based on prior work done by the authors in this area. Agility in general is defined [10] [11] as a formative construct comprised of the ability to sense a change, diagnose a change, select a response, and execute the response in real-time:

1) **Sense**: Ability to sense the stimuli for change (as they occur) in real-time;

2) **Diagnose**: Ability to interpret or analyze stimuli in real-time to determine the nature, cause, and impact of change;

3) **Respond**: Ability to respond to a change in real-time, further disaggregated

into *select* and *execute.*

a) Select: Ability to s*elect* a response in real-time (very short planning time) needed to capitalize on the opportunity or counter the threat.

b) Execute: Ability to *execute* the response in real-time.

Real-time is defined as the span of time in which the correctness of the task performed not only depends upon the logical correctness of the task performed but also upon the time at which the result is produced. If the timing constraints of the system are not met, system failure is said to have occurred [12].

Thus an Agile IS may be defined as one that has the ability to sense a change in real-time, diagnose the change in real-time, select a response in real-time, and execute the response in real-time. Due to the formative nature of the construct, several, or some, of these abilities might exist in the absence of others.

The IT industry over the last few years has made strides in enhancing IS agility. Perhaps the most important development has been in the area of Cloud computing with services like Infrastructure as a Service (IaaS), Platform as a Service (PaaS), Storage as a Service, Security as a Service, Database as a Service, and Software as a Service (SaaS), amongst others. In the area of software development, methodologies like eXtreme Programming (XP), SCRUM, Feature Driven Design, Microservices, and others have been implemented to facilitate continuous change to the software by incorporating new requirements as opposed to the freezing of requirements in the Waterfall methodologies. In the area of continuous deployment, DevOps has made great strides into the industry. However the adoption of these technologies and frameworks involves some learning curve and is not as rapid as anticipated. As per the ORACLE cloud agility survey, only 32% of respondents state that they fully understand what PaaS is, rising to 37% in the US, while 29% admit that they do not understand it at all. For those that say they do understand PaaS, only 31% cite reduced time frames for application development as a main benefit [13].

Having an agile IS is no simple task and needs a variety of abilities for sensing a change in real-time [14], diagnosing a change in real-time [15], and selecting a response and executing a response in real-time [16]. These abilities require a significant investment of resources in both the people and IT components of an IS. A relevant question then one may pose is what are the benefits of an agile IS? While many benefits may be apparent, it is still worthwhile to undertake an empirical investigation of this question. This is the research question addressed in this manuscript. It should be mentioned that there is literature specifically linking the role of IS to organizational agility [17]. The question explored here is specific to the benefits of IS agility, which may include both first order and higher order benefits.

2. Literature Review

Peer-reviewed academic literature alludes to several benefits of IS agility. While the authors clearly distinguish between flexibility and agility [11], the published literature often does not make this distinction and hence pertinent literature from both areas is examined. Also literature from other areas like supply chain management and manufacturing (which was and is at the forefront of the agility phenomenon) is also examined.

Based on the Resource-Based View (RBV) of the firm, we consider IS as a key resource of a firm. Even though many systems can be purchased from the marketplace, the use and customization of these systems is recognized as anchoring the IS competencies of the firm. [18] [19] view IS infrastructure as an IS competence, because not all the firms can equally capitalize on information technology (IT) without using a flexible IS infrastructure. Firm competencies inherit the following properties: they are valuable, rare, inimitable, and non-substitutable. These attributes cannot be easily imitated by competitors in the short-run because capabilities are deeply rooted in the history of the firm, and some capabilities could arise just by being in the right place at the right time [20]. Agility of an IS would further enhance an organization's competitive advantage.

Traditionally IS planning was conducted on an ad-hoc basis, because IS was considered as a support system performing back-end service functions. Therefore, the main function of IS management was to choose those systems that could perform back-end functions efficiently. Since the 1980s, however, IS planning started playing an important role in business planning. However, both business planning and IS planning exercises were done in isolation. Even though business managers acknowledged the key role of IS, they did not take notice of IS competencies [20] [21]. Today, we look upon IS in an agile manner that can add benefit to the organization through sensing, directing, executing and diagnosing information in real time. A model proposed by [22] proposes to examine how IT capabilities (*i.e.*, flexible IT infrastructure and IT assimilation) affect firm performance through absorptive capacity and supply chain agility, in the supply chain context [22]. Their research shows that absorptive capacity and supply chain agility fully mediate the influences of IT capabilities on firm performance.

There are many examples of agile IS in the literature. For example, Shin *et al.* [23] explored the nature and role of agility as a strategic intent and its influence on operational and firm performance. [24] claim that agile development has now become a well-known approach to collaboration in professional work life. Yanan *et al.* [25] believe that there has been a significant effect that the design of a plant can have on its agile and dynamic performance. Sangari *et al.* [26] contend that supply chain agility is a key determinant of competitiveness and they developed a practical evaluation framework that serves to identify critical factors for achieving supply chain agility. Gilgor *et al.* [27] feel that traditionally, researchers have claimed agility as an attribute closely tied to the effectiveness of strategic supply chain management that is closely associated with customer effectiveness. Goldsby *et al.* [28] claim that the relationship between agility and cost efficiency is not clear due to limited empirical scrutiny from researchers and shed light on the relationship between agility and efficiency. Narayanan *et al.* [29] demonstrate that several studies in the buyer-supplier relationship literature have addressed the impact of collaboration on agility performance and claim that some but not all studies have concluded that collaboration leads to beneficial effects while others have questioned the positive effects of collaboration on relationship performance. Chung *et al.* [30] examine how organizational workers improve their perceived job performance, while also investigating the impact of perceived organizational agility and location independence on technology acceptance. Sherehiy and Karwowski [31] believe that organizational agility requires development of an adaptable workforce that is able to deal with unexpected and dynamic changes in the business environment. They utilize an Agility Strategy Scale, Work Organization Scale, and Workforce Agility Scale to study autonomy at work as one of the most important predictors of workforce agility. Yang [32] developed and empirically tested a conceptual framework to investigate the antecedents of manufacturers' supply chain agility and the connection of their agility with performance. They postulated that technical (IT capability) and relational factors (information sharing and trust, and operational collaboration) are the antecedents of a manufacturer's supply chain agility.

Barthe-Delanoë *et al.* [33] propose that the modern business environment tends to involve a large network of heterogeneous people, devices, and organizations that engage in collaborative processes among themselves that lead to a high degree of interoperability between partner IS and that these processes need to be agile. Yusuf *et al.* [34] assesses the link between dimensions of an agile supply chain, competitive objectives, and business performance, and identify the most important dimensions and attributes of supply chain agility. Yusuf *et al.* [34] also researched the pressures that persist on organizations to master and profit from oil and gas energy. While most results suggest that clusters enhance and enable higher levels of agile practices, their findings indicate that there is no strong empirical basis to make a direct link between clusters and competitiveness. DeGroote and Marx [35] investigated the impact of information technology (IT) on supply chain agility measured by the ability to sense and respond to market changes, and the impact supply chain agility has on firm performance, and their results suggest that IT improves the supply chain's ability to sense market changes by improving the adequacy, accuracy, accessibility, and timeliness of the information flows among members of the supply chain. Balaji *et al.* [36] propose that Agility is perceived as the principal competitive medium for all organizations in an ambiguous and changing business environment and that enterprises are converging to a point where they need to be smarter, faster, flexible, and more reactive to changes in order to sustain in the demanding market. Seethamraju and Sundar [36] postulate that past research on the effect of ERP systems on agility is contradictory, and research on the post implementation effects of ERP systems on agility is limited and found that the inadequacies in implementation and poor process optimization prior to ERP implementation are restricting process agility. Galster and Avgeriou [37] investigate how variability facilitates the design of software products that can be adapted for a wide range of customers or contexts. They found that in agile development, software products begin to be built before the desired product is fully understood. Sheffield and Lemétayer [38] believe that there is considerable debate among practitioners and researchers on the nature of software development agility and conditions under which it is linked to project success. They found that software development agility was indicated by the project environment factor of organizational culture and a project factor of empowerment of the project team.

Krotov, *et al.* [39] identify several ways in which mobile technology is used to improve operational, customer, and partnering agility. A flexible IS infrastructure, according to Bharadwaj [18], is an integrated shared system that is built piece by piece over time. That means, as a firm learns to work with a system and gradually becomes proficient in using the system, it continually works to add other pieces in the infrastructure that can set it apart from other firms. A flexible IS infrastructure allows sharing of data and applications through communication networks (Wasko and Faraj [40]. It pertains to the arrangements of hardware, software, and networks so that data and applications can be accessed and shared within and between suppliers, customers, and vendors [41]. A flexible IS infrastructure helps in integrating disparate and geographically distributed systems and make IS applications cost effective in their operations and supports, therefore, flexible infrastructure becomes a critical source of advantage to the firm [42]. Weber *et al.* [43] pointed out that in both academics and industry, companies increasingly adopt process-aware information systems (PAISs), which offer promising perspectives for more flexible enterprise computing. Seebacher and Winkler [44] believe that recent economic developments indicated that greater flexibility in manufacturing is more important than ever and they present an applicable approach that shows exactly how to evaluate the manufacturing flexibility and how to measure an improvement of flexibility in business practice.

The literature points to several benefits of agility and more importantly the need for agility, in general, to an organization in areas like supply chain, enhanced partnership with customers, timely information, etc. Though the unit of analysis-IS within an organization, in this manuscript is different, several of these benefits may be rolled into higher order benefits of an agile IS.

3. Research Approach and Objectives

IS agility is an area where practitioners have taken the lead. In the practitioner literature, IS agility is equated to a set of technologies that enable seamless interconnection and collaboration between the IT components to achieve rapid configuration changes. The conceptualization of IS agility used in this study is much broader and more comprehensive in scope. To arrive at the benefits of an agile IS, a comprehensive survey of the practitioner literature was done. This included having Google alerts for the topic and continually refining the benefits. In addition, existing literature on agility was also examined to arrive at a list of benefits of an agile IS. Specifically, the following steps were taking to arrive at a list of benefits:

1) Arrive at a conceptualized set of benefits of an agile IS. Such benefits would arise due to the ability of an IS to respond to internal, organizational, and external changes through sensing a change in real-time, diagnosing the change in real-time, and selecting and executing a response in real-time (Pankaj, 2005).

2) Verify and refine the conceptualized set of benefits of an agile IS based on the feedback from practitioners and to arrive at a comprehensive set of benefits.

3) Validate the benefits through a survey.

4. Perceived Benefits of an Agile IS

As stated earlier benefits due to the ability of an agile IS to sense, diagnose, and select and respond in real-time are based on the comprehensive and continual review of the practitioner literature as well as published academic literature. The agility literature describes the benefits of agility as ranging from survival to enhancement of the competitive position. Since an agile IS contributes to the agility of an organization, the benefits of IS agility may span a similar range. The net effect of IS agility would be on the financial performance of the organization but it may have several other immediate or first order effects like reduction in the time needed for changing IS, etc. **Table 1** gives a list of benefits of an agile IS from the classical agility literature. It may be noted that most of these are higher order benefits. For the purpose of this manuscript, the focus is on first order benefits to

Table 1. Benefits of organizational agility.

Description	References
Enhanced value to customers	Vokurka, Zank, & III, [54]; Christian, Govande, Staehle, & Jr., [55]
Advantage from the changing situation; benefit from change	Yoffie & Kwak, [56]
Competitive advantage and/or competitive performance	Bessant, Francis, Meredith, & Kalinsky, [57]; Schonsleben, [58]; Cho, Jung, & Kim, [59]; Bal *et al.*, [3]; Vernadat, [60]; O'Connor, [61];
Profitable operations	Sahin, [62]; Vokurka & Fliedner, [63]; Vokurka *et al.*, [54]; Devor, Graves, & Miles, [64]; Noaker, [65]
Survive unprecedented threats, viability	Sharifi & Zhang, [7]; Cho *et al.*, [59]; Dove, [45];
Growth in a competitive market	Y. Y. Yusuf *et al.*, [34];
Capture new market	Vernadat, [59]
Leadership	Dove, [45]

ensure that the effects of investments in an agile IS are observable and not con-
founded by other variables.

Benefits of having an agile IS come from a real-time response to internal, organizational, and environmental changes. Internal changes in IS that are geared
for improvements, build spare capacity and enhance capabilities. Monitoring for
internal changes enables the IS to predict outages and other potential problems
and thus enables fast response by the IS to maximize the uptime and maintain
desired levels of services at all times. In case of outage, the properties of an agile
IS enable fast recovery and minimize downtime. An IS that changes easily in response to organizational changes ensures that the IS is aligned with the business
processes at all times thereby increasing the efficiency, productivity, and effectiveness of the business processes and related information processing tasks. The
efficiency and effectiveness may also lead to reduction in costs. An agile IS allows for rapid changes in the business processes thereby enabling the organization to maintain or enhance profits by countering the moves of competitors. The
ability to respond to an actual or anticipated IS innovation (environmental
change) in real-time enables an IS to provide the latest solutions for the business
processes thereby increasing the effectiveness of the business processes. It also
enables business process innovation through the use of the latest IS solutions,
and protects against technology obsolescence. Being responsive to the environment also enables the IS to protect itself and the organization against unfavorable events like expensive licensing terms, security vulnerabilities, cyber-attacks,
and viruses.

Overall, an agile IS will lead to a reduction in time for changing the IS. The
resulting changes would also be more robust [45]. The benefits of having an agile
IS for an organization are summarized in **Table 2**.

Table 2. Benefits of an agile information system.

---

1) Reduction in time to implement changes in IS.
2) Increase in the robustness of the implemented changes.
3) Benefits from response to internal changes.
   a) Increase in efficiency and effectiveness of the existing business processes.
   b) Increase in efficiency and effectiveness of information processing.
   c) Build spare capacity.
   d) Build enhanced capabilities for future use.
   e) Maintain the desired levels of service as per the service level agreements for the IS.
   f) Enable fast recovery in case of outages to minimize the down time.
4) Benefits from response to organizational changes.
   a) IS is aligned to business process requirements at all times.
   b) Business processes can change rapidly (in real time).
   c) Higher financial benefits to the organization.
5) Benefits from response to environmental changes.
   a) Avoid technology obsolescence through provision of needed latest IT/IS solutions.
   b) Allow business process innovation through incorporating the latest IS solutions.
   c) Protect the IS and the organization against unfavorable licensing terms and
   vendor induced situations.
   d) Allow rapid response to security threats like virus attacks, cyber-attacks, etc.

---

5. Improving and Refining the Benefits of an Agile IS

Ten executives were interviewed to elicit their opinions on the benefits of an agile IS. The interviews were comprehensive in the sense that they were introduced to the definition of IS agility, asked to validate it, comment on it, and discuss it, and then asked to comment on the attributes of an agile IS (published elsewhere). Subsequent to that they were asked about the benefits of an agile IS outlined in **Table 2**. They were requested to modify, add, and delete to and from the list. They were also requested to give a balanced perspective on different aspects of an agile IS ranging from organizational rules and policies to IT components. As per Bonoma's verification guidelines [46], multiple interviews were proposed for purposes of literal replication. The interviewees selected were participants in a discussion round table for a research center in a major university. The participants' organizations/companies were examined by the participating researchers and were deemed to have a need for IS agility based on an informal assessment of the antecedents of IS agility for these organizations [10].

The interviewees' demographics demonstrated diversity (industry and size; diversity in role and responsibilities; and diversity in organizations in terms of their approach to developing and managing IS). The interviewees' roles spanned from strategic, to a mix of strategic and technical, to more specialized technical roles.

Content analysis was done on the interviews [10]. Interviewees commented on the benefits of an agile IS but only the first order benefits of an agile IS were considered. Some of the first order benefits of IS agility mentioned were better recoverability, faster development of products and services, better responsiveness, higher availability of IS and conformance to Service Level Agreements (SLAs), cost savings on IS changes, use of IS as a strategic tool, targeted information for various tasks, increased problem resolution, better utilization of IS, availability of needed functionality in IS, process improvement, quick changes to operational processes, and alignment of IS with the business needs. Of these benefits, faster development of products and services and the use of IS as a strategic tool was not included in the original list of benefits and so these were included as a benefit of responding to organizational changes. Interviews also mentioned burnout effects resulting from changing too fast and too often. Changing fast and trying to be on the cutting edge of the technology may leave the organization with IS that use technologies that do not become mainstream, and a lot of new IS that stretch the IS staff. Poor vendor support for these cutting-edge technologies and their lack of maturity further aggravates the situation. As such, being agile does not necessarily mean that the IS should always use a cutting-edge technology. This aspect is stressed in the work that details the theory behind the definition of agility [10], where it has been mentioned that that a reconfiguration of an IS in response to change should result in a stable configuration. The criterion of stability will often preclude technologies that are not mature and proven, and are difficult to maintain. Most new and cutting-edge technologies share these characteristics, and so being agile may not necessarily mean being on the cutting-edge of technology, though such new technologies may often facilitate higher levels of IS agility.

Table 2 illustrates the perceived benefits of an Agile Information System. A refined set of attributes for sensing is presented in **Table 3**. New attributes have been italicized. These changes are meant to demonstrate how our study leads to improving and refining the original perceived benefits of an Agile IS. These refinements make a contribution to the literature and increase our understanding of the Agile IS construct. The benefits of an Agile IS will lead to optimization of enterprise performance with improved organizational knowledge, memory and learning. Our improved model leads to enterprise-wide intelligent information management principle adoption.

6. Survey Development & Administration

Survey development and administration was performed using the well-documented steps for survey development, administration and analysis [47] [48] [49] [50]. The development and validation of the survey was performed as per the guidelines by Churchill [51]: generate sample items, pilot test, and develop final measures.

The survey contained 18 items for benefits of an agile IS along with other items relating to sensing, diagnosis, selection and execution [14] [15] [16] [52]. The survey contained 6 items pertaining to demographics. There, demographic items were based on a sample of ten surveys designed by peer researchers. The demographic information collected included the title and department of the re-

Table 3. Post interview benefits of an agile information system.

---

1) Reduction in time to implement changes in IS.
2) Increase in the robustness of the implemented changes.
3) Benefits from response to internal changes.
    a) Increase in efficiency and effectiveness of the existing business processes.
    b) Increase in efficiency and effectiveness of the information processing.
    c) Build spare capacity.
    d) Build enhanced capabilities for future use.
    e) Maintaining the desired levels of service as per the service level agreements for the IS.
    f) Enable fast recovery in case of outages to minimize the down time.
4) Benefits from response to organizational changes.
    a) IS is aligned to business process requirements at all times.
    b) Business processes can change rapidly (in real time).
    c) Higher financial benefits to the organization.
    d) *Faster development of products and services.*
    e) *Ability to use IS as a strategic tool.*
5) Benefits from response to environmental changes.
    a) Avoid technology obsolescence through provision of needed latest IT/IS solutions.
    b) Allow business process innovation through incorporating the latest IS solutions.
    c) Protect the IS and the organization against unfavorable licensing terms and vendor induced situations.
    d) Allow rapid response to security threats like virus attacks, cyber-attacks, etc.

---

spondent, industry, the number of IS personnel, annual IS budget, and annual revenue. The draft survey was pilot-tested with four practitioners and three MIS researchers for assessing the understandability of the questions, clarity of the instructions, unambiguity in the wording of the items, and the overall format of the questionnaire. Though the questionnaire was a long, pilot-testers agreed that the survey could be completed within a reasonable time, and without extensive effort. It was suggested that items be grouped together. For example, items relating to personnel may be grouped together and items relating to the IT components may be grouped together. Additional changes suggested included the rephrasing of five items and the layout of the balloon graphic providing the definition of agility on the second page.

The pilot test for the web questionnaire was done using students and was oriented towards visual appeal, layout and design, and not content. The survey was tested on different browsers to verify that all the buttons and scripts worked and there were no run-time errors. The pause-and-resume functionality; clarity of the images and fonts; visual appeal of colors; amount of scrolling at standard resolution of 800×600; and download times were tested. Some changes in fonts and layout were done as a result of the tests.

Survey Administration

The survey was mailed to IS executives for self-administration. This list was purchased from a professional marketing company. The questionnaire was mailed to 2718 executives (IS staff strength of between 100 - 1500). The survey included a cover letter, a paper copy of the questionnaire and a prepaid return envelope. The only incentive for responding to the survey was to share the results of the survey. The cover letter specified that the survey could also be completed online if desired by the respondent. A reminder for the survey was mailed approximately three weeks after the original mailing. After mailing the questionnaires, emails were sent to about 30 potential respondents using referrals from IS executives known to the researchers. The emails contained an executive summary of the research concepts, a copy of the questionnaire, and a link to the web-based questionnaire. A second mailing of the survey was done. The survey was mailed to 2448 addresses and a reminder postcard was mailed approximately three weeks after the mailing.

7. Survey Analysis & Results

A total of 154 responses were received (105 paper and 49 web responses). 11 responses were likely from referrals. There were a total of 2539 solicitations (accounting for incorrect addresses). This gives a 5.7% response rate. This response rate was considered acceptable considering the questionnaire had 112 items (pertaining to sensing, diagnosis, selection, execution, benefits, and self-assessment), budgetary constraints on the survey, and the fact that these executives likely receive several surveys with some financial incentive (gift card) for completion.

All the data was entered into SPSS for analysis. The demographic data item categories (except for the title and department) were assigned numerical codes. The rating for all items for benefits and attributes were entered as marked on the questionnaire except for "Not Applicable" which was assigned a code of 0 (zero). To verify the correctness of data entry from the paper survey, a random sample of 20 questionnaires was selected and checked by a fellow researcher. No data entry errors were found. There were few missing values in the entire data set. Missing values were treated as pair-wise exclusive for correlational analyses like factor analysis. They were treated as list-wise exclusive otherwise, e.g. for purposes like calculating descriptive statistics.

7.1. Respondent Demographics

The demographics of the respondents are shown in **Tables 4-7**. Education, government, finance, healthcare, and information technology companies are prominently represented in the survey. 62% of the respondents had fewer than 250 IS personnel, 61% of the organizations had an annual IS budget between $1 million and $50 million, and 40% of the respondents had revenues between $1 billion and $25 billion.

Table 4. Industry distribution of survey respondents.

Industry	Frequency	Percent
Retail	3	2.0%
Finance & Insurance	23	15.0%
Government	24	15.7%
Information Technology	18	11.8%
Mining & Oil	1	0.7%
Manufacturing	9	5.9%
Education	32	20.9%
Recreation & Leisure	1	0.7%
Utilities	3	2.0%
Trading (Wholesale)	4	2.6%
Media/Publishing/Broadcasting	5	3.3%
Professional Services	3	2.0%
Healthcare	20	13.1%
Other	7	4.6%
Total Valid	**153**	**100.0%**
Missing	1	
Total	154	

Table 5. IS personnel distribution of survey respondents.

IS Personnel	Frequency	Percent	Cumulative Percent
1 - 100	39	25.3%	25.3%
101 - 250	56	36.4%	61.7%
251 - 500	29	18.8%	80.5%
501 - 750	12	7.8%	88.3%
751 - 1000	3	1.9%	90.3%
1001 - 1500	3	1.9%	92.2%
1501 - 2000	1	0.6%	92.9%
2001 - 5000	3	1.9%	94.8%
>5000	8	5.2%	100.0%
Total	154	100.0	

Table 6. Distribution of annual IS budget of survey respondents.

Annual IS Budget ($millions)	Frequency	Percent	Cumulative Percent
<0.5	11	7.2%	7.2%
0.5 - 1	10	6.5%	13.7%
1 - 50	93	60.8%	74.5%
50 -100	20	13.1%	87.6%
100 - 500 Million	15	9.8%	97.4%
500 - 1000	3	2.0%	99.3%
>1000	1	0.7%	100.0%
Total Valid	153	100.0%	
Missing	1		
Total	154		

Table 7. Distribution of annual revenue of survey respondents.

Annual Revenue	Frequency	Percent	Cumulative Percent
<$1 Million	8	5.5%	5.5%
$1 Million - $50 Million	18	12.4%	17.9%
$50 Million - $100 Million	9	6.2%	24.1%
$100 Million - $500 Million	25	17.2%	41.4%
$500 Million - $1 Billion	21	14.5%	55.9%
$1 Billion - $25 Billion	58	40.0%	95.9%
>$25 Billion	6	4.1%	100.0%
Total Valid	145	100.0%	
Missing	9		
Total	154		

In summary, the survey had respondents from various segments of the population and it captured opinions from a variety of organizations in different industries both small and large in terms of annual revenue, IS budget, and number of IS personnel.

7.2. Non-Response Bias

Since the survey was anonymous, it was not possible to test for differences between the respondents and the non-respondents. The respondents from the two mailings were, however, compared for differences. The number of responses for each medium and for each mailing is detailed in **Table 8**. The number of responses in the second mailing was about half of those in the first mailing.

Cross-tabulations on the demographic variables of industry, IS personnel, IS budget, and annual revenue were calculated and compared for differences. Chi-square tests were not conducted since many of the cells had an expected count of less than 5 and combining various categories led to mitigation of the differences with respect to the categories for the two mailings of the survey. There was no noticeable difference between the two mailings in terms of the demographic variables. The mean ratings of benefits of an agile IS from the responses of the two mailings were compared using independent sample t-tests. The means of the ratings were not different at a significance level of 0.01.

The 18 benefits of an agile IS were presented to the survey respondents for rating on a scale of 1 to 7, 1 being not important to 7 being very important. **Table 9** shows the frequency, mean, and standard deviation of the ratings of the benefits of an agile IS.

Benefits of an Agile IS

The item with the largest mean rating of 6.54 was "Rapid response to security threats like viruses and cyber-attacks", and indicating the emphasis that IS executives attach to security and quickly taking remedial actions to alleviate the threat. Security has been a constant focus in mainstream practitioner and academic literature recently, and so the expectation of an agile IS to excel in the area of security is understandable. In the same vein, "Recovery from failure" was rated as an important benefit of an agile IS (mean rating of 6.32). The benefit with the second highest mean was "Information systems changes are made in a timely fashion". This is the reason for having an agile IS and is an obvious benefit. The fact that it did not score as the top benefit is somewhat of a surprise but

Table 8. Paper and web responses for first and second survey mailing.

| | | Mailing | | Total |
		First	Second	
Type of Medium for Survey	Paper	67	38	105
	Web	36	13	49
Total		103	51	154

Table 9. Survey ratings of the benefits of an agile information system.

Benefit of an Agile IS	Frequency of Rating[1]								N	Mean[2]	Std. Dev
	1	2	3	4	5	6	7	N/A			
Rapid IS response to security threats like viruses and cyber attacks	0	1	0	2	13	23	114	1	154	6.61**	0.79
IS changes are made in a timely fashion	0	0	0	2	15	37	100	0	154	6.53**	0.73
Fast IS recovery from failures/outages	0	0	4	6	14	42	87	1	154	6.32**	0.98
Increase in efficiency and effectiveness of business processes supported by IS	0	1	0	6	22	54	71	0	154	6.21**	0.91
Effective information processing	0	2	3	9	23	54	61	2	154	6.02**	1.09
Alignment of IS with the business process requirements at all times	2	0	4	12	26	42	63	3	152	5.94**	1.23
Use of IS as a strategic business tool	0	1	7	10	26	54	54	2	154	5.89**	1.14
IS can meet the service level agreements (SLAs) for capacity and performance	0	1	6	8	42	52	42	3	154	5.75**	1.09
Quick building of capacity for handling peak loads and/or sudden loads	0	2	5	17	34	50	46	0	154	5.71**	1.78
Faster development of products and services	1	0	2	18	40	49	42	2	154	5.70**	1.10
Efficient information processing	1	2	4	18	38	43	47	1	154	5.66**	1.24
Increased financial benefits to the organization	2	2	6	12	33	52	44	3	154	5.68**	1.28
Rapid change in business processes	3	1	5	19	36	52	36	2	154	5.53**	1.29
Increased robustness of changes made to the IS	4	2	7	15	55	39	32	0	154	5.34**	1.34
Enhancement of IS capabilities	2	0	4	16	57	48	27	0	154	5.24**	1.11

Notes: [1]The shaded boxes show the rating with the highest frequencies. [2]Items are arranged in ascending order of mean rating. **Mean is significantly greater than 4 at 0.00 level of significance in a two-tailed test.

perhaps amply demonstrates the focus on security. Interestingly, "Quick building of capacity for handling peak loads and/or sudden loads" was not rated as one of the top benefits (it is 9th in the ranking) of an agile IS, yet this is the area where many IT providers are focused through various cloud initiatives like PasS, SaaS, IasS, etc. The low rating for "use of the latest technologies to avoid technology obsolescence", shows that the use of the latest technologies did not seem to be a priority for most IS organizations. Also, in spite of the trend towards applications service providers, off-the-shelf software products, outsourcing, and off-sourcing, managing vendor risk did not seem to be a major concern for most

IS executives, as denoted by the low rating on "protection of IS and the organization from vendor induced risks (bankruptcy, etc.)".

7.3. Exploratory Factor Analysis of Benefits of an Agile IS

An exploratory factor analysis (EFA) was conducted to identify possible dimensions underlying the benefits of an agile IS. Though broad categories were defined when arriving at attributes and it would be possible to do a confirmatory factor analysis, it was felt that an EFA is appropriate given the exploratory nature of the study. There were 18 items for benefits of an agile IS. Given the sample size of 154, the case-to-variable ratio is 8.55:1. This ratio satisfies the rule of thumb of 5:1 and thus the sample size was considered as acceptable for an EFA. Kaiser-Meyer-Olkin's Measure of Sampling Adequacy (KMO MSA) for the correlation matrix was 0.88. This is considered at meritorious level, signifying that the correlation matrix can be used for factor analysis.

An EFA was conducted using principal axis factoring since the objective was to identify underlying dimensions based on the common variance shared by the attributes. Varimax rotation was used to arrive at a simple factor structure. Other rotations including varimax, oblimin, quatrimax, and promax were tested. Varimax rotation provided the simplest and most interpretable structure. The number of factors to be extracted was based on a combination of the scree-test, eigen-value criterion, and simple structure. Simplicity of structure was given preference over parsimony. Initial factor extraction was based on the criteria of the eigen-value being greater than 1. Then, the scree plot was examined for a visible elbow such that all factors with an eigen-value of greater than 1 were included in the solution. The factor analysis was run again with the number of factors indicated by the elbow. Both solutions were examined and the factor structure that was simple and interpretable was chosen. The cut-off for factor loading was taken as 0.4. While no set criteria for the factor loading exist in the literature, guidelines suggest [53] loadings of greater than ± 0.3 to meet the minimal level while loadings of ± 0.40 are considered more important.

The criteria of eigen-values greater than 1 yielded four factors. The scree plot did not indicate a distinct elbow, though the slope seemed to decrease at factor 5. The five-factor solution was not superior in any sense to the four-factor solution and so the four-factor solution was retained. These four factors together explain 62% of the variance. **Table 10** depicts the factors: The strategic benefits factor reflects a top down approach and provides guidance for all levels of the organization's managers.

The first factor was labeled as the "Technology Leverage" factor. Though "protection of IS and the organization" and "increased robustness of changes" may be seen more as mitigating risks, these benefits in recent times have emerged due to the use of new and better technologies. In some cases, the benefits have arisen due to leveraging existing technologies and using them in an innovative way. The item "faster development of product and services" cross-

Table 10. Factors for benefits of an agile information system.

Benefit of an Agile IS	Factor			
	1 (Technology Leverage)	2 (Strategic Benefits)	3 (Cost Savings)	4 (Top Performance)
Use of the latest technologies to avoid technology obsolescence	0.795			
Business process innovation through use of latest IS technologies	0.719			
Protection of IS and the organization from vendor induced risks (bankruptcy, etc.)	0.663			
Increased robustness of changes made to the IS	0.569			
Enhancement of IS capabilities	0.483			
Alignment of IS with the business process requirements at all times		0.719		
Use of IS as a strategic business tool		0.652		
Faster development of products and services	0.449	0.541		
Rapid change in business processes		0.488		
Increased financial benefits to the organization				
Effective information processing			0.822	
Efficient information processing			0.717	
Increase in efficiency and effectiveness of business processes supported by IS			0.525	
Rapid IS response to security threats like viruses and cyber attacks				0.726
Fast IS recovery from failures/outages				0.551
IS can meet the service level agreements (SLAs) for capacity and performance				0.542
Quick building of capacity for handling peak loads and/or sudden loads				0.428
IS changes are made in a timely fashion				

loaded onto this factor. Faster development of product and services may be another benefit of leveraging technologies and hence the loading of the item could be considered appropriate. It must be understood that the technology leverage factor deals with improving the enterprise through technology attributes such as improved flexibility and expertise. This is often a bottom up phenomenon. The second factor was labeled as "Strategic Benefits". The item "faster development of products and services" that loaded on this factor and cross-loaded on the first factor may also be considered as a strategic benefit to the organization. The strategic benefits factor reflects a top down approach and provides guidance for all levels of the organization's managers. The third factor was labeled as "Cost Saving" since the items that loaded onto it primarily dealt with efficiency and effectiveness of information processing which would lead to cost savings and increase in revenues. The fourth factor was labeled as "Top Performance" and included rapid response to various situations and sustaining performance levels.

The only cross-loading was of "faster development of products and services" on two factors, both of which appear to be relevant. It may need to be further investigated.

Two of the items did not load on any factor. The first was "IS changes are made in a timely fashion". In the rating of the benefits, this particular item was consistently rated high. It deals with changes that are undertaken in a planned or proactive fashion and may just not be attributable to agility but other factors like good project management and may be more related to planning related attributes. In hindsight, the item is an obvious benefit of IS agility and may easily apply to more than one factor or all the four factors. It may need to be worded more specifically; in which case, it is more likely to load on the "Strategic Benefit" factor. The item loaded on to "Top Performance" factor with a loading of 0.305. The second item in question that did not load on to a factor was "increased financial benefits to the organization". This item had a near 0.4 (0.379) loading on "Strategic Benefit Factor" and greater than 0.3 loading on the "Cost Savings" and "Technology Leverage" factors. It is more of a higher order benefit as compared to others. In hindsight, this item sounds fairly generic and may be split into at least two or maybe three distinct items. First would be cost savings, second would be an increase in revenue due to leveraging of technology and third may be increase in revenue by successfully keeping up with changes in the marketplace. The item "faster development of product and services" may also be split into two items: one that deals with innovation in products and services and the second that deals with maintaining competitiveness through emulating competitors or making incremental changes. These suggestions may be explored in future research.

8. Limitations

There are some methodological limitations to this study which have alluded to earlier for example in the EFA section. Some items may need to be further refined to avoid cross-loadings and non-loading items in EFA. The response rate for the survey was 5.7% and though this response rate was considered acceptable for the purpose of this survey there is still room to improve the response rate. This could be done, for example, through collaboration with some special interest groups and research groups with an interest in the area of IS agility.

In view of the rapid evolvement of new paradigms like the cloud model and machine to machine communication the issues and benefits may shift since, like all research such as this, this research represents the state at a particular point in time. The research may need to be continually refreshed to be more meaningful with the times.

9. Summary and Comments

The survey data provides support to the hypothesized benefits of an Agile IS. The top benefit of an agile IS was "rapid IS response to security threats like viruses and cyber-attacks" and the third most important benefit was "fast IS recovery from failures/outages". Thus IS agility may be present in some form in most of organizations in the IS especially in the recovery area.

These empirically supported benefits may provide the justification for investment in initiatives to increase the agility of an IS. Specifically, investments in areas that enhance sensing a change in real time [14], diagnosing a change in real-time [15], and selecting a response and executing a response in real-time [52] may be undertaken.

It is unarguable that the current IT industry has come to accept the requirement for agility in the IS. The industry approach though is somewhat fragmented along applications, databases, infrastructure and so forth and may lack a holistic framework in line with what has been proposed in this study. This is somewhat understandable given the complexity and distributed vendor driven nature of these new paradigms. The empirically-justified benefits from this study may provide support for an organization to invest in these initiatives through both capital and labor expenditures. Over a period of time with the benefits that have been established in this study and other new benefits, agile ISs will become a mainstream in organizations.

References

[1]   ORACLE (2015) New Oracle Research Reveals That Businesses Are Unaware of Competitive Advantages of Cloud Agility.
https://www.oracle.com/corporate/pressrelease/oracle-cloud-agility-survey-na-082715.html

[2]   Bajgoric, N. (2000) Web-Based Information Access for Agile Management. *International Journal of Agile Management Systems*, **2**, 121-129.
https://doi.org/10.1108/14654650010337131

[3]   Bal, J., Wilding, R. and Gundry, J. (1999) Virtual Teaming in the Agile Supply Chain. *The International Journal of Logistics Management*, **10**, 71-82.
https://doi.org/10.1108/09574099910806003

[4]   Christopher, M. (2000) The Agile Supply Chain: Competing in Volatile Markets. *Industrial Marketing Management*, **29**, 37-44.
https://doi.org/10.1016/S0019-8501(99)00110-8

[5]   Hoek, R.I.V. (2000) The Thesis of Leagility Revisited. *International Journal of Agile Manufacturing Management Systems*, **2**, 196-201.

[6]   Mason-Jones, R. and Towill, D.R. (1999) Total Cycle Time Compression and the

Agile Supply Chain. *International Journal of Production Economics*, **62**, 61-73.
https://doi.org/10.1016/S0925-5273(98)00221-7

[7] Sharifi, H. and Zhang, Z. (1999) A Methodology for Achieving Agility in Manufacturing Organizations: An Introduction. *International Journal of Production Economics*, **62**, 7-22. https://doi.org/10.1016/S0925-5273(98)00217-5

[8] Yusuf, Y.Y., Sarahadi, M. and Gunasekaran, A. (1999) Agile Manufacturing: The Drivers Concepts and Attributes. *International Journal of Production Economics*, **62**, 33-43. https://doi.org/10.1016/S0925-5273(98)00219-9

[9] Boynton, A.C. (1993) Achieving Dynamic Stability through Information Technology. *California Management Review* (*Winter*), **50**, 58-77.
https://doi.org/10.2307/41166722

[10] Pankaj (2005) An Analysis and Exploration of Information Systems Agility. Ph.D. Thesis, Southern Illinois University, Carbondale.

[11] Pankaj, Hyde, M., Ramaprasad, A. and Tadisina, S. (2009) Revisiting Agility to Conceptualize Information Systems Agility. In: Lytras, M. and Pablos, P.O.D., Eds., *Emerging Topics and Technologies in Information Systems*, IGI-Global, Hershey, 19-54. https://doi.org/10.4018/978-1-60566-222-0.ch002

[12] Unknown (2002) Comp.realtime: Frequently Asked Questions (FAQs) 3.6.
http://www.faqs.org/faqs/realtime-computing/faq/

[13] IT-Online (2015) Are You as Agile as You Think?
http://it-online.co.za/are-you-as-agile-as-you-think/

[14] Pankaj, Hyde, M. and Rodger, J.A. (2013b) Sensing Attributes of an Agile Information System. *Intelligent Information Management*, **5**, 150-161.
https://doi.org/10.4236/iim.2013.55016

[15] Pankaj, Hyde, M. and Rodger, J.A. (2013a) Attributes for Change Diagnosis in an Agile Information System. *International Journal of Computers & Technology*, **10**, 2095-2109.

[16] Pankaj, C., Micki, H. and James, A.R. (2015) Attributes for Executing Change in an Agile Information System. *International Journal of Technology Diffusion* (*IJTD*), **6**, 30-58. https://doi.org/10.4018/IJTD.2015040103

[17] Blessing Mavengere, N. (2014) Role of Information Systems for Strategic Agility in Supply Chain Setting: Telecommunication Industry Study. *Electronic Journal of Information Systems Evaluation*, **17**, 100-112.

[18] Bharadwaj, A.S. (2000) A Resource-Based Perspective on Information Technology Competences and Firm Performance: An Empirical Investigation. *MIS Quarterly*, **24**, 28. https://doi.org/10.2307/3250983

[19] Rockart, J.F., Earl, M.J. and Ross, J.W. (1996) Eight Imperatives for the New IT Organization. *Sloan Management Review*, **38**, 13.

[20] Barney, J.B. (1991) Firm Resources and Sustained Competitive Advantage. *Journal of Management*, **17**, 24. https://doi.org/10.1177/014920639101700108

[21] Chakravarty, A., Grewal, R. and Sambamurthy, V. (2013) Information Technology Competencies, Organizational Agility, and Firm Performance: Enabling and Facilitating Roles. *Information Systems Research*, **24**, 976-997.
https://doi.org/10.1287/isre.2013.0500

[22] Hefu, L., Weiling, K., Kwok, K.W. and Zhongsheng, H. (2013) The Impact of IT Capabilities on Firm Performance: The Mediating Roles of Absorptive Capacity and Supply Chain Agility. *Decision Support Systems*, **54**, 1452-1463.

https://doi.org/10.1016/j.dss.2012.12.016

[23] Shin, H., Lee, J.N., Kim, D. and Rhim, H. (2015) Strategic Agility of Korean small and Medium Enterprises and Its Influence on Operational and Firm Performance. *International Journal of Production Economics*, **168**, 181-196. https://doi.org/10.1016/j.ijpe.2015.06.015

[24] Gren, L., Torkar, R. and Feldt, R. (2015) The Prospects of a Quantitative Measurement of Agility: A Validation Study on an Agile Maturity Model. *Journal of Systems and Software*, **107**, 38-49. https://doi.org/10.1016/j.jss.2015.05.008

[25] Cao, Y., Swartz, C.L.E., Baldea, M. and Blouin, S. (2015) Optimization-Based Assessment of Design Limitations to Air Separation Plant Agility in Demand Response Scenarios. *Journal of Process Control*, **33**, 37-48. https://doi.org/10.1016/j.jprocont.2015.05.002

[26] Sangari, M.S., Razmi, J. and Zolfaghari, S. (2015) Developing a Practical Evaluation Framework for Identifying Critical Factors to Achieve Supply Chain Agility. *Measurement*, **62**, 205-214. https://doi.org/10.1016/j.measurement.2014.11.002

[27] Gligor, D.M., Esmark, C.L. and Holcomb, M.C. (2015) Performance Outcomes of Supply Chain Agility: When Should You Be Agile? *Journal of Operations Management*, **33**, 71-82. https://doi.org/10.1016/j.jom.2014.10.008

[28] Goldsby, T.J., Griffis, S.E. and Roath, A.S. (2006) Modeling Lean, Agile, and Leagile Supply Chain Strategies. *Journal of business logistics*, **27**, 57-80. https://doi.org/10.1002/j.2158-1592.2006.tb00241.x

[29] Narayanan, S., Narasimhan, R. and Schoenherr, T. (2015) Assessing the Contingent Effects of Collaboration on Agility Performance in Buyer-Supplier Relationships. *Journal of Operations Management*, **33**, 140-154. https://doi.org/10.1016/j.jom.2014.11.004

[30] Chung, S., Lee, K.Y. and Kim, K. (2014) Job Performance through Mobile Enterprise Systems: The Role of Organizational Agility, Location Independence, and Task Characteristics. *Information & Management*, **51**, 605-617. https://doi.org/10.1016/j.im.2014.05.007

[31] Sherehiy, B. and Karwowski, W. (2014) The Relationship between Work Organization and Workforce Agility in Small Manufacturing Enterprises. *International Journal of Industrial Ergonomics*, **44**, 466-473. https://doi.org/10.1016/j.ergon.2014.01.002

[32] Yang, J. (2014) Supply Chain Agility: Securing Performance for Chinese Manufacturers. *International Journal of Production Economics*, **150**, 104-114. https://doi.org/10.1016/j.ijpe.2013.12.018

[33] Barthe-Delanoë, A.M., Truptil, S., Bénaben, F. and Pingaud, H. (2014) Event-Driven Agility of Interoperability during the Run-Time of Collaborative Processes. *Decision Support Systems*, **59**, 171-179. https://doi.org/10.1016/j.dss.2013.11.005

[34] Yusuf, Y.Y., Gunasekaran, A., Musa, A., Dauda, M.M., El-Berishy, N. and Cang, S. (2014) A Relational Study of Supply Chain Agility, Competitiveness, and Business Performance in the Oil and Gas Industry. *International Journal of Production Economics*, **147**, 531-544. https://doi.org/10.1016/j.ijpe.2012.10.009

[35] DeGroote, S.E. and Marx, T.G. (2013) The Impact of IT on Supply Chain Agility and Firm Performance: An Empirical Investigation. *International Journal of Information Management*, **33**, 909-916. https://doi.org/10.1016/j.ijinfomgt.2013.09.001

[36] Balaji, M., Velmurugan, V., Sivabalan, G., Ilayaraja, V.S., Prapa, M. and Mythily, V. (2014) ASCTM Approach for Enterprise Agility. *Procedia Engineering*, **97**, 2222-

2231. https://doi.org/10.1016/j.proeng.2014.12.466

[37] Galster, M., Weyns, D., Tofan, D., Michalik, B. and Avgeriou, P. (2014) Variability in Software Systems—A Systematic Literature Review. *IEEE Transactions on Software Engineering*, **40**, 282-306. https://doi.org/10.1109/TSE.2013.56

[38] Sheffield, J. and Lemétayer, J. (2013) Factors Associated with the Software Development Agility of Successful Projects. *International Journal of Project Management*, **31**, 459-472. https://doi.org/10.1016/j.ijproman.2012.09.011

[39] Krotov, V.V.K.A.A.A., Junglas, I.I.C.F.E. and Steel, D.S.U.E. (2015) The Mobile Agility Framework: An Exploratory Study of Mobile Technology Enhancing Organizational Agility. *Journal of Theoretical & Applied Electronic Commerce Research*, **10**, 1-17. https://doi.org/10.4067/S0718-18762015000300002

[40] Wasko, M.M. and Faraj, S. (2005) Why Should I Share? Examining Social Capital and Knowledge Contribution in Electronic Networks of Practice. *MIS Quarterly*, **29**, 35-57.

[41] Broadbent, M., Weil, P. and St.Clair, D. (1999) The Implications of Information Technology Infrastructure for Business Process Redesign. *MIS Quarterly*, **23**, 159-182. https://doi.org/10.2307/249750

[42] Clemons, E.K. and Row, M.C. (1991) Sustaining IT Advantage: The Role of Structural Differences. *MIS Quarterly*, **15**, 275-292. https://doi.org/10.2307/249639

[43] Weber, B., Reichert, M. and Rinderle-Ma, S. (2008) Change Patterns and Change Support Features—Enhancing Flexibility in Process-Aware Information Systems. *Data & Knowledge Engineering*, **66**, 438-467. https://doi.org/10.1016/j.datak.2008.05.001

[44] Seebacher, G. and Winkler, H. (2014) Evaluating Flexibility in Discrete Manufacturing Based on Performance and Efficiency. *International Journal of Production Economics*, **153**, 340-351. https://doi.org/10.1016/j.ijpe.2014.03.018

[45] Dove, R. (1995) Agile Benefits: Viability and Leadership. *Production*, **1**, 16-17.

[46] Bonoma, T.V. (1985) Case Research in Marketing: Opportunities, Problems, and a Process. *Journal of Marketing Research*, **22**, 199-208. https://doi.org/10.2307/3151365

[47] Bailey, J.E. and Pearson, S.W. (1983) Development of a Tool for Measuring and Analyzing Computer User Satisfaction. *Management Science*, **29**, 530-545. https://doi.org/10.1287/mnsc.29.5.530

[48] Goodhue, D.L. (1988) Supporting Users of Corporate Data. Ph.D. Doctoral, Massachusetts Institute of Technology, Boston.

[49] Ives, B., Olson, M.H. and Baroudi, J.J. (1983) The Measurement of User Information Satisfaction. *Communications of the ACM*, **26**, 785-793. https://doi.org/10.1145/358413.358430

[50] Ricketts, J.A. and Jenkins, A.M. (1985) The Development of an MIS Satisfaction Questionnaire: An Instrument for Evaluating User Satisfaction with Turnkey Decision Support Systems. Retrieved from Bloomington, Indiana:

[51] Churchill, G.A. (1979) A Paradigm for Developing Better Measures of Marketing Constructs. *Journal of Marketing Research*, **16**, 64-73. https://doi.org/10.2307/3150876

[52] Chaudhary, P., Hyde, M. and Rodger, J.A. (2015) Attributes for Executing Change in an Agile Information System. *International Journal of Technology Diffusion (IJTD)*, **6**, 30-58. https://doi.org/10.4018/IJTD.2015040103

[53] Hair Jr., J.H., Anderson, R.E., Tatham, R.L. and Black, W.C. (1995) Multivariate Data Analysis. Prentice Hall, Upper Saddle River, New Jersey.
https://doi.org/10.1108/eb046431

[54] Vokurka, R.J., Zank, G.M. and Lund III, C.M. (2002) Improving Competitiveness through Supply Chain Management: A Cumulative Improvement Approach. *CR*, **12**, 14-25.

[55] Christian, P.H., Govande, V., Staehle, W. and Zimmers Jr., E.W (1999) Advantage through Agility. *IIE Solutions*, **31**, 26-33.

[56] Yoffie, D.B. and Kwak, M. (2001) Mastering Strategic Movement at Palm. *Sloan Management Review*, **43**, 55-63.

[57] Bessant, J., Francis, D., Meredith, S. and Kalinsky, R. (2001) Developing Manufacturing Agility in SMEs. *International Journal of Technology Management*, **22**, 28-54. https://doi.org/10.1504/IJTM.2001.002953

[58] Schonsleben, P. (2000) With Agility and Adequate Partnership Strategies towards Effective Logistics Networks. *Computers in Industry*, **42**, 33-42.
https://doi.org/10.1016/S0166-3615(99)00059-7

[59] Cho, H., Jung, M. and Kim, M. (1996) Enabling Technologies of Agile Manufacturing and its Related Activities in Korea. *Computers and Industrial Engineering*, **30**, 323-335. https://doi.org/10.1016/0360-8352(96)00001-0

[60] Vernadat, F.B. (1999) Research Agenda for Agile Manufacturing. *International Journal of Agile Management Systems*, **1**, 37-40.
https://doi.org/10.1108/14654659910266709

[61] O'Connor, L. (1994) Agile Manufacturing in a Responsive Factory. *Mechanical Engineering*, **3**, 54-57.

[62] Sahin, F. (2000) Manufacturing Competitiveness: Different Systems to Achieve the Same Results. *Production and Inventory Management Journal*, **1**, 56-65.

[63] Vokurka, R.J. and Fliedner, G. (1997) Agility: Competitive Weapon of the 1990s and Beyond? *Production and Inventory Management Journal*, **38**, 19-24.

[64] Devor, R., Graves, R. and Miles, J.J. (1997) Agile Manufacturing Research: Accomplishments and Opportunities. *IIE Transactions*, **29**, 813-823.
ps://doi.org/10.1080/07408179708966404

[65] Noaker, P.M. (1994) The Search for Agile Manufacturing. *Manufacturing Engineering*, **113**, 5-11.

11

Agri-food Supply Chain Management

C. Ganeshkumar[1], M. Pachayappan[2], G. Madanmohan[3]

[1]Indian Institute of Plantation Management, Bengaluru, India
[2]Department of International Business, School of Management, Pondicherry University, Puducherry, India
[3]Department of Management Studies, School of Management, Pondicherry University, Puducherry, India
Email: gcganeshkumar@gmail.com, pachayappanvn@gmail.com, mathansaradha@gmail.com.

Abstract

The purpose of this paper is to present a critical review of prior literature relating to agri-food supply chain management. An in-depth analysis has been carried out to identify the influential information from the literature. This paper has identified gaps to be explored about agricultural supply chain management (SCM) practices which may be used by researchers to enrich theory construction and practitioners may concentrate on establishing the extent and frontiers of agri-food SCM. This research work is the first attempt to make a critical literature review of available literature on agri-food SCM practices for developing countries like India. The research articles and other materials related to the agri-food supply chain management were collected from online data bases like Scopus, EBSCO and Google Scholar for the period of 10 years (2006-2016). The study performs content analysis and is followed by descriptive analysis. In the next phase, the literature in the field of agri-food supply chain management is classified into four broad categories viz. general literature review of agri-food supply chain, policies affecting the segments of agri-food supply chain, individual segments of agri-food SCM (structure of supply chain segments and conduct of supply chain segments) and performance of supply chain segments. These four categories are comprehensively reviewed and elaborated the research gap in the literature based on agri-food supply chain management. Finally, potato supply chain of India is considered as a case example for comprehensive analysis and elaborated in detail.

Keywords

Agri-Food, Supply Chain Management, Literature Review, Nvivo, Perishable Food

1. Introduction

India is an agro-based economy with the agriculture sector providing employment for more than half of the country's massive population. However, the sector contributes only 18% to the nation's Gross Domestic Product (GDP) [1]. Though the sector is employing huge proportion of the country's population, economic contribution of the sector is declining for every year. India has got very good numbers as far as agriculture is concerned. However, these numbers are very discouraging if compared with other countries. For instance, India ranks second in the world in production of agro-based food items. These stats are highly encouraging. However, India's share in trading of food products at the world level is a mere 0.2%, which is astonishingly lower than the proportion of world trade accounted for by other developing countries such as Vietnam and Brazil [2]. The sector plays a significant part in socio-economic development of under-privileged masses of the country. The sector plays a decisive role in the progress of other sectors of the economy, particularly the manufacturing sector. However, it is a regrettable fact that India' first five year plan (1951-1956) alone placed utmost prominence on agriculture while all other plans and the economic reforms which followed, emphasized largely on non-agricultural sectors, disregarding agriculture. This paramount shift in policy-making resulted in colossal poverty and massive discrepancy and inequality distribution of wealth and income [3]. Despite the immense utility of agricultural sector to Indian economy, researches on India's agro-food industry in general and supply chain issues of Indian agriculture in particular, are very limited due to the vastly unorganized characteristic of the sector, complicating the process of primary data collection for researchers and policy-formulators. Hence, the task of data-driven decision-making regarding improvements in the total supply chain process of agro-food industry has assumed immense complexities [4].

The major food crops cultivated globally are rice, maize, wheat and potato. India occupies top positions in all these four crops. India is second largest cultivator of potato, next to China (FAO, 2011). Agri-food like potatoes is seed-based crops. It is indispensable to provide sophisticated warehousing with effective refrigeration facilities to store the vegetables for long term to fetch remunerative returns for farmers. Hence, agri-food supply chain management needs to be effective for adequate farmer remuneration. Hence, research on supply chain management will be of huge interest for the farming community and the country as a whole. This paper has attempted to review the studies on concerns regarding agri-food supply chain taken holistically and throw light on important findings discussed relating to supply chain policy like financial issues, mode of organizing/ performance of different components of supply chain. It represents all intermediate functions involved in the process of transforming inputs into output. Agricultural supply chain management engulfs set of value activities resulting in transforming agricultural commodities from their raw stage to consumption phase. These activities may embrace acquisition or procurement of agricultural raw materials, production course of agricultural commodities and the process of marketing, storing and dispensation of agricultural commodities. Important agencies partaking in this process are agriculturists and consumers, suppliers of raw inputs (farmers), processors and human resources engaged in transporting and storage activities, etc. [5].

Over the few decades, lot of research work on the issues in supply chain management has been carried out in manufacturing and service sectors but little attention given to agriculture sector and the flip side agriculture sector contributing major part of human livelihood in the country like India and raw material for other industry. Among the agricultural commodity, food item has least explored in the context of supply chain management (Samuel *et al.*, 2012) and there is not structured literature in supply chain management of food sector in the context of what has been explored and not explored in agri-food supply chain management so this literature review paper will address this limitation through structured review of agri-food supply chain management. This paper aims at critically appraising studies conducted on agricultural supply chain. To put on a nutshell, this paper shall discuss previous studies conducted pertinent to principles and policies regarding potato supply chain. Prior literature studying comprehensive agri-food supply chain analysis and various issues concerning individual components of agri-food supply chain shall be thoroughly and critically reviewed and appraised. Hence, this paper shall take a holistic look at issues relevant to agri-food like potato supply chain which includes economic and financial aspects of all its components. Further the rest of the paper is organized as follows. In the next section we brief the data collection procedure and filtering conditions. In the Section 3, the design of content and descriptive analysis is explored via word cloud to identify the frequency of the words present in the collected literature, pie-chart shows the distribution of source of materials, heat map defines the authors list with research domain, and finally word cluster analysis is implemented to identify the relationship between the words in the collected literature. The content and descriptive analysis is done by Nvivo software. Section 4 devoted to four broad categories viz. general literature review of agri-food supply chain, policies affecting the segments of agri-food supply chain, individual segments of agri-food SCM (structure of supply chain segments and conduct of supply chain segments) and performance of supply chain segments [6]. Section 5 presents a case example of potato supply chain in India and followed by Section 6 research gap. Finally, Section 7 provides the insights for future research and conclusion.

2. Review Methodology

Literature review is a sum up of available research studies with the motive of exploring the focal point, developments and issues concerning the subject covered [7]. The process comprise of assessing contents utilizing both quantitative and qualitative. A critical evaluation of prior work conducted on specific subject shall divulge interesting issues which might not be well captured or noticed.

The process of literature data collection began very broadly with searching for the keywords of supply chain management and agriculture and the process gradually assumed to specificity. Hence, this paper uses a blend of deductive and inductive approaches. First, literature like published peer-reviewed journal papers, white papers, MS and Ph.D. thesis reports, presentations made in conferences and industry manuals pertinent were collected from online and offline resources. The preliminary stage of data consists of more than thousands of research articles and other material. However, the primary motive is to review literature relevant to agri-food supply chain management are considered, many studies relating to agriculture and supply chains were collected.

In the next stage to identify the exact articles (materials) from the preliminary data collection a three way filtering conditions are adapted. First is based on period, the study considered papers published on agriculture supply chain management during the period of 2005-2015. Next is based on keywords used for searching articles and papers for the purpose include Supply Chain Management (SCM), Agri-food supply chain, agriculture supply chain, vegetable supply chain, fresh supply chain, perishable agriculture products, food products and potato supply chain. Final filter is carried out based on reputed publications available in three databases viz. Scopus, EBSCO and Google Scholar. Based on this conditions totally 116 articles are selected for the critical literature review.

The procedure suggested by [8] (**Figure 1**) has been utilized to conduct content validity of the articles collected. The four steps followed in this process were:

1) Material Collection: All papers satisfying the three criteria laid down as limiting factors were taken for scrutiny;

2) Descriptive Analysis: We segregated the selected papers using Nvivo 11 based on source of material and based on authors;

3) Category selection: We then categorized the papers like general literature review of agri-food supply chain, policies affecting the segments of agri-food supply chain, individual segments of agri-food SCM and performance of supply chain segments;

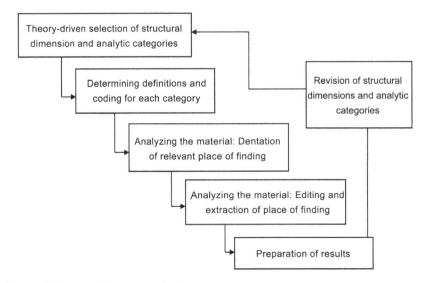

Figure 1. Process of content analysis.

4) Material evaluation: The filtered articles were scrutinized on the backdrop of the structural attributes and pertinent issues were analyzed to explore research gap in the prior literature [9].

Figure 1 portrays the entire process of content analysis ([10]). The figure highlights the process using a feedback loop. The study derived the structural attributes from extensive literature review and consultation with practitioners. Occurrence of errors have to be eliminated by following judiciously the third and fourth steps spelt out earlier which shall result in cautious revision of attributes and categories chosen for analysis.

3. Descriptive Analytics of Agri-Food Supply Chain Literature Using Nvivo Software

World Cloud (**Figure 2**) derived about literature on agri-food supply chain suggest that supply, market, farmers, chain, price, value, production, development, food and agriculture have been the frequently used words in these collected articles and also it is depict that there is no citation on business management related words so there is gap in the literature to discover the agri-food in the business management aspect like operations and supply chain management. From this bag of words it is clear that the selected research papers are more relevant to the proposed research work on agri-food supply chain management. The pie chart (**Figure 3**) provides the split of literature across outlets like journal articles, conference proceedings, books and other materials. In that 69.63% of journal articles, 5.76% of conference proceedings, 7.85% of book and thesis 3.15% are presents.

The Head Map (**Figure 4**) derived to review the prior literature about agri-food supply chain suggest that despite the thorough investigation of agri-food supply chain issues, studies on potato supply chain under Indian context is very limited.

Figure 5 shows the result of cluster analysis for exploring the relationship between different topics and context used by researcher in their articles and reports.

Figure 2. Word Cloud based on 116 articles.

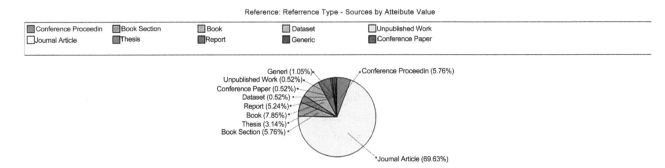

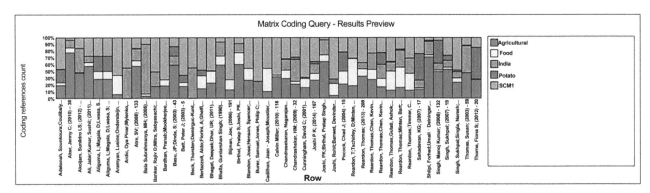

Figure 3. Split of literature.

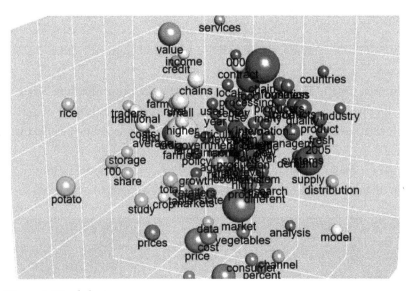

Figure 4. Authors list with research domain.

Figure 5. Word cluster.

There are six groups of cluster has formed based on the word citation in the review process, in the biggest cluster of black color depicts that researchers has explored the research in the context of quality, demand, contract, producer, country, industry and fresh of agriculture sector.

4. Literature Review Classification Based on Structure, Conduct and Performance (SCP) Paradigm

In this paper, the literature in the field of agri-Food supply chain management is classified into four broad categories as listed below:

1) General literature review of agri-food supply chain;
2) Policies affecting the segments of agri-food supply chain;
3) Individual segments of agri-food SCM;
4) Structure of supply chain segments;
5) Conduct of supply chain segments;
6) Performance of supply chain segments.

4.1. General Literature Review of Agri-Food Supply Chain

Cunningham [11] Scrutinized 123 peer reviewed journal articles published during 1987-2000 in seven commercial databases on the theme of agri-food supply chain management and exposed the possibility of conducting additional studies on all agri-food supply chain processes, particularly the fishery sector. Vasileiou and Morris [12] conducted a descriptive research based on primary data collected through exploratory interview of 240 potato cultivators, 17 potato merchants and 4 potato retailers and analyzed the data using non-parametric statistical tools. Results reveal that all participants of the supply chain were immensely concerned about sustaining their respective businesses and gaining comparative advantages and economic, market, social and environmental factors have great bearing on these endeavors. Vorst, *et al.* [13] conducted a simulation based study to explore SCM's effect on logistical performance indicators in food supply chain and found that uncertainty minimization drastically boosts service level. Frick, *et al.* [14] studied issues pertinent to supply chain of potatoes, lambs by interviewing cultivators and supply chain intermediaries. They found that entrepreneurship prospects were bright in supply chain of these commodities. However, they have cautioned that such prospects are highly dependent on efficient utilization of fuel and relationships between the components of the supply chain.

Taylor [15] conducted action research and used value stream analysis (VCA) involving farmers and a key processor and retailer and unearthed through a close scrutiny of lean supply chain mechanism that supply chain performance, efficiency, profitability and relationship between components of supply chain have got immense scope for improvement. Batt [16] studied potato supply chain issues in Vietnam by interviewing 60 potato cultivators, 10 traders and 25 retailers and used one-way ANOVA to explore the impact of various supply chain issues using transaction cost analysis and gap analysis. Results reveal that good interrelationship between different components of supply chain makes a significant positive contribution to enhance chances of innovation, thereby boosting probability of competitiveness and competence. Further, the author has pointed out that SCM and product diversification has been necessitated in developing countries due to the following reasons 1) Attainment of food security, 2) Increased urbanization, 3) Rise in standard of living and d) Preference for traditional food. These developments have enhanced farmers' income. .

Deshingkar, *et al.* [5] attempted to detect changes in cultivation pattern of Andhra Pradesh farmers. They found that larger farmers are engaged in cultivation of conventional vegetables such as onions, tomatoes, brinjals and cabbages while some of them have undertaken cultivation of hybrid vegetables of coriander and potatoes. The study also exposed the presence of small and marginal farmers making significant contribution to vegetable cultivation. Chandrashekar [17] analyzed fruits and vegetables SCM practices of Karnataka SAFAL market and exposed the prevalence of scope for better utilization of SCM concept to enhance productivity and efficiency. Hobbs [18] analyzed the current trends and future prospects of SCM of agri-food sector and established that enhanced attention on food security, free foreign trade reign, flow of foreign investments, heterogeneity of consumer choice and advancements in technology are important determinants driving modifications in SCM practices of agri-food sector. Moazzem and Fujita [19] analyzed the Bangladeshi potato SCM with a special emphasis on the marketing system. They found that time and finance constraints, too little productivity of potato cultivation, inadequate skill-level and shrinking rate of return from potato refrigerated warehousing business restricted the agriculturists and warehouse owners from undertaking trading activities. Despite these problems, investment in warehousing potatoes has been on the rise due to liberal credit offered by traders engaged in refrigerated warehousing.

Shukla and Jharkharia [10] undertook a review of 20 years (1989-2009) literature on fresh-produce-SCM. They classified the available literature based on problem milieu, methodology, product and other structural attributes. Their study revealed that fresh-produce-SCM papers have concentrated on maximizing revenue, customer satisfaction and minimization of post-harvest wastage. The other issues researched were disparity between demand and supply and inefficient demand predictions and the review revealed that majority of the articles available on fresh produce SCM is fragmented.

Fuglie [20] conducted an inter-country study on economics of potato warehousing in India, USA and Tunisia. This paper found that agriculturists might be exposed to lesser degree of market risk if a) they had access to market prices and stock details in time and b) forward and futures pricing mechanism existed. Beck and Demirguc-Kunt [21] analyzed research relating to access of finance for small and medium enterprises (SMEs) and suggested that factoring and leasing can play a significant role in providing finance for these enterprises in economies where financial institutions have not been well established. Sagheer, *et al.* [4] analyzed efficiency of agri-SCM of India at industrial and firm levels using Porter's Diamond and Momaya's Asset Process Performance (APP) Models respectively. Their study has revealed that human components (processors, government, producers, etc.) and non-human components (governing setup, food quality, etc.) significantly influence SCM competence.Minten, *et al.* [22] surveyed branding of agriculture commodities and SCM issues in Bihar. They found that brand materialization in agriculture commodities results in enhanced delineation in retailing segments. The authors have revealed shocking information for consumers that quality of branded commodities sold in packed materials are inferior when compared with those available in the market in loose lots. Hellin and

Meijer [23] scrutinized Ecuador SCM practices and found that consumer market requirements for processed potatoes is on the increase. They also found that increasing role of retailers and processors in potato SCM have successfully countered this demand spurt.

Punjabi [24] studied problems confronting SCM practices of fresh food and vegetable items in India by obtaining responses from corporate managers involved in the process. Her study exposed issues like insufficient refrigerated warehousing facilities, excessive competition among traders in conventional markets, contractual obligations of agriculturists and agro-business firms, dearth of standardization in agricultural commodities, non-compliance with APMC Act while procuring agricultural produce from agriculturists and improper handling of the postharvest produce due to lack of training. Ghai [25] conducted a descriptive research on financial aspects of components of agro supply chain using secondary data. The study has advocated that all components of supply chain should be interrelated and cooperate by ethically sharing benefits equally among themselves in order to sustain in the business through mutual coexistence. Bala Subrahmanya [26] conducted a research to expose various problems confronting the Indian small scale sector in the light of globalized scenario. His study has revealed that inefficient infrastructure, insufficient financial support due to low flow of formalized credit and outmoded technologies resulting in substandard quality and poor productivity and capacity utilization are the major issues adversely bothering Indian small-scale units.

Shilpa [27] analyzed the vegetables SCM practices in Bangalore and identified that inefficient recording of sales managed by agriculturists, procurement managed by middlemen, quantum sold to consumers and quantity remaining unsold and intra-day price variations are the major restrictions of vegetable SCM. KhairulIslam [28] analyzed Bangladeshi potato SCM through desk research and interviews and unearthed that Information Communication Technology (ICT) is the permanent solution to enable agriculturists in identifying various sources of qualitative inputs and enforcement of regulatory mechanism to check sale of substandard inputs in the market. Singh [29] analyzed potato SCM practices in Bihar and highlighted the major problem of agriculturists being exploited by middlemen who eat away lion's share of price paid by consumers, leaving the farmers a very little share. [30] conducted a descriptive study on financial aspects involved in SCM of rural entrepreneurship and advocated that financing SCM implies establishing link between financial institutions and all stakeholders in supply chain management. The author suggested that providing finance to facilitate flow of products and establishing relationships among different stakeholders of supply chain should immensely contribute to boost the efficiency of SCM practices.

4.2. Policies Affecting the Segments of Agri-Food Supply Chain

Driessen and Glasbergen [31] have compared efficiency of organic and generic farming. They have exposed some limitations of organic farming such as complexities associated with it and squat desire among consumers to use eco-friendly commodities. The study has revealed that governmental policies exert slender impact on potato SCM practices.

Cromme, *et al.* [32] endeavored to study ways of amplifying efficacy of potato SCM practices in developing countries by analyzing secondary data provided by UN's FAO (Food and Agriculture Organization) and exposed important problems confronted by potato SCM as dearth in support from both public and private parties, production initiatives, diversified fabrication clusters and market integration. Nations with minimum assortment in diet practices and those with high imports and exports are immensely benefitted by potato SCM.

Wei and Yanrong [33] have analyzed SCM practices of Melons and established that despite institutional scenario being supportive of SCM practices, social infrastructure has been the major cause of concern.Wheatley and Peters [34] analyzed the means and modes of enhancing efficacy of Agri-food SCM practices of Asian farm sector and recommended that innovation, supply chain intermediaries diversifying their activities to participate in other supply chains, precise consideration of different stakeholders in the supply chain and the mechanism of apportionment of cost and utility to these stakeholders shall enhance the efficiency of SCM practices.

Kumar, *et al.* [35] scrutinized 76 presentations made during eighteenth conference organized by NAARM covering SCM practices of agriculture items and its contribution to accomplishing food safety and eliminating poverty. Their study revealed that institutional framework comprising professional societies and national institutes might shoulder the responsibility of taking initiatives to develop sound theoretical concepts to strengthen SCM issues of agricultural food items.

Basu and Dinda [36] collected price movements of potatoes in West Bengal and applied co-integration test to highlight even transmission of trends in prices throughout. Basu [37] evaluated efficacy of Bengali potato SCM based on secondary data during July 2000 to December 2001 and has advocated intervention of private corporate in potato SCM to boost its efficacy. Rais, *et al.* [38] have conducted an in-depth scrutiny of India's food processing segment and its capacity to generate jobs. They stressed the importance of better government policies to institute proper infrastructure support for developing the industry that is engaging predominantly lesser skilled laborers. Jha, *et al.* [39] studied monthly data of 55 Indian wholesale commodity market segments during January 1970-December 1999 to test prevalence of integration among these segments. Their study has revealed the incompleteness of market integration among the segments due to excessive governmental intervention.

Joshi, *et al.* [40] examined trends of revenue from crops cultivation during 1980-1981 to 1999-2000 and have suggested better investment in agricultural R& encouraging marginal farmers to diversify into cultivation of high value crops through assistive institutional framework. Popkin [41] analyzed the trends of living pattern of developing countries and found that globalization has drastically altered pattern of energy usage and food habits of people in developing nations, leading to many health complexities. Sharma [3] has scrutinized trends in growth of India's sectors including agriculture and has established that despite the strong impact exerted by agriculture on progress of other sectors of economy and effectively addressing the menace of poverty, the sector has not been accorded due importance in the country's planning process, resulting in vast disparities of income and wealth distribution. U. Kleih [42] analyzed issues pertinent to providing financial assistance to small and medium agriculturists and fishermen and advocated that banks and financial institutions should educate these marginal sections of society about managing finance which will enhance their accessibility to finance. Rao, *et al.* [43] analyzed the nature of credit extended by 97 banks to SSI (Small-Scale Industry) sector and concluded that nonrepayment of loans obtained by SSI units resulted in banks being reluctant to accord credit to the sector. Tchale and Keyser [44] found that high farm prices in other nations, exploitation by middlemen, shrinking productivity and rising cost of inputs adversely affected the competitiveness of agricultural items such as rice, maize, cotton and tobacco in the international market. Smith [45] has suggested that those engaged in agro-based business can prosper only if consumers are educated about healthy food habits and encouraged to consume food harvested and preserved in their respective localities and accomplish a good and well sustained SCM practices in the agricultural sector. Trilochansastry [46] has suggested that effective SCM will lead to maximization of income and wealth for small and trivial farmers. A well-designed SCM warrants sufficient financing all components of supply chain, rendering modern technologies such as internet and cellular networks affordable and accessible to the intermediaries of supply chain, establishing agriculturists associations and providing expertise in all components of supply chain.

Swinnen and Maertens [47] have evaluated the influence of privatizing and globalizing the economy on agri-food SCM of Latin American and Central European nations in transitionary stage of economic development and found that the process has resulted in privatization and global integration of agri-food SCM practices of these nations. Gandhi and Namboodiri [48] studied the Ahmedabad's wholesale price and cost components of vegetables and fruits and found that marketing cost constituted nearly 8% of price paid by end-user in the case of former and 11% - 15% for the latter. Transportation and commission expenses constitute the bulk part of price paid by end-users while the agriculturists get only 48% and 37% of price paid by consumers in the case of vegetables and fruits respectively. Pal, *et al.* [49] scrutinized the Indian potatoes and groundnuts SCM practices and exposed the diversity of cultivation environment prevalent among states and within a state at some instances. Hence, they have advocated that regulations in seed legislations pertaining to compulsory registration or private participation might not hold valid for the entire nation. Naik and Jain [50] analyzed shift in the role of institutional infrastructure in farming sector of India and highlighted private sector, acting in coalition with public sector, gaining predominance in effecting growth of the agricultural sector at better pace, by better utilization of natural resources and knowledge. Reardon and Minten [51] have highlighted revolutionary changes drastically transforming Indian food SCM practices during past twenty years. Role of retailers is assuming immense significance with retail sales witnessing a whopping annual growth of 49%, penetrating both urban and rural markets, transforming lives of agriculturists.

Cromme, *et al.* [32] have studied the potato SCM practices in developing nations and advocated that effective private-public support, improving production process through formation of producer groups and integrating markets can strengthen potato SCM practices. Miller and Jones [52] analyzed issues pertinent to financing agri-food SCM practices. They suggested that financial institutions should carefully consider SCM dynamics while deciding about granting agricultural credit. Ghosh and Ganguly [2] have identified stumpy productivity as the key problem of Indian agriculture due to fragmented land holdings, irrational resources utilization, shrinking demand for food items, diminishing investments in the agri sector and inaccessible farm credit for petty and trivial agriculturists. Mancero [53] has hinted that rapid variance in requirements of agricultural sector due to fast changing economic conditions warrant petty agriculturists to adopt innovative SCM model by taking a consorted and coordinated approach. Gaiha and Thapa [54] have analyzed the comparative strengths and future opportunities for supermarkets and small players in Asian agri SCM practices and points out that the small players will not be affected by supermarkets if their constrictions are adequately addressed. They advocate that supermarkets and petty players can mutually benefit through partnership arrangements and strategic alliances.

4.3. Individual Segments of Agri-Food SCM

The individual segments of Agri-food SCM are classified into two categories viz. structure of supply chain segments and conduct of supply chain segments. These two categories are elaborated in this section.

4.3.1. Structure of Supply Chain Segments

Loader [55] analyzed Egyptian potato SCM practices and established that supply chain comprising of numerous processing players will result in complexity of inadequate intra-firm relationship. This might lead to businesses adopting vertical integration as growth strategy which can be managed by adequate dissemination of information among different SCM segments. Narrod, *et al.* [56] talks about petty Indian and Kenyan fruit and vegetable producers coping up with pressures of their profession and have advocated that effective SCM practices shall be the best solution. However, they have suggested that government has to play a facilitative role in correcting supply chain problems and not trying to control it. Beck and Demirguc-Kunt [21] have analyzed the problem of accessing finance for SMEs and have advocated conduct of more research at both micro and macro levels to arrive at better solution to this problem of enabling SMEs access to external finance. Howorth and Westhead [57] have established through their study that small firms concentrate much on managing their working capital for the goal of improving their returns.

Solér, *et al.* [58] analyzed the Swedish food SCM practices and found that consumers perceive information about the environment relating to food SCM distinctly and this distinct perception is affected by their location in the supply chain in relation to other stakeholders. Vorley [59] established that agricultural markets have undergone tremendous changes with wholesale markets replaced by closer SCM participants comprising of food processors, retailers and servicing personnel. Markelova, *et al.* [60] have recommended that petty agriculturists have to implement drastic alterations in organizing their producing and marketing mechanism to enhance their productivity and efficiency. Some of such initiatives may be adoption of sophisticated technology like spreading out producing processes, utilizing innovative means, enhancement of quality in processes, utilizing micro-irrigation mechanism and maintaining schedules of plantation and record of such schedule, quantum of plantation and expected productivity and likely date of harvesting. Ardic, *et al.* [61] analyzed the global flow of credit to SME sector and found that a total of 10 trillion $ credit is extended to SME sector in the world and OECD nations account for 70% of such credit. The study has revealed that credit to SMEs work out to 3% and 13% of GDP of developing and developed nations respectively. Pingali [62] has traced changes in Indian food habits during the preceding two decades and found that economic growth has transformed dietary habits of Indians which will adversely injure the interests of petty farmers engaged in subsistence agriculture. Adequate incentives and rational policies are needed to be provided for maintaining the livelihood of these agriculturists, integrating them to the world's food market. Bhalla [63] have highlighted the positive changes effected by sophisticated technology in Punjab agriculture in enhancing productivity of rice and wheat cultivation. Utilization of upgraded technologies in the agricultural sector has increased deployment of non-agricultural inputs in the sector, leading to intersectoral linkage.

McCullough, *et al.* [64] reported problems encountered by the stakeholders in agricultural SCM such as farmers, middlemen and consumers in Madhya Pradesh. The agriculturists encounter difficulties in production process of insufficient availability of human and financial resources, raw materials and other inputs, fertilizers and pesticides, information sharing and possibilities of burglary while they encounter difficulties in marketing such as deficient refrigerated warehousing, transporting and other infrastructure facilities, weak negotiating power, unjust share in consumer price and lack of grading and homogeny. Intermediaries encounter complexities such as lack of warehousing, grading and homogeneity, poor quality and highly perishable nature of agricultural produce, lack of consistency in demand and supply for agricultural produce and knowledge about prevalent consumer price. Complexities for consumers consist of low quality, poor warehousing causing seasonal fluctuations of supply resulting in abnormal swinging of prices, lack of standardization of agricultural commodities, deceitful weight measurements and weak bargaining power.

4.3.2. Conduct of Supply Chain Segments

Viator, *et al.* [65] conducted a study based on Philippines and Thailand to explore importance of business dealings and cold chain in food exports. They established that pricing of exports is significantly influenced by quality while opportunistic character of consumers may discourage flow of investment in cold chain segment that can be addressed only by winning assurance of the chain stakeholders for a longer period. Bertazzoli, *et al.* [66] conducted a research on 189 firms engaged in potato SCM, 187 in fruit SCM and 203 in cheese SCM and established that distribution creates 35% value in the cases of potato and fruit SCM while the contribution is a mere 13.6% in the case of cheese SCM. The study also revealed that over a five-year period, the value diminishes by 5% in the case of fruits and potatoes while the percent of diminishing is at a faster rate of 9%. Lack of effective coalition among all stakeholders of the supply chain of these three commodities has resulted in retailers gaining immense power at the cost of others.

McCluskey and O Rourke [67] evaluated the difficulties of SME agricultural firms of US and established that demands of retailers in the chain such as registration charges, utilization of upgraded technologies and food security examination complicates the survival of these SMEs. Rademakers and McKnight [68] have studied the Dutch potato SCM and established that globalization has resulted in a paramount change in preference of consumers towards better superiority and assortment of agricultural commodities and fair pricing. SCM practices of US agricultural firms have led to retailers gaining immense authority in European markets. Mmasa and Msuya [69] have analyzed the Tanzanian potato SCM practices by studying 150 intermediaries and established that agriculturists sell either directly to end-users or through retailing merchants or village petty sellers. They have also found that a shade above half of the agriculturists (50.7%) consider feedback from co-agriculturists to take pricing decisions while 44% of them adopt direct selling to consumers.

Singh [29] evaluated the effective usage of concept of CF (Contract Farming) by three Indian companies in raising three crops of potatoes, organic basmati paddy and mint. His study has revealed that the CF arrangement shall yield fruits for agriculturists and the economy in the very short and medium run if the arrangement is clear on contract expenses and promotes innovation and coordination. Birthal, *et al.* [70] have established the growing contribution of CF to small agriculturists gaining immense benefits by engaging in high value agricultural commodities by way of declining transaction expenses, enhanced market efficacy and higher reward for produce. Singgih and Woods [71] tried to explore the impact of culture on Indonesian and Australian SCM practices of bananas and established an adverse relation between the intermediaries of supply chains of these two countries. Indonesian rural areas were dominated by conventional systems while Australian villagers enjoyed more equity, amity and democracy. Nature of these relationships significantly influenced the mechanism of fixing prices and negotiating proclivity of farmers. Concepcion, *et al.* [72] surveyed all intermediaries in vegetables SCM of Philippines and established that agriculturists possess very little alertness about requirements of the vegetables market, resulting in them wrongly perceiving about demand characteristics and quality requirements of their commodities, leading to unavoidable wastage in SCM. Driessen and Glasbergen [31] explored the role of traders In linking Indonesian cocoa farmers and consumers and established that traders provide useful information to rectify quality issues. Hingley [73] analyzed nature of power politics existent in UK among fresh food SCM intermediaries comprising of supplying institutions, retailers and consumers. The study revealed that power politics always exist among the SCM components and such prevalence does not always result in adverse scenario. Relations-building may lead to power unevenness and weaker intermediaries are insensitive to such disparities.

Sohal and Perry [74] examined practices of comprehensive SCM of cereals in Australia. They found that factors such as pattern of demand influenced by globalization, complexities associated with nature of business, pricing mechanism, authority relations, vitality of timely and prompt deliveries, supply chain human resource needs, environmental situations affecting agricultural productivity, flow of useful and timely information and responsibility needs of industry significantly impact the environmental conditions of Indian agriculture. Fafchamps and Minten [75] assessed the utility derived by Maharashtrian agriculturists from RML (Reuters Market Light) providing agriculture-related information to their cell phones and came out that transmission of information through mobile services failed to make any impact on price managed by agriculturists for their produce, rational modification in agricultural practices or variety of crops and minimization of losses due to natural calamities. Minten, *et al.* [76] found in Delhi that organised contemporary retail outlets sell food items at price in par with or lower than the conventional retailers and hence, the former may play a decisive role in accomplishing food safety. Ramakrishnan [77] conducted a research on 605 retail grocery establishments in 2 Indian cities and found that even smaller retailers adopt unique operational tactics to boost efficiency and profitability. Banker and Mitra [78] studied an e-auction of coffee beans in India and established that e-selling of agricultural items may be successful under certain scenario only and state authorities can play a vital role in facilitating e-trade by enhancing negotiating skills of farmers and enhance confidence among consumers to buy directly from farmers.

Rodger [79] describes the structure of a Bayesian network from a real-world supply chain data set and then determines a posterior probability distribution for backorders using a stochastic simulation based on Markov blankets. Akoijam [80] established the positive contribution made by NABARD's micro finance programme implemented through self-help group linkage model in addressing rural poverty. He established the contribution of micro finance providing rural credit, which has provided an opportunity of sustained living for huge rural masses.Yogisha [81] conducted a study on   Karnataka commodities market and established that in the case of all crops studied (Groundnuts, onions, potatoes and Ragi) market price was shrinking during peak seasons and the prices of these crops displayed an inverse association.

Sikkel [82] explored the possibility of SMEs getting integrated with SCM practices at local and world levels and established that efficient utilisation of SCM practices and formation of association of small agriculturists lead to optimum capability utilisation and declining transaction expenses through economies of large scale operations, which capacitates even small agriculturists to access international markets. Fan [83] have established the role played by government spending on rural India in eradicating poverty. Such expenditure directly generates more jobs in villages while enhanced investment on education, infrastructure, health and R&D in villages results in stimulation of overall growth of the villages, resulting in more jobs and enhanced income of rural masses. HarbirSingh [84] have established that potatoes SCM suffer from irregularity in provision of timely information delinking public-private partnerships, warranting the necessity of effective R & D reconciliation to precisely study requirements and demand of market. Atre [85] established that existence of numerous intermediaries in agricultural supply chain drastically diminishes the agriculturists' share of price paid by the end-user.

4.4. Performance of Supply Chain Segments

Adetonah, *et al.* [86] surveyed 235 growers of good rice variety and vegetables in Benin and Mali and concluded that difficulties associated with accessing product market, poor availability of inputs comprising of seeds, fertilizers and petty tools, exorbitant cost of transportation, massive after-harvest loss and insufficient refrigerated warehousing facilities were complexities encountered by these agriculturists. Esterhuizen and Van Rooyen [87] have analyzed the efficacy of South African agro-business to venture into international markets and established that the comprehensive SCM of South African agro-business is not adequately qualitative to participate in global competition and quality of produce sold in local markets is so poor, disabling global participation. Gandhi and Namboodiri [88] analyzed the complexities confronting the wholesale vegetables and fruits markets of Ahmedabad, Chennai And Kolkata. They established that improvement in marketing infrastructure by enhancing quality of road transportation, refrigerated warehousing, convenient weight measurement and loading amenities made available and lucidity of operations will go a long way in boosting efficacy of these markets.

Ghezán, *et al.* [89] have examined the influence of MNCs on potato SCM by surveying managerial personnel of processing organizations and potato agriculturists. They have identified developments in potato SCM due to arrival of MNCs such as importance of wholesalers shrinking due to emerging supermarkets, novel SCM intermediaries such as expert wholesalers integrating with supermarkets gaining importance, advanced technologies and innovative strategies executed by SCM intermediaries shrinking the role of petty agriculturists. Mitra, *et al.* [90] established that Bengali middlemen in potatoes market swallowed 34%-89% of consumer price during 2008. Their study also revealed that information flow had no impact on margin levels but did exert an impact on traded volume. The traded volume had a direct relationship with information gained by agriculturists about wholesale price. Pocock [91] studied supply elasticity of Idaho potatoes and impact of contractual obligations on such potato cultivators. His study revealed that during the last three decades, supply elasticity of these potatoes has remained unaltered. The study has also established that price of potatoes which prevailed recently determine quantum of land used by agriculturists for potato cultivation. The study also revealed that potato cultivation had 3 - 3.5 year cycle. Sahadevan [92] studied the acuity of potato and mentha cultivators about commodities futures market and suggested that establishing agriculturists associations alone can improve efficiency of agricultural SCM and enhance partaking of petty agriculturists in commodities futures market. Thorne [93] assessed the impact of market factors on the volatile potato prices and applying ARCH technique. The study revealed that elasticity of demand for potatoes is high and increased demand for potatoes enhances their price while enhanced supply diminishes price. Morgan, *et al.* [94] have scrutinized the role of Indonesian vegetable supply chain intermediaries in serving interests of agriculturists in the light of food security and satisfying consumer aspirations. They established that supermarkets assist agriculturists by granting them steady orders well in advance, enabling them in scheduling their output.

Grigg and Walls [95] assessed the role of SQC (Statistical Quality Control) in assisting enhancement of quality of manufacture of food and drinks. Their study revealed that SQC resulted in good quality manufacturing process while this quality gradually diminishes due to interior and exterior environmental conditions [96] tried to assess the influence of cellular services on Niger's food grain prices. Utilizing time-series data and applying Linear Regression technique, the study established that cellular services during 2001-06 reduced grain prices dispersal by 10%-16%. Kinsey [97] assessed impact of market concentration and price movements on profits of US retail traders in food grain industry. His study revealed that price of dry groceries is on the upswing while that of refrigerated food items are witnessing a downward trend. The study further indicates that wholesale market concentration results in price decline while profit surges. Bardhan, *et al.* [98] evaluated the Heckscher-Ohlin model of North-South trade in benefitting intermediaries of agricultural SCM and overcoming problem of hazardous products. Their study has revealed that liberalized trading practices have disproportionately benefitted agricultural traders.

Thampy [99] assessed the benefits which shall accrue to Indian agriculturists in designing their products due to flow of information and established that cellular services can significantly influence rural economy by prospering agriculturists. Ghosh [100] evaluated the effect of reforming agriculture practices on spatially integrating agricultural markets. He applied the Optimum Likelihood technique of Co-Integration in this endeavour and established that reforms succeeded in strongly integrating the regional markets, satisfying the principle of uniform pricing throughout the region. Kuruvilla and Joshi [101] examined profile of some 3026 mall customers spread over 8 Indian cities. Their study revealed prevalence of significant difference in socio-demographic attributes, behavior, attitude and shopping preferences among heavy-shoppers. Ali and Kumar [102] have endeavoured to assess the decision-making competence of agriculturists and found that information flow to agriculturists through measures such as ITC (Indian Tobacco Company) sponsored e-Choupal can improve their decision-making skill and aptitude. However, such skill will also be affected by the socio-economic profile of agriculturists such as education, category, income and pattern of land ownership. Shilpi and Umali Deininger [103] surveyed 400 retailers and agriculturists spread over 40 villages and 20 wholesale markets in the year 2005 to assess the impact on marketing decisions of agriculturists and established that provision of facilities such as improved marketing infrastructure diminishing cost for agriculturists by way of declining travelling time to markets from residence, motivates agriculturists to boost their sales.

Kopparthi and Kagabo [104] have stressed the significant impact exerted by accessibility to supply chain financing on output and profitability of petty agriculturists based on surveying 122 agriculturists and personnel of Micro-finance institutions. Joshi, *et al.* [105] used FISM (Fuzzy Interpretive Structure Modeling) technique to arrive at two categories of that exists a group of inhibitors, one with dominant authority, maximum strategic dominance, attracting utmost attention and stumpy reliance while another group with exactly the opposite features.

Roy and Thorat [106] evaluated the performance of Mahagrapes agriculturists and they found that these agriculturists manage high returns due to enhanced qualitative output enabling them to access external markets also. Pingali and Khwaja [107] analyzed the impact of westernizing dietary trends in Asian countries on petty agriculturists and propagated that linking rural with urban economy through efficient infrastructural facilities such as effective transporting and communicating facilities, enhanced investments in rural market on R&D which shall lead to optimal utilization of resources and enhance output and foresighted strategy facilitating these petty agriculturists in getting transformed to commercial world shall enable them to sustain the assault of changing pattern of consumers. Gangadharappa [108] endeavored to analyze fluctuations in pricing potatoes in Karnataka commodities market by analyzing monthly arrival prices collected from KSAMB (Karnataka State Agricultural Marketing Board). He established the prevalence of fluctuating prices in all markets excepting Kolar market. Similarly, the trend in fluctuating prices is dissimilar among the different markets. Bhagat and Dhar [109] have scrutinized the SCM practices of agriculture and established that belief, dedication and transparency prevalent amidst SCM intermediaries determine the success of agriculture SCM by way of gaining good knowledge about uncertainties of agriculture, serving the rights of farmers and all stakeholders in supply chain, boosting responsibility and importance of petty players in SCM, inter-personal relations among intermediaries of supply chain resulting in lucidity and belief among them and SCM practices assuming consumer orientation.

Ramaswami, *et al.* [110] have found that though intermediaries in SCM of poultry business in Andhra Pradesh corner major portion of consumer price, CF practices have enabled poultry farmers to gain immensely due to low risk element and enhanced profitability. Khan [111] have found that production volume of Indian food grains segment is lower when compared with commercial crops such as sugar, oilseeds, vegetables and fruits. He has pointed out that agro-food industry is positively influenced by yield of agriculture, improved infrastructural facilities, modified pattern of consumption, foreign markets becoming accessible for agricultural commodities and assistive governmental policies. Naik and Jain [50] studied the efficiency of 6 Indian commodity futures markets and established that improper managing of risks and pricing mechanism have rendered these markets under-developed.

5. A Comprehensive Analysis of Agri-Food Like Potato Supply Chain in India

Upstream-Farm: 30% of medium sized cultivated farm lands in India account for almost 70% of potato cultivated farm lands. Rent and lease charges of farm lands are galloping at rapid rates making payment of rent for land equally strenuous like acquiring capital and paying interest for the same. Labor dearth is assuming significant proportions in India, hampering agriculture growth in the country and this problem has become more acute even in small farm lands. Government efforts of providing irrigation subsidies for potato cultivators is largely eaten away by the large farmers, incapacitating the small and marginal farmers from utilizing irrigation facilities for their small sized land holdings. Further, these small farmers do not have access to markets and are not aware about the remunerative prices prevalent in the market for their produce. As a result, they often end up being exploited by unscrupulous middlemen who acquire the potatoes at cheap rates from the farmers and sell at exorbitant prices in towns and cities. This problem can be solved only if farmers are made responsive to latest technologies in cultivation and market information for which the agriculturists should be facilitated to remain connected through the mobile technology.

5.1. Midstream-Refrigerated Warehousing and Traders

Providing easily accessible refrigerated warehousing facilities for potato farmers will contribute immensely to them from being exploited by middlemen and getting sizeable proportion of price paid by consumers for the potatoes. In short, a well accessible warehousing can almost eliminate the wholesale market for potatoes which will be highly rewarding for farmers. Enhanced logistics support to

farmers in the form of improved transport and warehousing facilities will contribute significantly to improve the lives of potato farmers. The main problem in
providing effective warehouse facilities is in shortage of power warranting enhanced investment in electricity generation. Further, farmers can also be saved
from traders delaying or defaulting payment for their produce.

5.2. Downstream-Retailers

Though retailers have contributed to quality enhancement of potatoes, packaging and branding of potatoes have not yet developed at all. Modern retail outlets
have uprooted in both rural and urban areas, posing severe threat to the traditional retail traders. Government's initiative of getting directly involved in aiding
potato retailing by establishing cooperative form in the retailing sector has
started penetrating the potato retail market, which is a positive sign.

5.3. Performance of the Potato Supply Chain-Rewards, Costs, and Margins

A whopping 71% of refrigerated warehousing cost is occupied by energy imply-
ing that almost 21% of the total supply chain cost and 11% of market price of
potatoes is directly accounted for by energy cost. Almost two-third of potatoes
cultivated is stored in refrigerated warehouses and hence, cost of power highly
influences potato price. Further, prevalence of market cost for marketing potatoes at the rate of 5% of total cost exerts almost 2% impact on potato price.
Another constituent of cost of potatoes is cost of transportation, which accounts
for 8% of total cost during harvest times and 11% during off-times. Considering
the different cost elements involved in potato supply chain, it can be said that
potato cultivators may get 57% of the retail price during harvest season and 52%
during off season. Since power occupy a significant proportion of cost and price
of potatoes, rational utilization of power or rise in power tariff will exert a telling
impact on potato prices, leading to inflation.

Recent efforts of government to develop refrigerated warehousing facilities,
investing more on research and development in rural areas, distribution of quality seeds at subsidized rates, providing irrigation and extension facilities, improving transportation facilities via road and rail, establishment of power grids
and provision of mobile services have contributed positively to enhancement of
economic standard of living of potato cultivators. Farmers have started utilizing
the refrigerated warehousing facilities for storing their produce, enabling them
to get remunerative prices while consumers can get potatoes perennially without
seasonal fluctuations. A Delhi-based potato supply chain study has revealed that
importance of wholesale market is shrinking drastically as almost farmers have
moved towards refrigerated warehousing, enabling them to sell in the open
market during any part of the year. Investors felt it highly remunerative to invest
in refrigerated warehouses, farmers felt it immensely beneficial to store their potato produce in these warehouses, traders used these warehouses to buy their
stock directly from farmers while consumers enjoyed perennial availability of

potatoes irrespective of season or off-season. Hence, a rational combination of all logistics support at various stages of potato supply chain has yielded fruits for all sections. In addition to provision of effective logistics support, if government efforts to provide agricultural subsidies reach the intended beneficiaries, all components of supply chain of agricultural commodities including that of potatoes, will flourish in the near future.

6. Research Gap

A close scrutiny of prior literature on agricultural supply chain management has revealed that lot of research literature exist on SCM practices of different agricultural commodities [112]. However, these studies have focused on problems encountered by different components of the supply chain management. Not much work has been conducted on examining the financial and energy aspects of all components comprising the entire supply chain management. Similarly, very few studies have been conducted on important aspects concerning the fresh food supply chain like potato under Indian context [6]. Furthermore, negligible quantum of studies have been conducted exploring problems confronted by different participants of potato supply chain, particularly the finance delivery mechanism available for agriculturists, agro-food processors and medium, small and micro enterprises (MSMEs). In the backdrop of this scenario, it shall be significantly important to conduct a research work on exploring the problem of accessing finance and energy aspects of each segment of agri-food supply chain management and arrive at concrete solution to assuage this serious problem [113].

7. Conclusions and Future Directions

The paper has identified gaps and issues in agricultural supply chain management (SCM) practices. A thorough scrutiny of the literature suggests that Indian agriculturists suffer seriously from the following problems: Stumpy bargaining capacity of farmers, putting them under the mercy of selfish traders and middlemen, who invariably exploit them to the core; very little fragmented land holdings; very little marketable surplus; exorbitant cost of cultivation and marketing; informal sector dominating the marketing process of agricultural produce; fragmented agricultural supply chain; poor marketing infrastructure installed for agricultural produce; imperfect market conditions for agricultural commodities; massive wastage of agricultural produce to the tune of 30% - 60%, due to ineffective warehousing and storing facilities; rapid perishability nature of high value commodities; non-availability of effective packaging, branding and certification; lack of adequate market information about remunerative returns available for cultivating particular crops; poor price-discovery means available to farmers, incapacitating them from getting the lion's share of price paid by consumers for their produce; soaring of risk ingredient to the tune of 60%-70%, associated with agricultural production and marketing process; low productivity yield resulting in truncated quantum of output; difficulty in accessing finance, particularly for working capital; inefficient crop insurance programmers; agro-firms existing for long period acquiring monophony; inadequate availability of information incapacitating farmers to comply with food security issues; non-availability of knowhow to utilize fertilizers and pesticides; lack of proficiency on the part of farmers in asset management, incapacitating them from effecting suitable portfolio modifications in the production process; lack of sophisticated technology reducing capacity utilization, leading to meager raising of output from inputs; excessive usage of chemical fertilizers having ruined land fertility; stumpy quality of produce; inadequate availability of power [114].

Combinations of majority of these problems magnify the inefficient functioning of agricultural sector in India. Variety of measures may be adopted to overcome these problems of Indian agriculture. Some of such measures may be: Farmers may be encouraged to form associations, consortiums, cooperatives and self-help groups which will enhance efficient utilization of resources. Contract farming is a good development towards this direction; marketing facilities for agricultural commodities should be improved; market for agricultural commodities needs to be improved; processing centers should be made more efficient; cautious execution of the model act; formulating and executing effective and relentless agricultural policies to establish favorable environment for rapid development of agriculture; sophisticated warehousing with effectual refrigeration facilities should be established to minimize wastage of agricultural produce; transportation needs to be developed vastly, particularly in rural areas; power shortages have to be urgently addressed by exploring generation of power through non-conventional sources such as solar, wind, etc. Banks and financial institutions should be encouraged to provide financial support to farmers by way of incentives to them for making investments in rural infrastructure and agriculture [115]. These measures may contribute to catalyze agricultural growth in India by improving the supply chain process. Agri-food supply chain management is an initiative towards this direction, which might serve a lot in overcoming problems encountered by Indian agriculture. The problems engulfing Indian agriculture are unique, complex and tough due to presence of majority of them among bulk of Indian agriculturists. Hence, advanced techniques need to be device to address these problems which warrant rapidly changing methodologies, technologies and management practices in the supply chain mechanism [116].

References

[1] Chandrasekaran, N. and Raghuram, G. (2014) Agribusiness Supply Chain Management. CRC Press, Boca Raton.

[2] Ghosh, G.N. and Ganguly, R. (2008) Development Challenges of Indian Agriculture. Background Technical Papers, The National Medium Term Priority Framework, Government of India and FAO.

[3] Sharma, V.P. (2012) Accelerating Agricultural Development for Inclusive Growth: Strategic Issues and Policy Options. *Vikalpa: The Journal for Decision Makers*, **37**, 1-17.

[4]   Sagheer, S., Yadav, S. and Deshmukh, S. (2009) Developing a Conceptual Frame-
        work for Assessing Competitiveness of India's Agrifood Chain. *International Jour-
        nal of Emerging Markets*, **4**, 137-159. https://doi.org/10.1108/17468800910945774

[5]   Deshingkar, P., Kulkarni, U., Rao, L. and Rao, S. (2003) Changing Food Systems in
        India: Resourcesharing and Marketing Arrangements for Vegetable Production in
        Andhra Pradesh. *Development Policy Review*, **21**, 627-639.
        https://doi.org/10.1111/j.1467-8659.2003.00228.x

[6]   Ahumada, O. and Villalobos, J.R. (2009) Application of Planning Models in the
        Agri-Food Supply Chain: A Review. *European Journal of Operational Research*,
        196, 1-20.

[7]   Meredith, J. (1993) Theory Building through Conceptual Methods. *International
        Journal of Operations & Production Management*, **13**, 3-11.
        https://doi.org/10.1108/01443579310028120

[8]   Cassell, C. and Symon, G. (2004) Essential Guide to Qualitative Methods in Organi-
        zational Research. Sage, Thousand Oaks.

[9]   Seuring, S. and Müller, M. (2008) From a Literature Review to a Conceptual Frame-
        work for Sustainable Supply Chain Management. *Journal of Cleaner Production*, **16**,
        1699-1710.

[10]   Shukla, M. and Jharkharia, S. (2013) Agri-Fresh Produce Supply Chain Manage-
        ment: A State-of-the-Art Literature Review. *International Journal of Operations &
        Production Management*, **33**, 114-158. https://doi.org/10.1108/01443571311295608

[11]   Cunningham, D.C. (2001) The Distribution and Extent of Agrifood Chain Manage-
        ment Research in the Public Domain. *Supply Chain Management: An International
        Journal*, **6**, 212-215. https://doi.org/10.1108/EUM0000000006040

[12]   Vasileiou, K. and Morris, J. (2006) The Sustainability of the Supply Chain for Fresh
        Potatoes in Britain. *Supply Chain Management: An International Journal*, **11**, 317-
        327. https://doi.org/10.1108/13598540610671761

[13]   Vorst, J., Beulens, A.J., Wit, W.D. and Beek, P.V. (1998) Supply Chain Management
        in Food Chains: Improving Performance by Reducing Uncertainty. *International
        Transactions in Operational Research*, **5**, 487-499.
        https://doi.org/10.1111/j.1475-3995.1998.tb00131.x

[14]   Frick, B., Vitins, G., Eisen, R., Oleschuk, M., Lipton, B. and Consulting, R.S. (2012)
        Local Food Supply Chains in Alberta: Case Studies from the Saskatoon, Potato and
        Lamb Sectors.

[15]   Taylor, D.H. (2005) Value Chain Analysis: An Approach to Supply Chain Improve-
        ment in Agri-Food Chains. *International Journal of Physical Distribution & Logis-
        tics Management*, **35**, 744-761. https://doi.org/10.1108/09600030510634599

[16]   Batt, P.J. (2003) Examining the Performance of the Supply Chain for Potatoes in the
        Red River Delta Using a Pluralistic Approach. *Supply Chain Management: An In-
        ternational Journal*, **8**, 442-454. https://doi.org/10.1108/13598540310500277

[17]   Chandrashekar, H. (2009) Supply Chain Management of Fruits and Vegetables in
        Karnataka—A Study of Safal Market, Bangalore, Karnataka, India. *Interdisciplinary
        Journal of Contemporary Research in Business*, **1**, 43.

[18]   Hobbs, J.E. (1998) Innovation and Future Direction of Supply Chain Management
        in the Canadian Agri-Food Industry. *Canadian Journal of Agricultural Econom-
        ics/Revue Canadienne d'Agroeconomie*, **46**, 525-537.
        https://doi.org/10.1111/j.1744-7976.1998.tb00977.x

[19]   Moazzem, K.G. and Fujita, K. (2004) The Potato Marketing System and Its Changes
        in Bangladesh: From the Perspective of a Village Study in Comilla District. *The De-

veloping Economies, **42**, 63-94. https://doi.org/10.1111/j.1746-1049.2004.tb01016.x

[20] Fuglie, K.O. (2002) Economics of Potato Storage: Case Studies. *Potato: Global Research and Development*, **2**, 6-11.

[21] Beck, T. and Demirguc-Kunt, A. (2006) Small and Medium-Size Enterprises: Access to Finance as a Growth Constraint. *Journal of Banking & Finance*, **30**, 2931-2943.

[22] Minten, B., Singh, K.M. and Sutradhar, R. (2013) Branding and Agricultural Value Chains in Developing Countries: Insights from Bihar (India). *Food Policy*, **38**, 23-34.

[23] Hellin, J. and Meijer, M. (2006) Guidelines for Value Chain Analysis. Food and Agriculture Organization of the United Nations (FAO), Rome, Italy.

[24] Punjabi, M. (2007) Initiatives and Issues in Fresh Fruit and Vegetable Supply Chains in India. Lotus Pang Suan Kaeo Hotel, Chiang Mai, Thailand, 115.

[25] Ghai, S. (2012) Value Chain Financing: Strategy towards Augmenting Growth in Agriculture Sector in India. *Journal of Economics and Sustainable Development*, **3**, 184-191.

[26] Bala Subrahmanya, M.B. (2006) Small Scale Industries in India under Globalization: Does Solace Lie in Technology and Innovation. *The First Max Planck India Workshop on Entrepreneurship, Innovation and Economic Growth*, IISc, Bangalore, 29-31 March 2006.

[27] Shilpa, K. (2008) Supply Chain Management in Vegetable Marketing: A Comparative Analysis. Master of Business Administration in Agribusiness, Department of Agribusiness Management, University of Agricultural Sciences, Dharwad.

[28] Islam, K. (2012) Learnings from the Potato Supply Chain Study. International Development Research Centre, Canada and the Department for International Development, UK and the ENRAP (Knowledge Networking for Rural Development in Asia Pacific) Programme.

[29] Singh, S. (2007) Leveraging Contract Farming for Improving Supply Chain Efficiency in India: Some Innovative and Successful Models. *ISHS Acta Horticulturae*, **794**, 317-324.

[30] Kit, I. (2010) Value Chain Finance beyond Microfinance for Rural Entrepreneurs. Royal Tropical Institute, Amsterdam, and International Institute of Rural Reconstruction, Nairobi.

[31] Driessen, P.P. and Glasbergen, P. (2008) Constraints on the Conversion to Sustainable Production: The Case of the Dutch Potato Chain. *Business Strategy and the Environment*, **17**, 369-381. https://doi.org/10.1002/bse.554

[32] Cromme, N., Prakash, A.B., Lutaladio, N. and Ezeta, F. (2010) Strengthening Potato Value Chains: Technical and Policy Options for Developing Countries. Food and Agriculture Organization of the United Nations (FAO).

[33] Wei, S. and Zhang, Y (2004) Supply-Chain Management and the "One Dragon" Approach: Institutional Bases for Agro-Industrialisation in China. Agri-Product Supply Chain Management in Developing Countries.

[34] Wheatley, C. and Peters, D. (2004) Who Benefits from Enhanced Management of Agri-Food Supply Chains? Agriproduct Supply-Chain Management in Developing Countries.

[35] Kumar, A., Singh, H., Kumar, S. and Mittal, S. (2011) Value Chains of Agricultural Commodities and Their Role in Food Security and Poverty Alleviation—A Synthesis. *Agricultural Economics Research Review*, **24**, 169-181.

[36] Basu, J. and Dinda, S. (2003) Market Integration: An Application of Error Correction Model to Potato Market in Hooghly District, West Bengal. *Indian Journal of*

Agricultural Economics, **58**, 742-751.

[37] Basu, J.P. (2010) Efficiency in Wholesale, Retail and Village Markets: A Study of Potato Markets in West Bengal. *Journal of South Asian Development*, **5**, 85-111. https://doi.org/10.1177/097317411000500104

[38] Rais, M., Acharya, S. and Sharma, N. (2013) Food Processing Industry in India: S & T Capability, Skills and Employment Opportunities. *Journal of Food Processing & Technology*, **4**, 260.

[39] Jha, R., Murthy, K. and Sharma, A. (2006) Market Integration in Wholesale Rice Markets in India. DSpace on 2011-01-05T08: 32: 54Z (GMT).

[40] Joshi, P.K., Birthal, P.S. and Minot, N. (2006) Sources of Agricultural Growth in India: Role of Diversification towards High-Value Crops. International Food Policy Research Institute (IFPRI).

[41] Popkin, B.M. (2006) Technology, Transport, Globalization and the Nutrition Transition Food Policy. *Food Policy*, **31**, 554-569.

[42] Kleih, M.K.U. and Yunus, K.B. (2010) Financial Services for SME Aquaculture and Fisheries Producers Tanzania Case Study. National Resource Institute.

[43] Rao, K.R., Das, A. and Singh, A.K. (2006) Commercial Bank Lending to Small-Scale Industry. *Economic and Political Weekly*, **41**, 1025-1033.

[44] Tchale, H. and Keyser, J. (2010) Quantitative Value Chain Analysis: An Application to Malawi.

[45] Smith, B.G. (2008) Developing Sustainable Food Supply Chains. *Philosophical Transactions of the Royal Society B: Biological Sciences*, **363**, 849-861. https://doi.org/10.1098/rstb.2007.2187

[46] Sastry, T. (2009) Extending Supply Chains to Create Wealth for the Poor. *The Wall Street Journal.*

[47] Swinnen, J.F. and Maertens, M. (2007) Globalization, Privatization, and Vertical Coordination in Food Value Chains in Developing and Transition Countries. *Agricultural Economics*, **37**, 89-102. https://doi.org/10.1111/j.1574-0862.2007.00237.x

[48] Gandhi, V.P. and Namboodiri, N. (2002) Fruit and Vegetable Marketing and Its Efficiency in India: A Study of Wholesale Markets in the Ahmedabad Area. Retrieved 25 April 2009.

[49] Pal, S., Mruthyunjaya, J., Joshi, P. and Saxena, R. (2003) Institutional Change in Indian Agriculture. National Centre For Agricultural Economics and Policy Research.

[50] Naik, G. and Jain, S.K. (2002) Indian Agricultural Commodity Futures Markets: A Performance Survey. *Economic and Political Weekly*, **37**, 3161-3173.

[51] Reardon, T. and Minten, B. (2011) The Quiet Revolution in India's Food Supply Chains. International Food Policy Research Institute, New Delhi.

[52] Miller, C. and Jones, L. (2010) Agricultural Value Chain Finance: Tools and Lessons. Food and Agriculture Organization of the United Nations (FAO). https://doi.org/10.3362/9781780440514

[53] Mancero, L. (2007) Potato Chain Study. Central Ecuadorian Sierra Region.

[54] Gaiha, R. and Thapa, G. (2007) Supermarkets, Smallholders and Livelihood Prospects in Selected Asian Countries. Occasional Papers: Knowledge for Development Effectiveness, 4.

[55] Loader, R. (1997) Assessing Transaction Costs to Describe Supply Chain Relationships in Agri-Food Systems. *Supply Chain Management: An International Journal*, **2**, 23-35. https://doi.org/10.1108/13598549710156330

[56] Narrod, C., Roy, D., Okello, J., Avendaño, B., Rich, K. and Thorat, A. (2009) Public-private Partnerships and Collective Action in High Value Fruit and Vegetable Supply Chains. *Food Policy*, **34**, 8-15.

[57] Howorth, C. and Westhead, P. (2003) The Focus of Working Capital Management in UK Small Firms. *Management Accounting Research*, **14**, 94-111.

[58] Solér, C., Bergström, K. and Shanahan, H. (2010) Green Supply Chains and the Missing Link between Environmental Information and Practice. *Business Strategy and the Environment*, **19**, 14-25.

[59] Vorley, B. (2001) The Chains of Agriculture: Sustainability and the Restructuring of Agri-Food Markets. WSSD Briefing Paper, IIED, London.

[60] Markelova, H., Meinzen-Dick, R., Hellin, J. and Dohrn, S. (2009) Collective Action for Smallholder Market Access. *Food Policy*, **34**, 1-7.

[61] Ardic, O.P., Mylenko, N. and Saltane, V. (2012) Access to Finance by Small and Medium Enterprises: A Cross Country Analysis with a New Data Set. *Pacific Economic Review*, **17**, 491-513. https://doi.org/10.1111/j.1468-0106.2012.00596.x

[62] Pingali, P. (2007) Westernization of Asian Diets and the Transformation of Food Systems: Implications for Research and Policy. *Food Policy*, **32**, 281-298.

[63] Bhalla, G.S. (1990) Agricultural Growth and Structural Changes in the Punjab Economy: An Input-Output Analysis. Free downloads from IFPRI.

[64] McCullough, E.B., Pingali, P.L., Stamoulis, K.G., Haas, R., Canavari, M. and Slee, B. *et al.* (2010) Small Farms and the Transformation of Food Systems: An Overview. Looking East Looking West: Organic and Quality Food Marketing in Asia and Europe, 47-83.

[65] Viator, C.L., Fang, W.Y.D., Hadley, J.L., Aiew, W.M., Salin, V. and Nayga, R. (2000) Infrastructure Needs Assessment for Distribution of Frozen Processed Potato Products in Southeast Asian Countries.

[66] Bertazzoli, A., Fiorini, A., Ghelfi, R., Rivaroli, S., Samoggia, A. and Mazzotti, V. (2011) Food Chains and Value System: The Case of Potato, Fruit, and Cheese. *Journal of Food Products Marketing*, **17**, 303-326. https://doi.org/10.1080/10454446.2011.548691

[67] McCluskey, J.J. and Rourke, A.D.O. (2000) Relationships between Produce Supply Firms and Retailers in the New Food Supply Chain. *Journal of Food Distribution Research*, **31**, 11-20.

[68] Rademakers, M.F. and McKnight, P.J. (1998) Concentration and Inter-Firm Co-Operation within the Dutch Potato Supply Chain. *Supply Chain Management: An International Journal*, **3**, 203-213. https://doi.org/10.1108/13598549810244287

[69] Mmasa, J.J. and Msuya, E.E. (2012) Mapping of the Sweet Potato Value Chain Linkages between Actors, Processes and Activities in the Value Chain: A Case of "Michembe" and "Matobolwa" Products. *Sustainable Agriculture Research*, **1**, 130. https://doi.org/10.5539/sar.v1n1p130

[70] Birthal, P.S., Joshi, P. and Gulati, A. (2007) Vertical Coordination in High-Value Food Commodities.

[71] Singgih, S. and Woods, E.J. (2004) Banana Supply Chains in Indonesia and Australia: Effects of Culture on Supply Chains. Agriproduct Supply-Chain Management in Developing Countries.

[72] Concepcion, S., Montiflor, M., Hualda, L., Migalbin, L., Digal, L., Rasco, E., *et al.* (2004) Farmers' Misconceptions about Quality and Customers' Preferences: Contributing Inefficiencies to the Vegetable Supply Chain in Southern Mindanao. In: Johnson, G.I. and Hofman, P.J., Eds., *ACIAR Proceedings* 119: *Agri-Product Su-*

pply-Chain Management in Developing Countries, Proceedings of a Workshop, Bali, Indonesia, 19-22 August 2003.

[73] Hingley, M.K. (2005) Power Imbalanced Relationships: Cases from UK Fresh Food Supply. *International Journal of Retail & Distribution Management*, **33**, 551-569. https://doi.org/10.1108/09590550510608368

[74] Sohal, A.S. and Perry, M. (2006) Major Business-Environment Influences on the Cereal Products Industry Supply Chain: An Australian Study. *International Journal of Physical Distribution & Logistics Management*, **36**, 36-50. https://doi.org/10.1108/09600030610642922

[75] Fafchamps, M. and Minten, B. (2012) Impact of SMS-Based Agricultural Information on Indian Farmers. *The World Bank Economic Review*, **26**, 383-414. https://doi.org/10.1093/wber/lhr056

[76] Minten, B., Reardon, T. and Sutradhar, R. (2010) Food Prices and Modern Retail: The Case of Delhi. *World Development*, **38**, 1775-1787.

[77] Ramakrishnan, K. (2010) The Competitive Response of Small, Independent Retailers to Organized Retail: Study in an Emerging Economy. *Journal of Retailing and Consumer Services*, **17**, 251-258.

[78] Banker, R.D. and Mitra, S. (2007) Procurement Models in the Agricultural Supply Chain: A Case Study of Online Coffee Auctions in India. *Electronic Commerce Research and Applications*, **6**, 309-321.

[79] Rodger, J.A. (2014) Application of a Fuzzy Feasibility Bayesian Probabilistic Estimation of Supply Chain Backorder Aging, Unfilled Backorders, and Customer Wait Time Using Stochastic Simulation with Markov Blankets. *Expert Systems with Applications*, **41**, 7005-7022.

[80] Akoijam, S.L. (2012) Rural Credit: A Source of Sustainable Livelihood of Rural India. *International Journal of Social Economics*, **40**, 83-97. https://doi.org/10.1108/03068291311283454

[81] Yogisha, G.M. (2005) Market Integration for Major Agricultural Commodities in Kolar District. MBA, Department of Agricultural Marketing, University of Agricultural Sciences, Dharwad.

[82] Sikkel, M.W. (2010) Integrating SMEs into the Global & Regional Value Chains. United Nations Economic and Social Commission for Asia and the Pacific (ESCAP).

[83] Fan, S. (1999) Linkages between Government Spending, Growth, and Poverty in Rural India. International Food Policy Research Institute.

[84] Singh, H. (2009) Linking Farmers to Markets through Agricultural Supply Chain.

[85] Atre, S. (2008) Retail Boom: New Opportunities in Agricultural Finance. *Financing Agriculture*, 9-11.

[86] Adetonah, S., Coulibaly, O., Sessou, E., Padonou, S., Dembele, U. and Adekambli, S. (2010) Contribution of Inland Valleys Intensification to Sustainable Rice/vegetable Value Chain Development in Benin and Mali: Constraints, Opportunities and Profitable Cropping Systems. *Poster presented at the Joint 3rd African Association of Agricultural Economists (AAAE) and 48th Agricultural Economists Association of South Africa (AEASA) Conference*, Cape Town, South Africa.

[87] Esterhuizen, D. and Van Rooyen, C. (1999) How Competitive Is Agribusiness in the South African Food Commodity Chain? *Agrekon*, **38**, 744-754. https://doi.org/10.1080/03031853.1999.9524885

[88] Gandhi, V.P. and Namboodiri, N. (2004) Marketing of Fruits and Vegetables in India: A Study Covering the Ahmedabad, Chennai and Kolkata Markets. Indian Insti-

tute of Management Ahmedabad, Research and Publication Department.

[89] Ghezán, G., Mateos, M. and Viteri, L. (2002) Impact of Supermarkets and Fast-Food Chains on Horticulture Supply Chains in Argentina. *Development Policy Review*, **20**, 389-408. https://doi.org/10.1111/1467-7679.00179

[90] Mitra, S., Mookherjee, D., Torero, M. and Visaria, S. (2012) Asymmetric Information and Middleman Margins: An Experiment with West Bengal Potato Farmers. Discussion Paper, Mimeo, Hong Kong University of Science and Technology.

[91] Pocock, C.J. (2004) Do Contracts for Potatoes Benefit Farmers?: A Look at the Potato Contracts Used in Idaho as Well as a Discussion of the Use of Quality Assurance Schemes in the United Kingdom. Utah State University, Department of Economics.

[92] Sahadevan, K. (2007) Advantages of Commodity Futures Trading through Electronic Trading Platform for Farmers of Uttar Pradesh: A Study of Potato and Mentha. A Report for Multi Commodity Exchange of India Limited.

[93] Thorne, F.S. (2012) Potato Prices as Affected by Supply and Demand Factors: An Irish Case Study. 123*rd Seminar*, Dublin, Ireland, 23-24 February 2012.

[94] Morgan, W., Iwantoro, S. and Lestari, I.A.S. (2004) Improving Indonesian Vegetable Supply Chains. *Agriproduct Supply-Chain Management in Developing Countries*.

[95] Grigg, N.P. and Walls, L. (2007) Developing Statistical Thinking for Performance Improvement in the Food Industry. *International Journal of Quality & Reliability Management*, **24**, 347-369. https://doi.org/10.1108/02656710710740536

[96] Aker, J.C. (2010) Information from Markets Near and Far: Mobile Phones and Agricultural Markets in Niger. *American Economic Journal: Applied Economics*, **2**, 46-59. https://doi.org/10.1257/app.2.3.46

[97] Kinsey, J. (1998) Concentration of Ownership in Food Retailing: A Review of the Evidence about Consumer Impact. Retail Food Industry Center, University of Minnesota.

[98] Bardhan, P., Mookherjee, D. and Tsumagari, M. (2009) Middlemen Margins and Globalization. Seminar organized by IFPRI, Mimeo.

[99] Thampy, A. (2010) Financing of SME Firms in India: Interview with Ranjana Kumar, Former CMD, Indian Bank; Vigilance Commissioner, Central Vigilance Commission. *IIMB Management Review*, **22**, 93-101.

[100] Ghosh, M. (2011) Agricultural Policy Reforms and Spatial Integration of Food Grain Markets in India. *Journal of Economic Development*, **36**, 15-37.

[101] Kuruvilla, S.J. and Joshi, N. (2010) Influence of Demographics, Psychographics, Shopping Orientation, Mall Shopping Attitude and Purchase Patterns on Mall Patronage in India. *Journal of Retailing and Consumer Services*, **17**, 259-269.

[102] Ali, J. and Kumar, S. (2011) Information and Communication Technologies (ICTs) and Farmers' Decision-Making across the Agricultural Supply Chain. *International Journal of Information Management*, **31**, 149-159.

[103] Shilpi, F. and Umali Deininger, D. (2008) Market Facilities and Agricultural Marketing: Evidence from Tamil Nadu, India. *Agricultural Economics*, **39**, 281-294.

[104] Kopparthi, M.S. and Kagabo, N. (2012) Is Value Chain Financing a Solution to the Problems and Challenges of Access to Finance of Small-Scale Farmers in Rwanda. *Managerial Finance*, **38**, 993-1004. https://doi.org/10.1108/03074351211255182

[105] Joshi, R., Banwet, D.K. and Shankar, R. (2009) Indian Cold Chain: Modeling the Inhibitors. *British Food Journal*, **111**, 1260-1283. https://doi.org/10.1108/00070700911001077

[106] Roy, D. and Thorat, A. (2008) Success in High Value Horticultural Export Markets

for the Small Farmers: The Case of Mahagrapes in India. *World Development*, **36**, 1874-1890.

[107] Pingali, P. and Khwaja, Y. (2004) Globalisation of Indian Diets and the Transformation of Food Supply Systems. *Indian Journal of Agricultural Marketing*, **18**, 1.

[108] Gangadharappa, H. (2005) A Statistical Study of Variation in Arrivals and Prices of Potato in the Selected Markets of Karnataka. University of Agricultural Sciences.

[109] Bhagat, D. and Dhar, U. (2011) Agriculture Supply Chain Management: A Review. *IUP Journal of Supply Chain Management*, **8**, 7-25.

[110] Ramaswami, B., Birthal, P.S. and Joshi, P.K. (2006) Efficiency and Distribution in Contract Farming: The Case of Indian Poultry Growers. MTID Discussion Papers, 91.

[111] Khan, A.U. (2005) The Domestic Food Market: Is India Ready for Food Processing. *Conference on SPS Towards Global Competitiveness in the Food Processing Sector*, Monday.

[112] Samuel, M.V., Shah, M. and Sahay, B. (2012) An Insight into Agri-Food Supply Chains: A Review. *International Journal of Value Chain Management*, **6**, 115-143. https://doi.org/10.1504/IJVCM.2012.048378

[113] Howieson, J., Lawley, M. and Hastings, K. (2016) Value Chain Analysis: An Iterative and Relational Approach for Agri-Food Chains. *Supply Chain Management: An International Journal*, **21**, 352-362. https://doi.org/10.1108/SCM-06-2015-0220

[114] Septiani, W., Marimin, M., Herdiyeni, Y. and Haditjaroko, L. (2016) Method and Approach Mapping for Agri-Food Supply Chain Risk Management: A Literature Review. *International Journal of Supply Chain Management*, **5**, 51-64.

[115] Dania, W.A.P., Xing, K. and Amer, Y. (2016) Collaboration and Sustainable Agri-Food Suply Chain: A Literature Review. *MATEC Web of Conferences*.

[116] Tell, J., Hoveskog, M., Ulvenblad, P., Ulvenblad, P.-O., Barth, H. and Ståhl, J. (2016) Business Model Innovation in the Agri-Food Sector: A Literature Review. *British Food Journal*, **118**, 1462-1476. https://doi.org/10.1108/BFJ-08-2015-0293

12

A Comparative Survey on Arabic Stemming: Approaches and Challenges

Mohammad Mustafa[1], Afag Salah Eldeen[2], Sulieman Bani-Ahmad[3], Abdelrahman Osman Elfaki[4]

[1]Department of Computer Information Systems, Faculty of Computers and Information Technology, University of Tabuk, Tabuk, SA

[2]Department of Computer Science, College of Computer Science and Information Technology, Sudan University of Science and Technology, Khartoum State, Sudan

[3]Department of Computer Information Systems, School of Information Technology, Al-Balqa Applied University, Salt, Jordan

[4]Department of Information Technology, Faculty of Computers and Information Technology, University of Tabuk, Tabuk, Saudi Arabia

Email: mmustafa@ut.edu.sa, afagsalah@hotmail.com, sulieman@bau.edu.jo, a.elfaki@ut.edu.sa

Abstract

Arabic, as one of the Semitic languages, has a very rich and complex morphology, which is radically different from the European and the East Asian languages. The derivational system of Arabic, is therefore, based on roots, which are often inflected to compose words, using a spectacular and a relatively large set of Arabic morphemes affixes, e.g., antefixs, prefixes, suffixes, etc. Stemming is the process of rendering all the inflected forms of word into a common canonical form. Stemming is one of the early and major phases in natural processing, machine translation and information retrieval tasks. A number of Arabic language stemmers were proposed. Examples include light stemming, morphological analysis, statistical-based stemming, N-grams and parallel corpora (collections). Motivated by the reported results in the literature, this paper attempts to exhaustively review current achievements for stemming Arabic texts. A variety of algorithms are discussed. The main contribution of the paper is to provide better understanding among existing approaches with the hope of building an error-free and effective Arabic stemmer in the near future.

Keywords

Arabic Language, Light Stemming, Root-Based Stemming, Co-Occurrence, Artificial Intelligence Stemming

1. Introduction

The major task of an Information Retrieval (IR) system is how to match between a searchable document representation (documents) and a user need, which is always expressed in terms of queries. The process of representing documents, in which keywords or terms are extracted, is called indexing. Indexing often goes through several operations, most of which are language-dependent. Among these operations, stemming stands as one of the major steps that every IR system must handle. Since documents and/or queries may have several forms of a particular word, stemming is the process of mapping and transforming all the inflected forms of that word into a common, shared and canonical form and, thereby, this canonical form would be the most appropriate form for indexing and for searching, as well. In other words, stemming renders different inflected and variant forms of a certain word to a single word stem. In monolingual IR, stemming appears to have a positive impact on recall more than precision [1]. This means that stemming helps to find more relevant documents but it is not able to provide the best ranking for the retrieved list.

Over the last decades, Arabic has become one of the popular areas of research in IR, especially with the explosive growth of the language on the Web, which shows the need to develop good techniques for the increasing contents of the language. This increasing interest in Arabic, however, is caused by its complex morphology, which is radically different from the European and the East Asian languages [2]. In addition, Arabic has complicated grammatical rules and it is very rich in its derivational system [3]. These features make the language challenging in computational processing and morphological analysis because in most cases, exact keyword matching between documents and user queries, is inadequate.

A number of studies have been devoted to stemming for a wide range of languages, including Arabic. Different approaches were proposed. For Arabic stemming [3] [4], examples include light stemming, morphological analysis, statistical-based stemming using co-occurrence analysis, N-grams or parallel corpora (collections). Some of these stemming approaches, especially those statistical ones, are language-dependent and are not tailored to Arabic only, while others provide more language independency. It is reported that stemming has a high positive effect on highly inflected languages, such as Arabic [5].

Among these techniques, two major approaches are the most dominant for Arabic stemming. These are light stemming (known also as affix removal stemming) and heavy stemming (morphological analysis stemming). The light stemming chops off some affixes—such as plural endings in English lightly from words, whereas the second technique, which is heavy stemming, performs heuristic and linguistic processes so as to extract the root of the word, the possible roots or the stem of the word. The stem in Arabic IR is the least form of the word without any prefixes and suffixes, whereas the root of the surface form is the basic unit which often consists of three letters. Technically, root base stemmers attempt always to analyze words and to produce their roots.

Other techniques such as the use of corpus-based statistics and lexicons (to determine most frequent affixes and employing genetic algorithms and neural networks) have been also reported in the literature. Approaches like co-occurrence techniques for clustering words together and the use of parallel corpora have been also investigated.

However, in spite of the significant achievements and developments of these Arabic stemming techniques, each of the proposed approaches has some pros and cons and it is yet unclear which technique is to be adopted for indexing and/ or stemming Arabic texts.

This paper attempts to review current techniques to Arabic stemming problem. It provides firstly a comprehensive examination to the features of the Arabic that make the language challenging to Natural Language processing (NLP) and Information Retrieval (IR). The paper also compares among a considerable number of stemmers and how each of them works and produces the stem and/or root from Arabic text. The strengths and the weaknesses of each technique are also provided.

The rest of this paper is organized as follows. Section two introduces the characteristics of Arabic language which makes it challenging to Arabic IR task. Section three is an in-depth coverage for the existing approaches to Arabic stemming. Several studies are presented in this section. In section four an intensive discussion on the current approaches and their limitations is conducted. In section five, the paper is concluded.

2. Why Arabic Is Challenging

Arabic is one of the Semitic languages, which also includes Hebrew, Aramaic and Amharic. It is the lingua-franca of a large group of people. It is estimated that there are approximately four hundred million first-language speakers of Arabic [3] [6]. Since it is the language of religious instruction in Islam, many other speakers from varied nations have at least a passive knowledge of the language. Arabic also is one of the six official languages of the (UN) and it is the fifth most widely used language in the world [2] [7].

Sentences in Arabic are delimited by periods, dashes and commas, while words are separated by white spaces and other punctuation marks. Arabic script is written from right-to-left while Arabic numbers are written and read from left-to-right. Script of Arabic consists of two types of symbols [3] [8]: these are the letters and the diacritics (known also as short vowels), which are certain orthographic symbols that are usually added to disambiguate Arabic words. Cited in [2], Tayli and Al-Salamah stated that the Arabic alphabet has 28 letters, and, unlike English, there is no lower and upper case for letters in Arabic. An additional character, which is the HAMZA (ء), has been also added, but, usually it is not classified as the 29th letter.

Arabic words are classified into three main parts-of-speech: nouns (including adjectives and adverbs), verbs and particles. Particles in Arabic are attached to verbs and nouns. Words in Arabic are either masculine or feminine. The feminine is often formed differently from the masculine, e.g., مُبرمج and مُبرمجة (meaning: single masculine programmer and single feminine programmer, respectively). The same feature appears also in both nouns and verbs in literary Arabic in order to indicate number (singular, dual "for describing two entities" and plural) as in مُبرمجان ,مُبرمج and مُبرمجون (meaning: singular programmer, two programmers and more than two programmers, respectively).

Arabic has a complex morphology. Its derivational system is based on 10,000 independent roots [9]. Roots in Arabic are usually constructed from 3 consonants (tri-literals) and it is possible that 4 consonants (quad-literals) or 5 consonants (pent-literals) are used. Out of the 10,000 roots, only about 1200 are still in use in the modern Arabic vocabulary [10]. Words are formed by expanding the root with affixes using well-known morphological patterns (known sometimes as measures). For example, **Table 1** shows some different forms derived for the word أخلاء, which is the plural of the word خليل (meaning: a close friend) after being attached to different affixes. All words are correct in Modern Standard Arabic (MSA). This feature causes Arabic to have more words that can occur only once in text, compared to other languages, e.g., English [2] [11].

Words and morphological variations are derived from roots using patterns. Grammatically, the main pattern, which corresponds to the tri-literal root, is the pattern فعَل (transliterated as f-à-l). More regular patterns, adhering to well-known morphological rules, can be derived from the main pattern فعل (f-à-l). Examples of some patterns are أفَاعِيل ،فعَل، فِعَال, transliterated as f-à-l, f-i-à-l and a-f-à-i-l, respectively.

Different kinds of affixes can be added to the derived patterned words to construct a more complex structure. Definite articles—like ال (its counterpart is the definite "the"), conjunctions, particles and other prefixes can be affixed to the beginning of a word, whereas suffixes can be added to the end. For example, the word لنجْمَعَنّهم (meaning: we will surely gather them) can be decomposed as follows: (antefix: ل, prefix: ن, root: جمع, suffix: ن and postfix: هم). For the purpose of understanding stemming, all Arabic affixes are listed in **Table 2**, quoted in Kadri and Nie [12].

Antefixes, whether they are separated or not, are usually prepositions added to the beginning of words before prefixes. Prefixes are attached to exemplify the present tense and imperative forms of verbs and usually consist of one, two or three letters. Suffixes are added to denote gender and number, for examples in dual feminine and plural masculine. Postfixes are used to indicate pronouns and to represent the absent person (third person), for example. Usually this morphology is used to create verbal and nominal phrases. **Table 3** illustrates several lexical words derived from the root حسب, which corresponds to the main pattern

Table 1. Different affixes attached to Arabic word أخلاء (meaning: the plural of the word خليل, which means "a close friend").

Word
أخلاء
أخلانه، أخلاؤه، أخلاءه، أخلانهم، أخلاؤهم، أخلاءهم، أخلانهن، أخلاؤهما، أخلاءهما، أخلاءنا، أخلاؤنا، أخلاننا، أخلاؤنا، أخلانكم، أخلانك، أخلاءك، أخلاؤها، أخلانها، وأخلائي، أخلائي،أخلاي، الأخلاء، بالأخلاء، بأخلاء، بأخلانهم ... إلخ

Table 2. Affixes in MSA (Arabic is read from right to left).

Antefixes	Prefixes	Suffixes	Postfixes
وبال، وال، بال، فال، كال، ولل، ال، وب، ول، لل، فس، فب، فل، وس، ك، فـ، ب، ل	ا، ن، ي، ت	تا، وا، ين، ون، ان، ات، تان، تين، يون، تما، تم، و، ي، ا، ن، ت، نا، تن	ي، ه، ك، كم، هم، نا، ها، تي، هن، كن، هما، كما
Prepositions meaning respectively: and with the, and the, with the, then the, as the, and to (for) the, the, and with, and to (for), then will, then with, then to (for), and will, as, then, and, with, to (for)	Letters meaning the conjugation person of verbs in the present tense	Terminations of conjugation for verbs and dual/plural/female/male marks for nouns	Pronouns meaning respectively: my, his, your, your, their, our, her, my, their, your, their, your

Table 3. Different derivatives from the root حسب..

Arabic Word	Pattern Transliterated	Meaning
حسب	f-$\grave{a}$-l	Compute (a tri-literal root)
يحسب	y-f-$\grave{a}$-l	He computes
حسبنا	f-$\grave{a}$-l-n-a	We compute
حسبن	f-$\grave{a}$-l-n	They compute (plural feminine)
يحسبون	y-f-$\grave{a}$-l-o-n	They compute (plural masculine)
حسبا	f-$\grave{a}$-l-a	They compute (dual masculine)
حاسوب	f-a-$\grave{a}$-o-l	Computer (Machine name)
حسّب	f-$\grave{a}$-$\grave{a}$-l	He computes (for intensifying verbs)

فعل (f-$\grave{a}$-l), according to some different patterns, in which some letters are added to the main pattern.

Affixes in Arabic may include also some clitics. Clitics, which have been used in the proposed stemmers and can be proclitics or enclitics according to their locations in words, are morphemes that have the syntactic characteristics of a word but are morphologically bound to other words [13]. Thus, clitics are attached to the beginning or end of words. Such clitics include some prepositions, definite articles, conjunctions, possessive pronouns, particles and pronouns. Examples of clitics are the letters ك (pronounced as KAF) and ف (pronounced as FAA), which mean as and then, respectively.

Arabic also has three grammatical cases, as well. These cases are: nominative, accusative and genitive. For example, if the noun is a subject, then it will have the nominative grammatical case; if it is an object, the noun will be in the accusative case; and the noun will be in a genitive case if it is an object for a preposition. These grammatical cases cause Arabic to derive many words from a single noun (*i.e.* adjective) because it often results in a different form of the word. Note that adjectives in Arabic are nouns. For example, the different forms that can be derived from the adjective مزارع (meaning: farmer) according to their both grammatical forms may include words like: مزارعة (for singular feminine in nominative, accusative and genitive cases), مزارعان (for dual masculine in nominative case), مزارعَين (for dual masculine in accusative and genitive cases), مزارعتان (for dual feminine in nominative case), مزارعتين (for dual feminine in accusative and genitive cases), مزارعون (plural masculine in nominative case), مزارعِين (for plural masculine in accusative and genitive cases) and مزارعات (for plural feminine in nominative, accusative and genitive cases).

Morphology adds a level of ambiguity that makes the exact keyword matching mechanism inadequate for retrieval. Morphological ambiguity can appear in several cases. For example, clitics may accidentally produce a form that is homographic or homogenous (the same word with two or more different meanings) with another full word [2] [3] [14]. For example, the word علم (meaning: science) can be joined with the clitic (ي) to construct the word علمي (meaning: my knowledge) which is homographic with the word علمي (meaning: scientific). Additionally, Arabic grammar contributes to the morphological ambiguity. For example, according to some Arabic grammar rules, sometimes vowels are removed from roots. The set of the vowel letters in Arabic consists of three letters: ALIF, YAA and WAW (أ، ي ، و). These letters have different rules that do not obey the derivational system of Arabic and make them very changeable. For instance, the last letter YAA is removed in a word like امشي (meaning: go), resulting in امش, if it appears in an imperative form.

Besides the complex morphology, Arabic also has a very complex type of plurals known as broken plural. Plurals in Arabic do not obey morphological rules. They are similar to cases like: *corpus* and *corpora*; and *mouse* and *mice* in English, but differing in that there is no rule-based morphological syntax to the broken plurals. Broken plurals constitute 10% of Arabic texts and 41% of plurals [2] [15]. Unlike English, the plural in Arabic indicates any number higher than two. The term broken means that the plural form does not resemble the original singular form. For example, the plural of the word نهر (meaning: river) is أنهار (rivers). In the simple cases of broken plurals, the new inflected plural has some letters in common when it is compared to the singular form, as in the previous example. But in many cases the plural is totally different from the original word, e.g., the plural of the word إمراة (meaning: woman) is نساء (women).

Diversity in broken plurals makes them highly unpredictable. In most cases knowing the singular form does not assist to deduce the plural, and vice-versa. This fact shows how much broken plurals lead to a mismatch problem in Arabic IR.

Arabic also has very diverse types of orthographic variations. They are very common and present real challenges for both Arabic IR and NLP systems. Examples include, but they are not limited to *Typographical Variations*, which merely caused by the Arabic letters ALIF with its different glyphs (أ, إ, آ and ا) and YAA with its dotted and un-dotted forms (ي and ى) and HAA with the forms ه and ة. In most cases, one of the glyphs of a certain letter is altered/dropped, initially, medially or finally, with another glyph of the same letter when writing text [16]. **Table 4** shows some examples of different typographical variations in MSA. Sometimes the typographical variant changes the meaning of the original word significantly, for example the قرآن (meaning: the Holy Quran) is typographically changed to قران (meaning: marriage contract), when the letter ALIF MADDA glyph in the middle is changed to bare ALIF.

3. Stemming in Arabic

Since Arabic is an inflectional language, a large number of studies have been devoted to the analysis of the best approach to index Arabic words. The process of producing index terms often goes through several operations, most of which are language-dependent. *Normalization* and *stemming* are among these major processes.

Normalization is the process of producing the canonical form of a token and/or a word in order to maximize matching between a query token and document collection tokens. In its simple form normalization pre-processes tokens to a single form, but very lightly. This is often done in several pre-processing stages so as to render different forms of a particular letter to a single Unicode representation, e.g., replacing the Arabic letter un-dotted ى with a final dotted ي, when this letter appears at the end of an Arabic word.

In its complex forms, normalization is used to handle morphological variation and inflation of words [17]. This is called stemming. Stemming is the process of rendering different inflected and variant forms of a certain word to a single term, known as *stem*. For instance, words like participating, participates, participation and participant may all be rendered to a common single stem *participat*.

Since documents and/or queries may have several forms of a particular word, stemming should map and transform all the inflected forms of a word into a common shared form and, thereby, this shared form would be the most appropriate form for indexing the representations of documents and for searching as well.In monolingual IR, stemming appears to have a positive impact on recall more than precision [5]. Furthermore, stemming shows a high positive effect on highly inflected languages, such as Arabic [5]. An additional advantage for the

Table 4. Illustrates some examples for typological variants in Arabic.

MSA	Variant	Gloss	Typographical Occurrence
امتحان	إمتحان	Exam	The final bare ALIF is changed to ALIF HAMZA below
صفاء	صفا	Purity	The final HAMZA is dropped
قرآن	قران	The Quran	ALIF MADDA in the middle is altered to bare ALIF
علاء	علا	A proper noun	They compute (plural feminine)
نافذه	نافذة	Window	The final letter HAA is altered to a different letter, which is TAA MARBOOTA
زراعي	زراعى	Agricultural	The final dotted YAA is changed to un-dotted YAA

stemming is that it also reduces the size of the index since many words are grouped together in a single canonical form.

In Arabic IR, the word is the surface form which is often obtained by tokenizing the text (*i.e.* tokenizing text on white space and punctuations). Thus, the word in Arabic in its complete structure is a concatenated form of letters consisting of prefixes, morpheme and suffixes, e.g., وألعابهم (meaning: and their games or their toys). From that perspective, the issue of whether Arabic index terms should be roots or stems has always been a major question. Cited in [13], some studies claimed that the lemmatized form of words in Arabic is the stem, while others argue that the lemma of the language is the root and the stem is only a manifestation to the root. By the term lemma [1] [3], it is meant the single dictionary entry form of the several inflected derivatives of a word. Nevertheless, there is an implicit assumption in NLP and IR that the stem in Arabic IR is the least form of the word without any prefixes and suffixes or their attached clitics, but possibly having extra letters medially. In the case of verbs in Arabic language, this is often the third person, perfective (past) and singular forms of verbs, whereas the stem is the singular form in the case of nouns (including adjectives). For instance, the stem of the word وألعابهم above is ألعاب in which both prefixes and suffixes from the beginning and ending of the word is truncated.

On the other hand, it is known in Arabic linguistics community that the root of the Arabic surface form is the basic unit, which usually rhymed and/or patterned by the pattern فعَل as it was described earlier. Accordingly, if an Arabic root is to be extracted from a surface form, all the affixes that appear in that word, even they are written medially, should be stripped-off.

Accordingly indexing Arabic words has two different paradigms [3] [13] [14]: either to index stem or root. Stem indexing paradigm attempts to remove only a few common numbers of prefixes and suffixes from words and without attempting to identify the patterns of words or their roots. On the other hand, root indexing technique attempts to analyze the words, which often contain root, patterns, prefixes and suffixes, so as to produce the root or all the possible roots of a word.

In order to achieve the goal of indexing the most adequate Arabic term (stem or root) from a word/token, several approaches have investigated from the use of lexicons and dictionaries to morphological analysis and combination of different techniques. Each method has its pros and cons and the studies investigated exhaustively what is the best technique to index Arabic words.

Due to large number of the studies in this specific area, researchers attempt to classify the techniques according to their algorithmic behaviors. Larkey, *et al.*, [4] clusters the techniques into four categories:

- Manually constructed dictionaries, in which words with their roots and their possible segmentations are stored in a large lookup table.
- Affix truncation techniques which often attempt to stem the words lightly by removing common suffixes and prefixes.
- Morphological analyzers, in which the root is extracted using morphological analysis.

- Statistical stemming which is based on clustering similar words in documents together.

In spite of the good classification of these techniques, but in the opinion of the authors this classification needs to be extended so as to include newer techniques. The new extended classification is shown in **Figure 1**.

Before delving into the details of each of the employed technique, it is important first to cover simple normalization. This is because stemming is in fact a complex normalization technique as it was illustrated earlier. In addition, the majority of the techniques perform some normalization technique firstly. Next sections explain normalization and stemming techniques in details.

3.1. Normalization

Before normalization, the majority of the Arabic stemming techniques process texts. Preprocessing in Arabic includes removal of non-characters, normalization of letters and removal of stopwords. Removal of non-characters [2] [18] includes the removal of punctuation marks, diacritics and *Kasheeda*, known also as *Tatweel*, which is an Arabic stylistic elongation of some words for cosmetic writing. For example, the word عادل (a proper noun) can be written with kasheeda as عـــــادل.

As it was shown earlier, normalization in Arabic is used to render different forms of a letter with a single Unicode representation. This is important to moderate the orthographic variations. Since there are only few Arabic letters that are the sources for orthographic variations of words, most stemming approaches handle them in a similar way. Accordingly, the majority of the stemming techniques normalize documents and queries using some or all of the following normalization [2] [12] [19].

Main Stemming Techniques for Arabic-Language Text							
Root-based and Morphological analysis	Affix truncation and light stemming		Statistical Stemming		Simple POS Tagging and Combined Techniques	Artificial Intelligence	
	Light Stemming	Linguistic Removal using corpus statistics	N-grams methods	Co-occurrence analysis	Clustering words using corpora		Neural networks	Genetic Algorithms

Figure 1. Classification of stemming techniques according to their algorithmic behaviors.

- Replacing ALIF in HAMZA forms (ALIF combined with HAMZA that is written above or below the ALIF like in "أ and إ") and ALIF MADDA (آ) with bare ALIF (ا).
- Replacing final un-dotted YAA (ى) with dotted YAA (ي).
- Replacing final TAA MARBOOTA (ة) with HAA (ه).
- Replacing the sequence ءى with ئ.
- Replacing the sequence ءي with ئ.
- Replacing ؤ with bare ALIF (ا).

In spite of the wide use of these normalization steps, Abdelali, *et al.*, [18] stated that some of these normalizations may conceal word characteristics and create ambiguity. For instance, it is not always correct to unify all glyphs of ALIF to a plain ALIF as it may lead to invalid words. Similar trends were also shown by Daoud and Hasan [20] who showed that normalization of Arabic letters, especially in the middle of words can result in incorrect words. For instance, normalizing ALIF MADDA (آ) with bare ALIF (ا) in the Arabic word قرآن (meaning: the Quran) results in the word قران (meaning: marriage contract).

To address the impact of Arabic challenges on both monolingual and crosslingual retrieval and the problem of orthographic resolution errors, such as changing the letter YAA (ي) to the letter ALIF MAKSURA (ى) at the end of a word, the studies in Xu, *et al.* [21] [22] used two different techniques to normalize spelling variations. The first technique is the normalization, which replaces all occurrences of the diacritical ALIF, HAMZA (أ،إ) and MADDA (آ), with a bare ALIF (ا). The second technique is the mapping, which maps every word with a bare ALIF to a set of words that can potentially be written as that word by changing diacritical ALIFs to the plain ALIF. All the mapped words in the set are equally probable, each of which obtains 1/n probability. The study of Xu and his team concluded that there is little difference between mapping techniques and normalization techniques for orthographic resolution.

The use of normalization techniques is almost similar in Arabic and it seems that in order to increase matching, the penalty paid is to normalize Arabic letters before stemming the words in which they occur.

3.2. Arabic Stemming Approaches

As it was illustrated earlier, we extended the classification of the employed approaches for stemming Arabic texts. The next section describes the techniques in this classification in details.

3.2.1. Root-Based and Morphological Analyzers

With the premise that the basic unit in Arabic is the root, root—based stemming technique attempts to perform heuristic and linguistic morphological analysis so as to extract the root of a word. For example, root-based algorithms produce the root عمل for the word وأعمالهم (meaning: and their works) because all affixes are removed. To achieve this goal of obtaining roots, researchers employ the use of Arabic morphological analyzers.

Khoja stemmer [23] is one of the most famous root-based stemmers. The algorithm was widely used in Arabic IR. It renders inflectional forms of words to produce their roots by removing their longest prefixes and suffixes, at first. For instance, the prefix ي and the suffix ون are firstly removed, using Khoja stemmer, if the input word is يلاعبون (meaning: they are playing with). The resulted word (in this case the word لاعب) is then matched with some predefined patterns and some list-driven roots. The selected pattern depends on the length of the extracted word. For example, for the word لاعب in our example the pattern فاعل may be chosen. By this matching process the root is produced as لعب (meaning: play) since the pattern فاعل is already predefined in the language that is has a bare letter ALIF (ا) added medially to the tri-literal pattern فعل. Finally, in the algorithm, the extracted root is compared to a list of roots to check its validity.

One advantage of Khoja stemmer is that it has the ability to detect letters that were deleted during the derivational process of words. For instance, the last letter YAA is removed in a word like امشي (meaning: go), resulting in امش, if it appears in an imperative form. As another example, the last letter ALIF in the root نما (meaning: grew) will be modified to WAW in the present form of this root and thus it will be نّمو instead of نّما. Using Khoja stemmer, it is possible to handle such cases.

However, in spite of its superiority and its wide use, the algorithm has a major drawback, that is the over-stemming in which the stemmer may erroneously cluster some semantically different words into a single root. This is because a tremendous number of Arabic words may have different semantic meanings although they share the same root, leading to low precision and high level of ambiguity. For example, both the words مقاتلات (meaning: fighters) and يتقاتلون (meaning: they are fighting each others) are originated from the canonical root قتل (meaning: to kill). Examples also include words like طفيليات (meaning: parasites) and لعوب (meaning: irresponsible) in which the produced roots using Khoja stemmer are طفل and لعب. Both stems are semantically different from the original word.

Additionally, sometimes the algorithm removes some affixes that are parts of words (known as mis-stemming), such as in the word مدرسه (meaning: schools) which will be stemmed to the root درس (meaning: lesson or learn in past tense). Khoja stemmer may also result in truncating some letters that are parts of the word. It is clear that removal of prefixes and suffixes blindly causes the stemmer to erroneously remove some original letters from the root. For instance, chopping-off suffixes and prefixes blindly from a word like بالغات (meaning: feminine adults) will result in removing the letters بال, which will be handled in the algorithm as a prefix although they are original letters of the root بلغ (meaning: to attain or to accomplish).

In his study for the Holy Quran, Hammo [24] stated that most of the failing cases of Khoja when it was used to stem words of the Holy book, were occurred when stemming proper names such as the names of Prophets, angels, ancient cities, places and people, numerals, as well as words with the diacritical mark shadda.

Darwish [25] developed Sebawai, a root-based analyzer that is based on auto-matically derived rules and statistics. Sebawai has two main modules. At first, a list of "word-root" pairs *i.e.* (وذهابهم, ذهب), which means (go, and they gone), had been constructed. The word-root pairs list was constructed using an old mor-phological analyzer called ALPNET. Then by comparing the root to the word, Sebawai extracts a list of prefixes, suffixes and stem templates. For example, given the pair (وذهابهم, ذهب) in the example above, the system produces و (meaning: and) as the prefix, هم (meaning: theirs) as the suffix and "CCAC" as the stem template (C's represent the letters in the root). During this phase of training, the frequency of each of the generated item (*i.e.* suffix) is computed and hence the probability that a prefix, suffix or stem template would occur is computed. For example, if the total number of occurrences of a certain prefix is 100, and the list of the gener-ated word-root pairs is 1000, then a probability of value 0.1 is assigned to that prefix. As a result to this training phase probability tables are obtained for the suffixes, prefixes and stems of the training corpus (word-root pairs).

For the root detection phase, Sebawai takes the input word and produces all the possible combinations among prefix, suffix and template, which could result in forming that word. Once a possible combination is obtained, its product pro-bability (with the independence assumption) is computed according to the pre-viously estimated probabilities. The higher probability computed of a certain com-bination, its root is detected and matched against 10,000 roots to check its valid-ity.

Sebawai has some limitations stated by its developer. First, it cannot stem trans-literated words such as entity names (*i.e.*, انجلترا, which means England) because it binds the choice of roots to a fixed set. Second, Sebawai cannot deal with some individual words that constitute complete sentences, like لَنَهْدِيَنَّهُم (meaning: we will surely guide them) because the appearance of such words is very rare and thus, low probabilities are assigned. Additionally, since Sebawai is a root-based stemmer, it results in the same problem of over-stemming as in Khoja.

Buckwalter [26] developed a stem-based morphological analyzer which is one of the most popular and respected analyzers that were used widely in the TREC experiments.

Unlike, Khoja for example, Buckwalter produces a single stem or all the possi-ble stems of the input word. The basic idea is similar to the one presented by Sebawi. At first, manually constructed tables are collected. The tables are based on three groups (prefixes, possible stems and suffixes). In addition, the valid combinations of each pair of the three groups (prefix/stem pairs, prefix/suffix pairs and stem/suffix pairs), are also stored in form of truth tables. Thus during the root detection phase, Buckwalter algorithm, which is coded in a program called Ara Morph, divided input word into three sub-strings (potential prefix, stems and suffix), with all its possibilities. The produced sub-strings are generated according to the pre-constructed tables. Following this, a matching process is performed for each possible combination of prefix, stem and suffix that could yield the input word. Hence using the truth tables pairs and if the first sub-string is a correct prefix, the second sub-string is a legitimate stem, the third sub-string is a legitimate sub-string and if the combination of all of them is valid then the second sub-string will extracted as a stem for the input word. If more than one stem is obtained then all of them will be listed.

Buckwalter is not just a stemmer. Instaed, it also tags the words with its possible POS and provides all the possible translations in English for that word. For example, for the word تعمل (tEml in Buckwalter transliteration), a version of the Buckwalter analyzer provided many solutions, two of them are presented in **Figure 2**.

One deficiency of Buckwalter's analyzer is that some words may not be stemmed because they may not be included in the stem table. In addition, broken plurals are not managed by the Buckwalter stemmer [21]. Attia [13] lists 11 cases where the Buckwalter analyzer failed to get their stems. One of the listed shortcomings is that Buckwalter failed to stem clitic question morpheme because of lack of coverage for such cases, e.g., أعادل (meaning: Is it correct that Adil).

Based on Buckwalter analyzer and the fact that the analyzer lists all the possible stems, Xu, *et al.*, [21] attempt to resolve ambiguity when more than one stem are returned. This is done by using a probabilistic model (as part of the retrieval task in that study) to accommodate ambiguity, which arises when equally probable probabilities are assigned to each of the obtained stems (when more than one stem is returned by the algorithm). Results showed that using one stem is somewhat better than using all the stems even they are in the IR task, but the improvement is not statistically significant. Abdelali [18] concluded that their approach may fail to eliminate ambiguous words. Since the same probability is assigned to both valid stem and possible stems, noise may be introduced.

```
Processing token : تعمل
Transliteration :   tEml

SOLUTION #1
Lemma  :  Eamil
Vocalized as :      taEomal
Morphology :
        prefix : IVPref-hy-ta
        stem : IV
        suffix : Suff-0
Grammatical category :
        prefix : ta          IV3FS
        stem : Eomal         VERB_IMPERFECT
Glossed as :
        prefix : it/they/she
        stem : work/function/act

SOLUTION #2
Lemma  :  taEam~ul
Vocalized as :      taEam~ul
Morphology :
        prefix : Pref-0
        stem : N/At
        suffix : Suff-0
Grammatical category :
        stem : taEam~ul      NOUN
Glossed as :
        stem : mannerism
```

Figure 2. Two solutions for the word تعمل using the Buckwalter.

Ghwanmeh, *et al.*, [27] follows similar technique to Khoja to detect root. However, the algorithm is only used for those words whose lengths are greater than three letters. Accordingly, the algorithm takes the input word and leaves it as it appears if its length is less than four letters. Otherwise, the algorithm begins to remove the longest prefixes and suffixes and follows the she step by comparing the extracted stem to a list of pre-defined patterns. If the pattern length is equivalent to the generated stem, the algorithm chooses that pattern and extracts the root. The Algorithm was tested using a small dataset extracted from a small abstracts taken from Arabic proceedings of the Saudi conferences. Accordingly, results deemed to be indicative.

Recently, Al-Kabi, *et al.*, [28] have developed a novel approach for root detection using an extended version of Khoja stemmer. As in khoja, the algorithm in that study begins with the removal of suffixes and prefixes in the input word. However, the main difference between the two algorithms is that Khoja stemmer depends on matching the extracted stem (words after stripping off suffixes and prefixes) with patterns the in terms of their lengths, whereas in Al-kabi study the pattern is chosen according to its length and according to the common letters between the stem and the pattern. For example, given the word المنتجات (meaning: products), the algorithm removes the suffixes and prefixes at first, resulting in the stem استغفار (meaning: amnesty or forgiveness). During the matching task, threeverb patterns can be identified according to the length of that stem, these are: افتعالي, انفعاليand استفعال (transliterated as: *i-f-t-à-a-l-i, i-n-f-à-a-l-i* and*i-s-t-f-à-a-l*). However, the only pattern that have the highest number of common letters with the stem is the verb pattern استفعال (its shares four letters at positions 1, 2, 3 and 6) and thus, the pattern استفعال is chosen as the valid verb pattern for the stem منتج. As the pattern is selected, the root can be easily extracted from the matched pattern.

Results reported in Al-Kabi study showed that the proposed algorithm yields higher accuracy when it was compared to Khoja stemmer. One of the cons of the developed stemmer, however, is that it fails to extract roots from words whose lengths are less than 4 letters. In addition, the dataset that have been used in study is extremely small. It only contains 6081 Arabic words. Therefore, the results of the study can be considered as indicative rather than conclusive.

3.2.2. Light-Based Stemming and Affix Truncation

To mitigate the impact of the major drawback of root-based algorithms, which is losing stem semantics, light stemming for Arabic was also proposed. Light stemmers chop off some affixes such as plural endings in English lightly from words and without performing deep linguistic analysis. From that perspective, the majority of the approaches attempt to strip off the most frequent prefixes (*i.e.* definite articles), suffixes (*i.e.* possessive pronouns) and any antefixes or postfixes that can be attached to the beginning or endings of words. For example, light stemmers generate أعمال (meaning: works) because only prefixes (including antefixes) and suffixes (including postfixes) are removed. The decision of removing any affixes, however, is usually controlled by some heuristic rules derived from common use of these antefixes. Examples of such types of stemmers include, but are not limited to, Al-stem by Darwish and Oard [19], Aljlayl and Frieder stemmer [29], Kadri and Nie linguistic stemmer [12] and Chen and Gey stemmer [30] from California Berkeley team.

Al-stem is a light stemmer, presented by Darwish and Oard [20], which lightly chops off the following prefixes but in order from right to left (،بت ،بال ،فال ،وال) plus the following (ابا ،لا ،فا ،وا ،وا ،في ،لل ،ال ،فم ،كم ،وم ،لم ،بم ،نت ،ست ،وت ،مت ،لت ،يت) suffixes starting from right to left, too (ية ،ها ،هن ،هم ،كم ،تم ،ته ،تي ،ان ،وه ،ون ،وا ،ات ا ،ي ،هـ ،ة ،يه ،ين ،نا ،تك). Darwish and Oard used Al-stem in their experiment to develop a technique for Arabic-English cross-language information retrieval at TREC 2002. By the term cross-language IR, it is meant the query is written in a language that is different from documents' language. In that study, Al-Stem was compared to light8 stemmer, which will be illustrated later in this section. Results concluded that the there almost no difference statistically between the two stemmers when they were tested using TREC 2001 data. Later, Al-Stem has been modified by David Graff from the Linguistic data Consortium (LDC) to strip-off the suffixes (تا and ا) and the prefixes (سي and تت) from the list of suffixes in Al-Stem.

Based on the assumption that light stemming preserves the meaning of words, unlike root-based techniques, Aljlayl and Frieder [29] proposed an algorithm to stem Arabic words lightly. The algorithm strips the most prevalent suffixes (*i.e.* possessive pronouns), prefixes (*i.e.* definite articles), antefixes or postfixes that can be affixed to the beginning of the prefixes or the end of suffixes. Aljlayl and Frieder, however, did not list their removable sets of prefixes and suffixes explicitly. The removal of affixes, however, in Aljlayl's work had been controlled by an algorithm depending on the remaining numbers of letters in the word under stemming.

After the input word is fed to the algorithm, the stemmer truncates the letter و (pronounced as WAW and it means and) only if the length of the word is greater than or equal to 3. Following this, articles are truncated from the beginning of words. If the length is of the input word is still greater than or equal to 3, longest suffixes are removed if and only if the remaining letters are 3 or more. Next, the algorithm truncates prefixes from the produced word in the previous step, but, if and only if the remaining letters are also greater than or equal 3. The last step is repeatedly performed until the stem is obtained. In some cases the algorithm uses a normalization technique for words as well as removing all the diacritical marks except the diacritical mark shadda. This is because shadda is a sign for a duplication process of a consonant and thus it exemplifies a letter that could be lost if shadda is removed. One advantage of the algorithm is that it can deal with some arabicized words according to a predefined list. Arabicization referred to Arabic transliterated, rather than translated, words that are borrowed from other languages e.g., كمبيوتر (meaning: computer). Arabicized words in Arabic are often nouns and terminology derived from other languages. However, entries in such an arabicized list would probably be limited in its coverage. Aljlayl and

Frieder concluded that their light stemming algorithm outperforms root-based algorithms, in particular the Khoja stemmer.

Larkey, Ballesteros and Connell [31] proposed several light stemmers (light 1, light 2, light 3 and light 8) based on heuristics and some strippable prefixes and suffixes. The affixes to be removed are listed in **Table 5**. In the implementation, the algorithms of these different versions of light stemming perform the following steps:

- Peel away the letter و (meaning: and) from the beginning of words for light 2, light 3, and light 8 only if there are 3 or more remaining letters after removing the و. Such condition attempts to avoid removing words that start with the letter و.
- Truncate definite articles if this leaves 2 letters or more.
- Remove suffixes, listed in table below from right to left, from the end of words if this leaves 2 letters or more.

In monolingual and cross lingual experiments, developers of light 8 concluded that it outperforms the Khoja stemmer, especially after removing stopwords with or without query expansion. Actually, Larkey, Ballesteros and Connell concluded that removing stopwords results in a small increase in average precision, which is statistically significant for light 2 and light 8, but not for raw (the case of no stemming or normalization) and normalized words. In the same experiments, Larkey, Ballesteros and Connell used co-occurrence analysis, based on a string similarity metric, to refine some simple stemmers that are light stemmers followed by removal of vowel letters plus HAMZA (ء). From the experiment, it is concluded that a repartitioning process consisting of vowel removal followed by refinement using co-occurrence analysis performed better than no-stemming or very light stemming. In contrast, light8 stemming followed by vowel removal and the co-occurrence analysis is not better that light8 with stop word removal.

Larkey, Ballesteros and Connell [4] expanded their previous studies by adding another light stemmer called light 10. In fact, among the set of the Arabic light stemmers, the most famous, and yet the most elegant and heavily used one, is light 10 [4]. Light 10 is an extension to Larkey's light stemmers set and in particular it is the latest update of light 8 in her set. Light 10 has been identified as the best ever developed stemmer for Arabic language. In light-10, Larkey and her team proposes to lightly chops off the prefixes (ال، وال، بال، كال، فال، لل، و) from the beginning of words plus the suffixes (ها، ان، ات، ون، ين، يه، ية، ة، هـ، ي) from the end. However, the removal of affixes in the algorithm is controlled with three rules:

Table 5. Strippable strings removed in light stemming.

Light stemmer type	Removing from front	Removing from end
Light1	ال، وال، بال، كال، فال	none
Light2	ال، وال، بال، كال، فال، و	none
Light3	ال، وال، بال، كال، فال، و	هـ، ة
Light8	ال، وال، بال، كال، فال، و	ها، ان، ات، ون، ين، يه، ية، ة، هـ، ي

1) Peel away the letter و (meaning: and) from the beginning of words if there are 3 or more remaining letters after removing the و.

2) Truncate definite articles if this leaves 2 letters or more.

3) Remove suffixes, starting from right to left, from the end of words if this leaves 2 letters or more.

The robust feature of light 10 and in light stemming approaches in general, is that the stemmer minimizes the impact of the over-stemming problem. Since only few prefixes and suffixes are removed then the semantic meanings of words will be preserved. Consider the word الطفيليات. If the word is lightly stemmed, then the resulted stem is طفيل (as only the definite article prefix ال and the plural feminine suffix ات will be eliminated according to the algorithm). It is noticed that both the word and the stem have the same semantic meaning. In general, this is a very strong feature for light-stemming approaches. In the experiments, the developers of light 10 showed that it outperforms Khoja stemmer and the difference is statistically significant.

In the same study, the produced stems using light10 was also compared to the generated stems after words were processed using both Buckwalter and Diab analyzers [26] [32]. Diab Analyzer [32] is an Arabic morphological software developed to resolve the tokenization, POS tagging and Base Phrase Chunking problem of MSA. The analyzer utilized a supervised learning approach that uses training data taken from the Arabic Tree Bank and is based on using SVM (Support Vector Machines). The assumption made here is that   problems like tokenization and part of speech tagging, for examples, can be considered as some types of classification problems in which the task is to predict the tag of the token's class, based on a trained number of features that are extracted from a predefined linguistic context. Thus, in the experimental setup of the experiments conducted by Lareky and her team [31], Diab analyzer was used to tag words and then according to this tagging process several runs were tested. For example, by referring to tags of words that are generated by Diab analyzer, light 10 determines either to truncate suffixes or to truncate only some of these suffixes. For instance, if the tagger tags a word as dual or plural proper nouns or plural nouns, light10 truncates only dual and plural endings from input words. In the study, results concluded that light 10 outperformed both Buckwalter and Diab analyzers and the differences are statistically significant.

In spite of the above stated conclusion about light 10, but yet the stemmer still have major drawbacks that can be identified. The obvious one is the under-stemming problem, in which words with the same meanings may be clustered into different groups. For instance, the stemmer fails to group the words اقتتل (meaning: they are fighting hardly with each others), which is stemmed to اقتتل, and القاتل (meaning: the killer), which is stemmed to قاتل, although both words are semantically similar. As a result, the stemmer may result in low recall as many relevant documents will not be retrieved. Under-stemming is limited to light 10 only and it appears in every light stemmer in Arabic studies.

Inspired by the drawbacks of both light and heavy stemming techniques, Kadri and Nie [12] proposed a new stemming technique known as linguistic-stem. The developers employed Arabic morphological rules to produce possible stems of words. The task consists of two phases. In the first phase, which is the training, 523,359 different tokens in the TREC collection were firstly extracted so as to create corpus-based statistics. The role of these statistics is to determine the most common stems because the latter can resolve easily any ambiguity occurring when words are stemmed. Accordingly, in the training phase, every word in the corpus has been decomposed according to some rules to produce all the possible stems. Thus, a corpus of stems with their occurrence frequencies was built and the most common stems are listed with their frequencies. However, the developers didn't list the rules that were applied in the study. In the second stage of the study, which is the stemming, Kadri technique truncates the most common prefixes and suffixes (as in other light stemmers) that were obtained from corpus statistics. So, if there is only one stem, the stem is returned; otherwise, the algorithm chooses the most appropriate stem depending on the pre-estimated statistics. In the same study, which was implemented using Arabic TREC collection, another light stemmer that was developed by the same author, was compared. In that light stemmer, the same argument of computing some corpus statistics but, for antefixes rather than for stems was also used. The used prefixes were (فب ,و ,ا ,ال ,ب ,ل ,وال , بال , وب ,ول ,فال ,كال ,ولل ,فل ,وبال) and the list of suffixes contains(ا ,ه ,ن ,ي ,ت ,ها , ين,و ,ان ,ات ,ون ,هم ,نا ,آ ,وا ,هما ,تي). Results reported in the study showed that the proposed linguistic stemmer yields better results than the used light stemmer and the difference in performance is statistically significant. However, it is noticed that the complete details for how the rules have been applied was not provided in the study.

Chen and Gey [30] from California Berkeley team follow the same technique to stem Arabic words with the ability to remove 26 prefixes and 22 suffixes. The two lists were identified manually according to grammatical roles that these affixes play in language. Additionally, corpus based statistics (occurrence of affixes frequencies), empirical evaluation for the previous experiments of TREC and English translations of the affixes.

The algorithm that handles affixes removal is well controlled in the Berkeley team work.

For the removal of prefixes, the algorithm checks the length of the input word and according to that length; a specific rule will be applied. If the length is:

- At least 5 characters, truncate the first 3 characters if and only if the first three letters of the word is in the list (لال ,سال ,اال ,مال ,ولل ,كال ,بال ,وال).
- At least 4 characters, truncate the first 2 characters if and only if the first two letters of the word is in the list (فا ,كا ,ول ,وي ,وس ,سي ,لا ,وت ,وم ,لل ,بال). However, if the word begins with the letter و, remove that letter.
- At least 4 characters and the initial letter in the word is ب or ل, then truncate the occurring letter if and only if the produced word (after the letter ب or ف is being truncated) is in the TREC 2002 Arabic collection.

For stripping-off suffixes, the algorithm also checks the length of the word (before removing the suffix but after the removal of the prefix). If the length is:

- At least 4 characters long, truncate recursively the following letters according to their occurrences in the list: (ها, ية ,هم ,وا ,نا ,وا,ما ,يا , ني ,هن ,كم, كن ,تم, تن, (ون ,ات ,ان ,ين).

- At least 3 characters long, truncate recursively the following one-character suffixes that appear in the list: (ة, ه,ي , ت).

The results reported by Chen and Gey study, showed that the algorithm was very beneficial to retrieval performance.

Inspired by the fact that some light stemmer may result in removing some affixes that are parts of the original words, Nwesri, *et al.*, [33] [34] proposed some heuristic algorithms to strictly and lightly strip-off prefixes, which are conjunctions and prepositions as described earlier. The developed algorithms are based on how to identify prepositions from conjunctions like ف and ل (pronounced as: FAA and LAM). The algorithms consist of several steps and they make use of some Arabic lexicons and spelling checkers with more than 15 million Arabic words. The experiments, which were tested using TREC 2001, showed that the improvement of in performance was statistically significant.

Ababneh, *et al.* [35] developed a new rule-based stemmer which firstly matches the input word with a single pre-defined list of some Arabic patterns, e.g., فاعل. This is performed firstly in the study so to take a decision whether to remove possible prefixes from words begin with them or not. For instance, consider the word كامل (meaning: the proper noun Kamil). Since the word matches the pattern فاعل then the prefix كا will not be removed as the prefix would be a part of the word. Thus, the word in which the prefix occurs would be retained as a stem. In the algorithm, if the word does not match any pattern, then the possible combinations between prefixes and suffixes in the word are examine—according to some compatibility table. If the combination is not valid then the word is preserved and returned as a stem; otherwise some heuristic rules that are based on counting the length of words after and/or before truncating affixes, are applied. The experiments reported in Ababneh and his team [35], however, were conducted with a sample term lists containing only 21 words.

Very recently, Sameer [36] developed an approach for stemming Arabic words using similar techniques to those in light stemming. The algorithm is really simple. It depends on pre-defined and ordered lists of suffixes and prefixes. During the algorithm, the developers remove occurring suffixes and prefixes according to their order in their corresponding table. The algorithm was not tested sufficiently as only 14 words were used to test the algorithm.

Morphological analyzers for dialectal Arabic have been also proposed. It is known that fro Arabic language, there is a continuum of spoken dialects varying geographically, but also by social class, which are native languages. These dialects differ phonologically, lexically, morphologically and syntactically from one another [2] [37]. Regional variation problem is one of the challenging problems to Arabic IR and NLP. Examples for such analyzers are ADAM (Analyzer for Dialectal Arabic Morphology) [38]. AbuAtta and Al-Omari [39] also attempts to produce stem for words written in Gulf dialect. As in ADAM, the authors developed a set of morphological rules to remove suffixes and prefixes from Arabic Gulf dialect texts. As in MSA stemmers, the algorithm implements also some rules for truncation that are based on word length. The results indicated that MSA stemmers were not able to extract the stems of Arabic Gulf text unless their rules are modified. Therefore, the developed stemmer yields better results than MSA stemmers. Results were tested using small collection.

3.2.3. Statistical Stemming

Motivated by the fact that the stemming technique is a language-dependent process, statistical-based stemmers that demonstrate as language-independent techniques to conflation were also proposed for Arabic IR. Examples of statistical stemmers are those based on corpus analysis [31] [40]. The basic principle made here is that since conflated words in a given corpus tend to co-occur together in the same corpus, then the relationship between words, which is usually computed using some similarity measure (*i.e.* Mutual Information or Dice Coefficient), can be utilized to prevent, for example, two semantically different words that have the same stem to be grouped together even if the stemmer produces a single stem for those conflated words. For example, the words طفيليات and أطفال should not be grouped in the same stem (or as in English the words police and policy) because making use of co-occurrence statistics would result in distinguishing words from each others.

From that perspective, using co-occurrence statistics and association relationship measures (*i.e.* Mutual Information) between word pairs, makes it possible to determine which words are semantically different and which are similar, even if the words have the same letters. For instance, consider the Arabic word. ذهب the word is a polysemous as two meanings can be provided: go and gold. Accordingly, by making use of co-occurrence statistics, the two words should be stemmed to different clusters if the context in which they appear indicates such distinctive meanings. Reported results by Xu and Croft [40] and by Larkey, *et al.* [31] showed that the approach is effective for improving stemming but, yet it was not found to be better than light-10.

The use of association similarity measures to words level has been also used for Arabic IR stemming. The premise here is that segmenting each word into a set of 3-grams for example, and computing a similarity measure, using Dice Coefficient for example, between the set of the 3-grams of that word and the set of the possible 3-grams of the query word would result in a similarity value that might allow clustering the word in a specific class. The major advantage for the use of N-grams models is that they are able to capture broken plurals. In spite of that broken plurals do not get conflated with their singular forms because they preserve some affixes and internal differences, but, yet, the singular form and broken plural of a certain word have some common letters in many broken plurals. Accordingly, segmenting the word in its singular and plural forms would probably capture the shared letters and hence, the plural and also different inflected forms of words are thus, clustered.

Using these arguments, Mustafa and Al-Radaideh [41] stated that the use of a di-gram method for Arabic IR offers better performance than tri-grams with respect to precision and recall ratio but, the method is not an effective solution to corpus-based Arabic word conflation because the language richness.

The same technique had been also used by Khreisat [42], who used both Dice similarity and Manhattan dissimilarity coefficients. The contribution of this study is that it showed that the use of similarity measures is much better than using dissimilarity coefficients. In the study the used N-grams was the tri-grams. The total number of the used documents in Khreisat was not provided in the study.

Hmeidi, et al., [43] followed a similar approach to Khreisat. They used the same similarity and dissimilarity measures, which are Dice and Manhattan coefficients. They concluded that the use of bi-grams Arabic tokens is efficient to extract Arabic roots regardless of their length (i.e. trilateral or quadliteral roots). The algorithm was tested with only 242 abstract plus the texts of the Holy Quran. As in Khreisat work, the results concluded that the use of similarity measure yield better results than the use of dissimilar measure.

Xu, et al. [22] combined Arabic monolingual N-gram retrieval with stemmed words. The study showed that the use of tri-grams combined with stemming, improved retrieval, though this improvement is not statistically significant. The study also experimented with bi-grams and di-grams, instead of tri-grams. Results indicated that both of them do not outperform tri-grams because bi-grams are very short with little context while di-grams are similar to word or stem-based retrieval. In the study, the use of the N-grams was able to detect broken plurals.

The same authors extended their study to include spelling normalization [22] In that study, spelling normalisation (variants in spelling) was implemented to detect the confused cases of some letters (i.e. YAA and ALIF). In the experiments, Xu and his colleagues concluded that the use of spelling normalisation for orthographic variation with 3-grams and stemming improves Arabic retrieval performance significantly by 40%. Surprisingly, in this experiment, Xu and his colleagues stated that stemming and spelling normalisation have a small impact on cross language information retrieval, unlike the results by the developers of the light10 stemmer, who used the same TREC 2001 data. With respect to stemming, Larkey, et al., [19] explained that Xu, et al., [44] used a parallel corpus, extracted from a UN corpus, so their bilingual lexicon contains several variants of Arabic words. However, Larkey, Ballesteros and Connell used a bilingual lexicon derived from an online dictionary, so it contains fewer variants. This means that query terms were not matched against the dictionary entries unless they were stemmed.

Chen and Gey [30] implemented a new approach for Arabic stemming using statistical stemmers that make use of parallel corpora (several monolingual corpora translated in more than one language). Chen and Gey used an English stemmer to stem English words in an English-Arabic parallel corpus. Then, Arabic words are clustered together into a stem category depending on their mappings/translations to English stems in the corpus after being aligned and processed with GIZA++ [45], which is a statistical MT toolkit that was designed for alignment in parallel corpora. Results showed that the increase in performance was substantial when it was compared with Al-stem.

3.2.4. Simple Tagging Based Stemming

Stemming based on light/simple tagging has been also utilized for Arabic texts. The idea is to lightly tag words into some different tags so as to use different types of stemming techniques. Al-Shammari and Lin [46] used a list of 2200 stopwords to classify verbs from nouns with a hypothesis that some stopwords precede nouns, e.g., من (meaning: from or to) whereas others precede verbs e.g., لم (لم is an Arabic conjunction means never and is used for the negation of the verb that follows). In the study, the Khoja stemmer was applied to stem verbs while light stemming is applied to nouns. Using two samples of data, in particular 47 medical documents with 9435 words and 10 sports articles (7071 words), Al-Shammari and Lin evaluated their stemmer, which was called Educated Text Stemmer (ETS) and they concluded that their stemmer was able to generate 96% correct stems. In addition, they stated that the ETS stemmer produces better results when more documents are contained in the stemming process.

Mansour *et al.* [44] presented an auto-indexing approach to build indices for Arabic documents. In their indexing process, the algorithm firstly tagged every word into verbs and nouns using morphological rules. The process was managed by a set of predefined rhythms (patterns). Secondly, the algorithm removes stopword and stop-list phrases. Thirdly, the algorithm identifies nouns and verbs depending on the preceding word, as it illustrated in the stemming section in this chapter. Fourthly, the algorithm extracts stems from the rhymed/patterned words. In particular, some morphological rules were used to extract stems from both nouns and verbs. For instance, verbs were checked firstly against some exceptional grammatical rules for Arabic verbs. If such scenario fails, then verbs are checked against the "ten-verb-additions" rule (grammarians of Arabic stated that the derivative system of any verb has 10 known different formats) after being heavily investigated to remove non-essential letters and thus the stem of any verb is obtained. Finally, Mansour and his colleagues assign weights to the stemmed words relative to their documents, depending on some statistical factors like the frequency of occurrence of a word in its containing document. Thus, all the possible stems of a word will be sorted according to their weights. Developers concluded that their method is very useful and obtain an average recall of 46% and an average precision of 64% when it is tested with 24 arbitrarily selected general-purpose texts with various lengths.

Both methods of Mansour and Al-Shammari seem reasonable but the experiments were not comprehensive as small and non-standard sets were used (only 24 texts were used by Mansour).

3.2.5. Artificial Intelligence Approaches to Stemming

Inspired by the fact that Neural Networks (NN) can be applied to a large number of applications, Alserhan and Ayesh [47], proposed the use of Back-Propagation Neural Network (BPNN) for stemming Arabic text. The work was motivated by the fact that the majority of the current root-based approaches employed relatively large morphological rules, which could have a real impact on storage and time required to access. The classification is based on the frequent appearance of the letters in Arabic language. So, in the study, Alserhan and Ayesh classified Arabic letters into four different classes that represent Arabic affixes. Each class is assigned a value of a three binary digits. During training stage, the neural network was trained using 250 words with their correct roots. Results reported by the study, showed that the use of neural networks in Arabic stemming could yield the correct root with an accuracy of 84%. The major advantage of Alserhan and Ayesh study is that it does not depend on any morphological rules but, yet, the study has two major drawbacks. First, it was limited to Arabic words with a maximum of length 4. Second, the results were only tested by 1000 words.

Boubas, *et al.*, [48] proposed the use of Genetic Algorithms (GA) to handle problem of Arabic stemming. The population in the study is built with 3089 solutions, which represent all possibilities that can be produced from a single root after being combined with suffixes and prefixes. However, during building the morphological system, only tri-laterals were used and thus, only addition and removal of prefixes and suffixes are applied, but not their substations or replacements. The possible combinations, with their examples, were fed to the system, in terms of learning patterns, during learning phase so as to generate morphological rules for verb patterns. During root-extraction phase, the system performs string matching so as to match input word with the morphologically extracted rules. The authors claimed that their machine learning system is able to produce roots from any Arabic word. In spite of the novelty of the proposed approach, the developers didn't prove how the system is tested. In addition, they didn't illustrate how the complete system works (*i.e.* fitness function employed).

4. Discussion

It is apparent that in highly morphological languages such as Arabic stemming could have a significant impact on retrieval. This is very evident in the majority of the studies provided in the paper. It is also clear that heavy and light stemming approaches are the most dominant ones among the existing approaches for stemming Arabic but, it can be concluded from the reported studies that light-based stemming is better than heavy-based stemming. But, each of the two paradigms has some pros and cons. On one hand, heavy stemming often results in overstemming, leading to a low precision. This is especially true in morphologically rich languages, as Arabic, which are often rich of polysemous words in which a single word could have multiple meanings. So, rendering infected forms of words into a single root would probably results in returning large number of irrelevant documents.

On the other hand, light stemming may not succeed to cluster semantically similar words together (under-stemming), resulting in low recall. However, in spite of this major drawback, light 10 is the best known algorithm for indexing Arabic texts. It has been identified as a fashionable solution to Arabic stemming problem. Therefore, light 10 has been added to the most famous IR systems like the Lucene and the Lemur toolkit.

It is true that light stemming preserves the meaning of words, unlike root-based techniques, and achieves the goal of retrieving the most pertinent documents, but in the opinion of the authors of this paper, the major reason behind the success of light-based stemming over root-based stemming is that the strippable affixes in the former approach are those appearing in Arabic nouns and adjectives (*i.e.*, وال، بال، كال، فال) and the belief is in Arabic nouns and adjectives are much larger than verbs. In fact, there are only few morphological rules, known as "ten-verb-addition", to formulate verbs from roots. In contrast, root-based stemming techniques, which often attempt to produce root, focus on verbs and handle even nouns and adjective in the same context. It is evident that it is not always correct to produce the root of proper nouns or nouns in general. Let's consider the following nouns: السعودية, المكاني, المهرجان, باراك أوباما and الستائر (meanings respectively: Saudia, the festival, spatial, the US leader Barak Obama). Using a root based stemmer like Khoja, the stems are سعد, كني, هرج, برا وبا and ستر, respectively. All of the stems are either chaotic or/and do not have similar semantic meanings to their original words. These two facts are the main causes for why light stemming techniques outperform root-based st.

However, in IR the most semantically clustered words, the better retrieval task. Therefore, in spite of the achievements of light stemming techniques, in general (and light 10, in particular), the belief is that they are not the best paradigm for indexing Arabic texts. In addition, it is obvious that in a rich language like Arabic, the process of relatively blind removal of affixes (*i.e.* prefixes and suffixes) could have a significant impact on words and may lead to mis-stemming and ambiguity problems, in which some letters that are original in words are erroneously stripped-off. In fact, light stemming techniques are really simple as they depend solely on the removal of affixed and some controlled rules devised experimentally.

When it comes to Arabic English CLIR, in which the query language is different from the language that presents in document collection, the belief is that it may result in some relatively high OOV (Out-of-Vocabulary) words. This refers to that the majority of the Arabic-to-English dictionaries (not the opposite) list their entries in terms of roots. In fact, whenever Arabic native speakers need to translate an Arabic word into English, they always render Arabic words to their roots to increase the possibility of capturing the translation senses. This is an accredited point for root-based techniques.

In the opinion of the authors, the only way to avoid ambiguity that may occur due to blind removal of affixes (when a letter or some consecutive letters are not parts from words), is to use some statistical data extracted from corpora. It is very evident (as in Kadri and Nie study above) that such corpus statistics are very useful for handle such ambiguity because the removal decision of affixes depends on the distribution of that affixes in the corpus and whether it is most frequent or not and thus, our certainty about the removal process is handled and estimated, which could help a lot in the final decision.

Nevertheless, the use of corpus statistics just imposes burden of removal ambiguity to domain and size of that certain corpus. The belief of the authors is that there is always a possibility of undesirable behavior and/or poor performance once moving from one domain to another domain and/or when the corpus size changes. This is not surprising because using statistics depends solely on the size and the domain from which data is sampled. Consider, for example, Arabic technical words in computer science. There are a considerable number of words that are borrowed from other languages (*i.e.* English). So, using of corpus statistics to avoid removal ambiguity, with a corpus of computer science may result in dropping performance of some technique radically because news collections, for examples, may have unique features that may not be found in other genres.

It is also noticed in the reported studies in Arabic stemming, that a considerable number of the developed approaches had been tested using small collections, rather than using standard corpora (*i.e.* TREC 2001 and 2002). This is a major drawback in the developed approaches because their results deemed to indicative rather than conclusive in this case. It is not guaranteed to get the same achieved results, when such techniques are tested using standard test beds.

The majority of the developed techniques didn't show how they handle broken plurals in Arabic. In fact, only few studies addresses the problem in terms of statistical stemming and/or using some clustering approaches or translation techniques using an aligned corpora as it has been described earlier in this paper. As illustrated earlier, broken plurals represent 10% of Arabic texts. It is not avoidable and the belief is that the problem should be handles within stemming techniques.

The use of simple part of speech tagging, statistical stemming and artificial intelligence are very useful to Arabic stemming task. Statistical stemming (*i.e.* N-grams models) and artificial intelligence techniques, for examples, have the ability to detect broken plurals of Arabic words, unlike root and heavy based techniques. They also have the ability of cluster words that are related together and to minimize polysemy impact (*i.e.* when a word have multiple meanings, clustering could distinguish between these meanings). Nevertheless, the use of such techniques increases performance penalty needed to identify clusters and/or detect tag-of-speech of words. In addition, simple POS tagging techniques rely on a hypothesis that does not always holds, which is the preceding words. In fact, the majority of the Arabic words cannot be determined by only preceded words. This is may be the major reason for using only small text collections for reported experiments which used such technique.

Orthographic variation in Arabic and various writing of some letters could also have a significant, because incorrect normalization may yield a stemmed word that does not share the meaning with the original word. Such orthographical differences should be handled carefully within stemming techniques. In the belief of the authors of this paper, Arabic stemming task should not be dependent on a specific approach. This is the only method to develop an accurate and error-free Arabic stemmer.

5. Conclusions

Arabic language is an extremely rich with its morphology, derivational system and grammatical rules. For such a language, stemming techniques could have a significant impact on improving retrieval performance. This paper reviews a considerable number of studies that have been conducted to resolve Arabic stemming problem. Several studies are presented and the causes for why Arabic language is challenging and its implications on NLP and IR have been well analyzed in the paper.

However, in spite of the achievements, it is yet not apparent which approach is the best for indexing Arabic texts. It is true that in NLP and IR research, community light stemming techniques have been widely adopted for their simplicity and their ability to preserve words meanings. But, yet, they are still far from the optimal accuracy. Root-based stemmers may result in higher recall but, many irrelevant documents may be retrieved because they cluster words in different classes. Additionally, light stemmers focus on nouns and hence, they perform relatively poor for nouns. Morphological analyzers, as Khoja stemmer which firstly tokenizes the input text, could result in incorrect tokenization and in stemming consequently. Additionally, they have been adopted to focus on verbs rather than nouns. Tagging techniques could improve performance but in an ad-hoc task like IR they are not the optimum. Statistical techniques could contribute to resolving broken plural problem but, they depend solely on corpus statistics, which could be changed as we move from a specific domain to another. We can conclude that there is no optimal solution yet for the problem of how to index Arabic terms.

References

[1]	Manning, C.D., Raghavan, P. and Schutze, H. (2008) Introduction to Information Retrieval. Cambridge University Press, Cambridge. https://doi.org/10.1017/CBO9780511809071

[2]	Mustafa (2013) Mixed-Language Arabic-English Information Retrieval. PhD Thesis, University of Cape Town, Cape Town.

[3]	Darwish, K. and Magdy, W. (2014) Arabic Information Retrieval. *Foundations and Trends in Information Retrieval*, **7**, 239-342. https://doi.org/10.1561/1500000031

[4]	Larkey, L., Ballesteros, L. and Connell, M. (2007) Light Stemming for Arabic Information Retrieval. In: Soudi, A., van den Bosch, A. and Neumann, G., Eds., *Arabic Computational Morphology*, Springer, Berlin, 221-243. https://doi.org/10.1007/978-1-4020-6046-5_12

[5]	Pirkola, A., Hedlund, T., Keskustalo, H. and Järvelin, K. (2001) Dictionary-Based Cross-Language Information Retrieval: Problems, Methods, and Research Findings.

Information Retrieval, **4**, 209-230. https://doi.org/10.1023/A:1011994105352

[6]   Mirkin, B. (2010) Population Levels, Trends and Policies in the Arab Region: Challenges and Opportunities. Arab Human Development, Report Paper 1.

[7]   Cheung, W. (2008) Web Searching in a Multilingual World. *Communications of the ACM,* **51**, 32-40. https://doi.org/10.1145/1342327.1342335

[8]   Habash, N. and Rambow, O. (2007) Arabic Diacritization through Full Morphological Tagging. *Human Language Technologies: The Conference of the North American Chapter of the Association for Computational Linguistics,* Rochester, 22-27 April 2007, 53-56.

[9]   Manzour, I. (2017) Lisan Al-Arab. www.lesanarab.com

[10] Hegazi, N. and El-sharkawi, A. (1985) An Approach to a Computerized Lexical Analyzer for Natural Arabic Text. Proceedings of the Arabic Language Conference, Kuwait, 14-16 April 1985.

[11] Mustafa, M. and Suleman, H. (2011) Building a Multilingual and Mixed Arabic-English Collection. 3*rd Arabic Language Technology International Conference,* Alexandria, 17-18 July 2011, 28-37.

[12] Kadri, Y. and Nie, J.Y. (2006) Effective Stemming for Arabic Information Retrieval. *Proceedings of the Challenge of Arabic for NLP/MT Conference,* London, 23 October 2006, 68-74.

[13] Attia, M.A. (2008) Handling Arabic Morphological and Syntactic Ambiguity within the LFG Framework with a View to Machine Translation. PhD Thesis, The University of Manchester, Manchester.

[14] Attia, M.A. (2007) Arabic Tokenization System. *Proceedings of the* 2007 *Workshop on Computational Approaches to Semitic Languages: Common Issues and Resources,* Prague, 28 June 2007, 65-72. https://doi.org/10.3115/1654576.1654588

[15] Goweder, A., Poesio, M., De Roeck, A. and Reynolds, J. (2005) Identifying Broken Plurals in Unvowelised Arabic Text. *Proceedings of Human Language Technology Conference and Conference on Empirical Methods in Natural Language Processing,* Vancouver, 6-8 October 2005, 246-253.

[16] Buckwalter, T. (2004) Issues in Arabic Orthography and Morphology Analysis. *Proceedings of the Workshop on Computational Approaches to Arabic Script-Based Languages,* Geneva, 28 August 2004, 31-34.
       https://doi.org/10.3115/1621804.1621813

[17] Levow, G.A., Oard, D.W. and Resnik, P. (2005) Dictionary-Based Techniques for Cross-Language Information Retrieval. *Information Processing & Management,* **41**, 523-547. https://doi.org/10.1016/j.ipm.2004.06.012

[18] Abdelali, A. (2006) Improving Arabic Information Retrieval Using Local Variations in Modern Standard Arabic. PhD Thesis, New Mexico Institute of Mining and Technology, New Mexico.

[19] Darwish, K. and Oard, D.W. (2003) CLIR Experiments at Maryland for TREC-2002: Evidence Combination for Arabic-English Retrieval.

[20] Daoud, D. and Hasan, Q. (2011) Stemming Arabic Using Longest-Match and Dynamic Normalization. 3*rd Arabic Language Technology International Conference,* Alexandria, 17-18 July 2011, 54-59.

[21] Xu, J., Fraser, A. and Weischedel, R. (2001) TREC 2001 Cross-Lingual Retrieval at BBN. *Text Retrieval Conference,* Gaithersburg, 13-16 November 2001, 68-78.

[22] Xu, J., Fraser, A. and Weischedel, R. (2002) Empirical Studies in Strategies for Arabic Retrieval. *Proceedings of the* 25*th Annual International ACM SIGIR Conference on Research and Development in Information Retrieval,* Tampere, 11-15 August

2002, 269-274. https://doi.org/10.1145/564376.564424

[23] Khoja, S. and Garside, R. (1999) Stemming Arabic Text. Computing Department, Lancaster University, Lancaster.

[24] Hammo, B.H. (2009) Towards Enhancing Retrieval Effectiveness of Search Engines for Diacritisized Arabic Documents. *Information Retrieval*, **12**, 300-323. https://doi.org/10.1007/s10791-008-9081-9

[25] Darwish, K. (2002) Building a Shallow Arabic Morphological Analyzer in One Day. *Proceedings of the ACL Workshop on Computational Approaches to Semitic Languages*, Morristown, July 2002, 1-8. https://doi.org/10.3115/1118637.1118643

[26] Buckwalter, T. (2002) Buckwalter Arabic Morphological Analyzer Version 1.0. Linguistic Data Consortium, University of Pennsylvania, Philadelphia.

[27] Ghwanmeh, S., Kanaan, G., Al-Shalabi, R. and Alrababah, S. (2009) Enhanced Algorithm for Extracting the Root of Arabic Words. *6th International Conference on Computer Graphics, Imaging and Visualization*, Tian Jin, 11-14 August 2009, 388-391.

[28] Al-Kabi, M., Kazakzeh, S., Abu Ata, B., Al-Rababah, A.S. and Izzat, A.M. (2015) A Novel Root Based Arabic Stemmer. *Journal of King Saud University—Computer and Information Sciences*, **27**, 94-103. https://doi.org/10.1016/j.jksuci.2014.04.001

[29] Aljlayl, M. and Frieder, O. (2002) On Arabic Search: Improving the Retrieval Effectiveness via Light Stemming Approach. *Proceedings of the 11th ACM International Conference on Information and Knowledge Management*, Illinois, 4-9 November 2002, 340-347. https://doi.org/10.1145/584792.584848

[30] Chen, A. and Gey, F. (2002) Building an Arabic Stemmer for Information Retrieval. *Text Retrieval Conference*, Gaithersburg, 19-22 November 2002, 631-639.

[31] Larkey, L.S., Ballesteros, L. and Connell, M.E. (2002) Improving Stemming for Arabic Information Retrieval: Light Stemming and Co-Occurrence Analysis. In: *Proceedings of the 25th Annual International ACM SIGIR Conference on Research and Development in Information Retrieval*, Tampere, 11-15 August 2002, 275-282. https://doi.org/10.1145/564376.564425

[32] Diab, M., Hacioglu, K. and Jurafsky, D. (2004) Automatic Tagging of Arabic Text: From Raw Text to Base Phrase Chunks. *Proceedings of the Human Language Technology Conference of the North American Chapter of the Association for Computational Linguistics*, Boston, 2-7 May 2004, 149-152. https://doi.org/10.3115/1613984.1614022

[33] Nwesri, A.F.A., Tahaghoghi, S.M.M. and Scholer, F. (2005) Stemming Arabic Conjunctions and Prepositions. *Lecture Notes in Computer Science*, **3772**, 206-217. https://doi.org/10.1007/11575832_23

[34] Nwesri, A., Tahaghoghi, S.M.M. and Scholer, F. (2007) Arabic Text Processing for Indexing and Retrieval. *Proceedings of the International Colloquium on Arabic Language Processing*, Rabat, 18-19 June 2007, 18-19.

[35] Ababneh, M., Al-Shalabi, R., Kanaan, G. and Al-Nobani, A. (2012) Building an Effective Rule-Based Light Stemmer for Arabic Language to Improve Search Effectiveness. *International Arab Journal of Information Technology*, **9**, 368-372.

[36] Sameer, R. (2016) Modified Light Stemming Algorithm for Arabic Language. *Iraqi Journal of Science*, **57**, 507-513.

[37] Habash, N. and Rambow, O. (2006) MAGEAD: A Morphological Analyzer and Generator for the Arabic Dialects. *Proceedings of the 21st International Conference on Computational Linguistics and the 44th Annual Meeting of the Association for Computational Linguistics*, Sydney, 17-21 July 2006, 681-688.

https://doi.org/10.3115/1220175.1220261

[38] Salloum, W. and Habash, N. (2014) ADAM: Analyzer for Dialectal Arabic Morpho-logy. *Journal of King Saud University—Computer and Information Sciences*, **26**, 372-378. https://doi.org/10.1016/j.jksuci.2014.06.010

[39] Abu Ata, B. and Al-Omari, A. (2014) A Rule-Based Stemmer for Arabic Gulf Dia-lect. *Journal of King Saud University—Computer and Information Sciences*, **27**, 104-112.

[40] Xu, J. and Croft, W.B. (1998) Corpus-Based Stemming Using Cooccurrence of Word Variants. *ACM Transactions on Information Systems*, **16**, 61-81. https://doi.org/10.1145/267954.267957

[41] Mustafa, S.H. and Al-Radaideh, Q.A. (2004) Using N-Grams for Arabic Text Sear-ching. *Journal of the American Society for Information Science and Technology*, **55**, 1002-1007. https://doi.org/10.1002/asi.20051

[42] Khreisat, L. (2006) Arabic Text Classification Using N-Gram Frequency Statistics a Comparative Study. *Proceedings of the* 2006 *International Conference on Data Mi-ning*, Las Vegas, 26-29 June 2006, 78-82.

[43] Hmeidi, I.I., Al-Shalabi, R.F., Al-Taani, A.T., Najadat, H. and Al-Hazaimeh, S.A. (2010) A Novel Approach to the Extraction of Roots from Arabic Words Using Bi-grams. *Journal of the Association for Information Science and Technology*, **61**, 583-591.

[44] Mansour, N., Haraty, R.A., Daher, W. and Houri, M. (2008) An Auto-Indexing Me-thod for Arabic Text. *Information Processing & Management*, **44**, 1538-1545. https://doi.org/10.1016/j.ipm.2007.12.007

[45] Och, F.J. and Ney, H. (2003) A Systematic Comparison of Various Statistical Align-ment Models. *Computational Linguistics*, **29**, 19-51. https://doi.org/10.1162/089120103321337421

[46] Al-shammari, E.T. and Lin, J. (2008) Towards an Error-Free Arabic Stemming. *Pro-ceedings of the* 2*nd ACM Workshop on Improving Non English Web Searching*, Napa Valley, 26-30 October 2008, 9-16. https://doi.org/10.1145/1460027.1460030

[47] Al-Serhan, H. and Ayesh, A. (2006) A Triliteral Word Roots Extraction Using Neu-ral Network for Arabic. *International Conference on Computer Engineering and Systems*, Cairo, 5-7 November 2006, 436-440. https://doi.org/10.1109/icces.2006.320487

[48] Boubas, A., Leena, L.L., Belkhouche, B. and Harous, S. (2011) GENESTEM: A Novel Approach for an Arabic Stemmer Using Genetic Algorithms. *International Confe-ren-ce on Innovations in Information Technology*, Abu Dhabi, 25-27 April 2011, 77-82. https://doi.org/10.1109/innovations.2011.5893872

Permissions

List of Contributors

Che-Jen Chuang and Chih-Feng Ko
Department of Tourism and Leisure Management, Vanung University, Taiwan

Jeng-Jong Lin
Department of Tourism and Leisure Management, Vanung University, Taiwan
Department of Information Management, Vanung University, Taiwan

Sai Ji and Rongheng Li
Key Laboratory of High Performance Computing and Stochastic Information Processing, Department of Mathematics, Hunan Normal University, Changsha, China

Yunxia Zhou
Department of Computer, Hunan Normal University, Changsha, China

David J. Webb
Axalta Coating Systems, Front Royal, Virginia, USA

Wissam M. Alobaidi and Eric Sandgren
Systems Engineering Department, Donaghey College of Engineering & Information Technology, University of Arkansas at Little Rock, Little Rock, Arkansas, USA

Kazuma Kuroda
Data Marketing Laboratory, Tokyo, Japan

Antonio Di Leva and Emilio Sulis
Department of Informatics, University of Torino, Torino, Italy

Manuela Vinai
QRS SocCoop — Consorzio Sociale Il Filo da Tessere, Biella, Italy

Wissam Alobaidi and Eric Sandgren
Systems Engineering Department, Donaghey College of Engineering & Information Technology, University of Arkansas at Little Rock, Little Rock, USA

Entidhar Alkuam
Department of Physics and Astronomy, College of Arts, Letters, and Sciences, University of Arkansas at Little Rock, USA

Vivian Vimarlund
International Business School, Jönköping University, Jönköping, Sweden
Department of Computer and Information Science/Human-Centered Systems, Linköping University, Linköping, Sweden

Craig Kuziemsky
University of Ottawa, Ottawa, Canada

Christian Nøhr
Aalborg University, Aalborg, Denmark

Pirkko Nykänen
University of Tampere, Tampere, Finland

Nicolas Nikula
Post-Nord, Stockholm, Sweden

Saleh Almuayqil
College of Computer Sciences and Information, Aljouf University, Sakaka, KSA
School of Computing and Digital Technologies, Staffordshire University, Stoke-on-Trent, UK

Anthony S. Atkins and Bernadette Sharp
School of Computing and Digital Technologies, Staffordshire University, Stoke-on-Trent, UK

Pankaj Chaudhary, Micki Hyde and James A. Rodger
Information Systems and Decisions Sciences Department, Eberly College of Business & IT, Indiana University of Pennsylvania, Indiana, USA

C. Ganeshkumar
Indian Institute of Plantation Management, Bengaluru, India

M. Pachayappan
Department of International Business, School of Management, Pondicherry University, Puducherry, India

G. Madanmohan
Department of Management Studies, School of Management, Pondicherry University, Puducherry, India

Mohammad Mustafa
Department of Computer Information Systems, Faculty of Computers and Information Technology, University of Tabuk, Tabuk, SA

Afag Salah Eldeen
Department of Computer Science, College of Computer Science and Information Technology, Sudan University of Science and Technology, Khartoum State, Sudan

Sulieman Bani-Ahmad
Department of Computer Information Systems, School of Information Technology, Al-Balqa Applied University, Salt, Jordan

Abdelrahman Osman Elfaki
Department of Information Technology, Faculty of Computers and Information Technology, University of Tabuk, Tabuk, Saudi Arabia

Index

A

Agent Based Modeling, 68-69, 73
Agent Based Simulation, 42, 68-70, 73
Agile Information System, 136, 143, 145, 152, 155, 157
Agri-food Supply Chain, 159-165, 167, 179-181, 187
Arabic Stemming, 188-190, 196-197, 208, 210-213, 216
Arbitrary Release Times, 19-20, 27
Artificial Intelligence, 44, 50, 84, 188, 210, 212

B

Bin Packing, 68, 70, 75-76, 80, 82, 84
Breakdown Diagnosis, 1, 17
Business Process, 137, 143, 145, 152, 157

C

Coding Scheme, 6-7
Competence, 139, 165-166, 176
Computation Time, 29-30, 34-35, 41

D

Data Mining, 50, 115, 124, 132
Decision Support, 29-30, 42-43, 68, 70-71, 73-75, 82-83, 132, 155-157
Decision Support Problem, 71, 74, 82
Decision Support System, 70
Diabetes Mellitus, 115-119, 123-125, 130-133
Diabetes Self-management, 117-118, 123, 125-126, 131-133

E

E-health Market, 103-105, 107-108, 110-112
Ensemble Approach, 48, 50
Ensemble Method, 44-45, 49-50
Evolutionary Algorithm, 43, 50, 69, 82
Evolutionary Approach, 29-30, 37, 50
Evolutionary Optimization, 42-43, 68-71, 73-74, 79, 83, 85
Explicit Knowledge, 115-116, 119-120, 122, 125, 134

F

Fitness Function, 5-7, 14, 210
Fuzzy Logic, 1-2, 16-18
Fuzzy Logical Equation, 2-3, 15-16
Fuzzy Relation Matrix, 2, 8, 11-13
Fuzzy Truth Value, 8, 10-11

G

Genetic Algorithm, 1-2, 16, 29-31, 33-41, 44, 46-47, 50, 68, 74, 82, 84
Genetic Optimization, 29-30, 33-34, 36, 42-43, 68, 70, 76, 82
Goal Programming Approach, 70, 72

H

Healthcare Delivery, 103, 119
Heuristic Algorithm, 20

I

Information Retrieval, 188, 190, 202, 208, 213-215
Information System, 136, 143, 145, 152, 155, 157
Information Systems Agility, 136, 155
Intelligent Agent, 42, 68, 80, 82
Intelligent Diagnosis System, 1-2, 10, 18
Inverse Fuzzy Inference, 1-2

K

Knowledge Discovery, 116, 124, 132, 135
Knowledge Management, 115-116, 119, 125, 132, 134-135, 215

L

Light Stemming, 188-189, 201-204, 206, 209-211, 213, 215
Light-based Stemming, 201, 210-211

M

Machine Learning, 17, 42, 44, 50, 210
Manufacturing Process, 1-2, 16, 84, 175
Mathematical Formulation, 71, 73
Maximum Completion Time, 19-20
Maze Navigation, 29-30
Medication, 118-120, 124-127, 129, 131, 133-134

N

Neural Network, 17, 44, 50, 210

O

Ordinal Algorithm, 19, 28

P

Parallel Machine, 19-20, 28
Parallel Machines, 19-20, 28

Peg Game, 68, 70-72, 74-75, 82

Potato Supply Chain, 159, 161-163, 165, 177-179, 182, 184

R

Resource Allocation, 29, 69

Root-based Stemming, 188, 211

S

Scheduling Problem, 19-20, 27

Search Algorithm, 2

Seci Model, 115-117, 121-123, 125-128, 130-132, 135

Self-management, 115-119, 123, 125-126, 131-133

Service Industry, 103-106, 108, 111-112

Simulated Annealing, 76

Small and Medium Enterprises, 103-104, 156, 166

Social Innovation, 109, 113

Socialization, 116, 126

Statistical Stemming, 196, 207, 212

Supply Chain Management, 139, 158-165, 167, 179-184, 187

Supply Chain Process, 160, 180

T

Trading Agents, 44-50

Traditional Genetic Algorithm, 29-30,34, 37, 39, 41

Traveling Salesman, 30, 43, 85

Traveling Salesman Problem, 30, 43, 85

V

Virtual Broker, 109

W

Web Tool, 128-130

Worst Case Ratio, 19-20

Printed in the USA
CPSIA information can be obtained
at www.ICGtesting.com
JSHW051415221024
72173JS00006B/1360